**THE TRIUMPHANT CONCLUSION
TO THE SAGA OF TWO FAMILIES
WHOSE DREAMS WERE THE
DESTINY OF A NEW LAND**

"A BLOCKBUSTER SERIES . . .
Its considerable strengths are its meticulous
historical fidelity and its interesting, lively
characters."

West Coast Review of Books

"A CRACKLING GOOD ROMANCE"
Ottawa Citizen

"ADAIR AND ROSENSTOCK
KNOW HOW TO TELL A STORY . . .
Fans seeking historical fiction and romance
will find plenty to keep them turning the pages
. . . physical violence, personal turmoil, battles, sex, narrow escapes . . . action fast and fu-
rious."

Toronto Quill and Quire

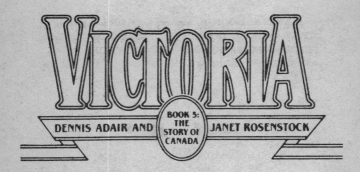

VICTORIA

DENNIS ADAIR AND **BOOK 5: THE STORY OF CANADA** JANET ROSENSTOCK

AVON
PUBLISHERS OF BARD, CAMELOT, DISCUS AND FLARE BOOKS

VICTORIA: THE STORY OF CANADA: BOOK 5 is an original publication of Avon Books. This work has never before appeared in book form.

AVON BOOKS
A division of
The Hearst Corporation
1790 Broadway
New York, New York 10019

A GOLDEN MUSE PRODUCTION
Published by arrangement with the authors
Library of Congress Catalog Card Number: 83-91102
ISBN: 0-380-85134-2

First Avon Printing, November, 1983

AVON TRADEMARK REG. U. S. PAT. OFF. AND IN OTHER COUNTRIES, MARCA REGISTRADA, HECHO EN U. S. A.

Printed in the U. S. A.

WFH 10 9 8 7 6 5 4 3 2 1

ACKNOWLEDGMENTS

Among the reference books used in preparation of this novel were: *James Douglas: Servant of Two Empires* and *Victoria the Fort* by Derek Pethick; *The Fraser* by Bruce Hutchison; *British Columbia: A History* by Margaret Ormsby; *The Gold Rush Trail and the Road to Oregon* by Todd Webb; *Short Portage to Lillooet and other Tails and Trails* by Irene Edwards; *Washington, a Bicentennial History* by Norman H. Clark; *Sepass Poems, The Songs of Y-AIL-MIHTH* recorded by Eloise Street.

The authors would also like to acknowledge Frieda, our Olympia EX 100, our cover artist A. Johnson for his fine work, and our editor, Paul Dinas. We give special thanks to Avon Canada and all who work there.

FOREWORD

There was a West before Confederation, and in the 1850s the small, sophisticated, but isolated Colony of Vancouver began to grow and strive for self-government. The Colony of Vancouver was established on Vancouver Island and consisted of Fort Victoria and its surrounding community. A major port for the British Pacific Fleet, it steadily grew in importance during the Crimean War and the gold rush that followed.

In the 1850s, British North America consisted of the United Provinces of Canada East (today Quebec), Canada West (today Ontario), the Maritimes (today the Atlantic provinces: New Brunswick, Newfoundland, Prince Edward Island, and Nova Scotia), Rupert's Land (today Manitoba, Saskatchewan, and Alberta), New Caledonia (today British Columbia), and the Colony of Vancouver (subsequently part of the Province of British Columbia).

During the historic period in which *Victoria* is set, the giant Hudson's Bay Company controlled much of Rupert's Land and New Caledonia. It lost its trading license in 1858 when the license was not renewed by the British Crown, but the company continued to have a strong influence in the developing commerce of both New Caledonia and Rupert's Land.

In 1846, the American President James Polk signed the Oregon Boundary Treaty with Britain. This treaty extended the border between the United States and British North America, the 49th parallel, to the Pacific Ocean.

But in spite of the border, travel, commerce, and communication between the Colony of Vancouver and the Washington and Oregon territories continued. The native inhabitants of both areas shared common tribal cultures; the Indians cared little for the lines Europeans drew on maps.

Following the brutal extermination of the Yakima and Puget Sound tribes by Governor Stevens in the Yakima War of 1855 to 1858, the chief of the Yakima, Kamiakan, escaped to seek refuge among the tribes in British North America.

CHAPTER I

April 1, 1855

Margot Macleod, the only daughter of Ronald Macleod of Lochiel, paused briefly to look in the window of the general store as she made her way down the street toward the town square of Niagara-on-the-Lake. It was not the merchandise that intrigued her, but her own reflection in the glass.

She was a reasonably tall girl with a fine figure and a striking angular face. Her long black hair was done up in a severe bun and hidden prudently beneath her large gray bonnet. She smiled at herself. Everyone said her coloring was unusual; few girls had green eyes and jet-black hair. She wore a prim gray suit, a gray jacket, and a white blouse with a high ruffled collar. It was a modest outfit, carefully tailored to emphasize her figure without being in any way revealing. It was certainly the kind of costume she believed Ernest McGrath would find acceptable.

Not that Margot had the slightest evidence that the young Reverend Ernest McGrath even knew she was alive. But he will, Margot vowed. I shall always sit as close to the front of the church as I can. I shall be more pious than any other young woman and I shall work harder as well. I shall campaign for temperance and I will fight against moral corruption. He will see, she told herself. And when I am eighteen in four months, he will take note of all the work I have done. He will begin to see me for the helpmate I can be to him and then . . . then we could work together to save wayward souls.

With that thought firmly in her mind, she continued down the street and across the well-kept lawn of the town square toward the white clapboard chapel.

It's a wonderful day, Margot thought. A wonderful, wondrous spring day! It often rained in April and sometimes it even snowed as late as May. But this year spring had truly come early. The grass was already green, and jackrabbits hopped through fields which would soon be planted. The large weeping willows on the lawn in front of the church rustled gently in the breeze as Margot Macleod climbed the steps and hurried into the chapel. The church was nearly full, but seeing it so crowded was hardly a surprise. Today was a special day. Today the senior Reverend McGrath, Aloysius McGrath, had invited Dr. Simon Templeton Hobart of the United Missionary Society to give a special talk.

Margot squeezed into the third pew from the front. She glanced across the aisle and waved discreetly at her cousins, the MacLeans. Then she leaned back and adjusted her skirt. She sat prim and proper, her hands folded in her lap.

Upon a signal from the elder Reverend McGrath, the congregation rose and sang the hymn of the day, *Blest Be the Tie that Binds*. Margot sang in a clear voice, but her mind was not entirely on the hymn. Her eyes searched the dignitaries sitting directly beneath the pulpit. No, she thought sadly, the young Reverend McGrath was not among them. Surely, though, he would not miss today's service.

When the singing of the hymn was finished, Reverend McGrath led the congregation in prayer and when Margot opened her eyes, she was relieved to see that Ernest had taken a seat near an unfamiliar man. She assumed the stranger to be the famous guest preacher.

Aloysius McGrath held his arms outstretched, and in the tones of every great Shakespearian actor since Richard Burbage, introduced Dr. Hobart.

"Ah, my friends, my good friends! My brothers and sisters in the faith! I thank you for inviting me here today. I thrill in the taking of communion with you! I thrill in celebrating our beliefs!" Dr. Hobart paused and gulped some water from the glass that had been placed on the pulpit. He had a booming voice and was even more dramatic than the elder Reverend McGrath.

"Today," he began, "I have come to tell you a magnificent story—a story of great sacrifice and stamina, a story of gifted people inspired by our faith and led by the Holy

Spirit. They ventured across this vast continent into a wilderness to bring peace and comfort, yea love and salvation, to the poor miserable savages who make their wretched lives on the far Pacific shore of our great and magnificent land!

"This is a tale of great bravery—an inspirational story of a beautiful, God-fearing woman and her handsome, brave, dedicated husband. It is a tale to bring tears to the eyes and resolve—yes, my friends, resolve—to the heart and soul of each and every true believer."

Simon Templeton Hobart paused again to take some water. Margot glanced at Ernest and he smiled at her. She shivered slightly. Ernest had never smiled at her before! Perhaps he did, after all, know she was alive.

"My story is the tale of Narcissa Prentiss Whitman and her beloved husband, Marcus Whitman. Friends, let me carry you back to the year eighteen-thirty-six—a full nineteen years ago—a full twelve years before the California gold rush when greed—yes, my friends, greed—took evil men across the Rocky Mountains in search of gold. But, my friends, you know—you know because you know the words of our faith—you know that money is the root of all evil and you know what sins greedy men can commit. But no! Mrs. Narcissa Prentiss Whitman and her good husband were not of the gold rush generation, they were not of the evils born of greed, but of the love born of faith! Why, Narcissa herself, a mere slip of a girl, a beautiful young woman, alone and unafraid, applied to go West to help Christianize the savages. But of course we could not let her go! We could not allow this brave, beautiful woman—not even considering her strength and her faith—to go among the savages alone."

Margot leaned forward in her pew. Her eyes roamed no more to Ernest, but were now riveted on Dr. Simon Templeton Hobart. His tale compelled her to listen. She conjured in her mind the image of Narcissa Prentiss and she saw in Narcissa's eyes the burning fire of conviction. Margot shuddered. Sometimes—no, not just sometimes, but all the time when the young Reverend Ernest McGrath gave the Sunday sermon—she herself felt a spiritual desire, doubtless the same desire Narcissa Prentiss had felt.

"But Narcissa Prentiss' desire to fulfill her faith was not to be thwarted!" Dr. Hobart continued. "God was to deliver unto her a mate; a man with whom she could join in matrimony; a man who burned with the same fire as she; a man who would take her into the wilderness to minister the faith to the savages and to help her realize her dream of bringing those miserable creatures to the glory of the salvation!

"Thus did Miss Narcissa Prentiss and Dr. Marcus Whitman marry. Theirs was a perilous journey into the hinterland, but they went bravely. Three months and fifteen hundred miles later, the Whitmans arrived at Fort Boise, where poor Mrs. Whitman, now heavy with child, wrote that she was able to wash clothes for the third time in all the three months of their ordeal. And we all know that cleanliness is next to Godliness! Imagine her pain, if you can. The pain of a pious woman as she traveled through the dark valleys of decision and climbed the mountains of despair! She wrote of the boils suffered—yes, my friends, boils like the ones suffered by Job! Boils caused because the travelers could not wash their clothes!"

A hum of disbelief and revulsion rippled through the congregation.

"And she wrote that many suffered dysentery and many died of cholera. She wrote of how the weary travelers had to arm themselves against the marauding buffalo and wolves, and that many shot one another by accident, thinking the noises they heard in the dark were some beastly intruder. And oh, the tragedies! Weary little children would fall asleep in the hot afternoon sun and tumble off the seats of their wagons to be run over by the great iron wheels of the next wagon. And Narcissa's good husband Marcus performed wondrously. He insisted on taking his wagon beyond Fort Laramie, my friends. No wagon had ever been taken beyond Fort Laramie. At every obstacle, Narcissa and Marcus had to unload and disassemble the wagon; then they had to reassemble and reload it. A trial, my friends! It was a

4

trial of the spirit, a trial which Marcus passed, bless his dear departed soul!

"But not without pain! Not without fatigue! Narcissa wrote that Marcus lost near a third of his body weight. But he persisted, he persisted because he and Narcissa were driven West by their faith, not by mere lust for gold!

"And the wagon was abandoned only at Fort Vancouver, where the good factor, Mr. McLoughlin, offered the Whitmans his meager hospitality. But the Whitmans had arrived, and true to their belief they built their mission in Waiilatpu, on the River Walla Walla, among the heathen tribes known as the Cayuse and Yakima."

Many of the women in the congregation sighed and wiped tears from their eyes. Margot blinked back her own tears and bit her lower lip as she continued to lean forward, enraptured with Dr. Simon Templeton Hobart's inspiring tale of faith and sacrifice.

"But of course that is not the end of the story, my friends. The last chapter is one of Christian martyrdom. Oh, not the martyrdom claimed by the Papists, but true martyrdom—a martyrdom in the wilderness, a martyrdom without witnesses. But not before, no, not before Marcus Whitman had returned to the east to convince the faithful of the need for more funds and the continued support of missions for the heathen savages. Then, Marcus Whitman acted as guide and advisor on the Great Migration trek in 1843, a migration that took good, brave men and women into the wilderness of the Oregon country. And because of Marcus Whitman and his brave Narcissa, the Oregon Territory became a part of the United States, and a border between British North America and the United States was recognized. But then, as fate would have it, horror struck! On November 29, 1847, Narcissa and Marcus Whitman and eleven others were brutally murdered by those very heathens whom they so dearly loved! And when the good, brave Narcissa was found, her body, which had been put in a shallow grave, was ravaged by wolves!"

The congregation gasped and Dr. Hobart allowed the

shock of his story to have its desired effect. Timing, he well knew, was everything.

"Ah, my friends! That is the story and it is God's own truth! But the tale is not quite over. The godless heathen Indians, indeed the godless heathen Cayuse whose lands span both the United States and British North America, those dreadful wretches, are still without salvation! Still without the faith! And some, heaven save us, are still without proper coverings for their bodies! More missionaries are needed and we are willing to send the qualified. But we need funds! We need money to buy bibles and supplies in order to bring love, decency, and faith to the heathens. So I ask you, I ask you personally, in the name of Narcissa and Marcus—our friends—to donate to the United Missionary Society which will, if God is willing and he finds a wife, send your very own Reverend Ernest McGrath West on the same trail followed by Narcissa and Marcus."

In absolute unison a wave of whispers filled the chapel. Margot sat bolt upright and looked at Ernest McGrath. So, in fact, did every young woman in the congregation.

"Next year, God and funds willing, the young Reverend McGrath will begin, if he has a wife, the very same trip West—a fitting manner in which to celebrate the faith of the Whitmans on the 20th anniversary of their historic trek!"

Margot sank back in her pew. A year, she had a year! Somehow, she thought, I must make Ernest see what a perfect wife I would make. Oh, to be the spiritual equal of Narcissa Prentiss! I will become another Narcissa, she vowed. And Ernest will become another Marcus! What a glorious life we will have together, dying for our faith!

A gentle breeze swept a low, thick fog in from Lake Ontario. The heavy mist wrapped itself around the neat two-story brick and clapboard buildings that lined the main street of Niagara-on-the-Lake. Such nights, some said, were nights for ghosts, for the distressed spirits of those who died violent deaths in the War of 1812. "On nights like this," claimed old Mary, who ran the local inn, "you can hear the hoofbeats of General Brock's horse, Alfred, and you can see the distinguished gentleman himself, dressed fit as a king and riding off to fight the American intruders. See his picture there on the wall? Watch it carefully. The eyes move, you know . . ."

But in Mary's inn, a crowd of merry-makers drank whiskey and rum and gathered 'round a fiddler who played old Scottish songs. They were undisturbed by the old woman's tales; they came to drink and to be entertained. Ronald Macleod tapped his foot to the music and sang along happily. He did not come often to the inn, but when he did he enjoyed himself immensely. Though his daughter Margot, he thought, would certainly disapprove, dedicated as she was to the belief that good brew was evil.

There was, to be sure, an element of immorality to be found in the inn, he conceded to himself. Old Mary kept voluptuous young women to wait table, and if they occasionally disappeared upstairs with a customer, she did not complain as long as she received a fraction of the fee charged. But, Ronald reasoned, such activity was inevitable given the ratio of men to women. Old Mary's "girls" performed a useful function. But he himself came to the inn for the sole purpose of being with old friends and singing and drinking with them.

Ronald's friends were gathered near the large stone fireplace. Their songs were interspersed with conversation on topics that ranged from the weather and crops to politics and religion.

At the far end of the room, a group of Americans gathered together. Theirs was a constant presence at the inn, and though their names varied there was a certain sameness about the men. Some were travelers who were simply passing through on the way to Toronto, others were traders who came with some regularity to offer goods. But they remained apart from the Canadians, choosing to drink alone and talk alone. And in general they were more raucous. They drank more, swore more, and talked louder. When they had political arguments they were noisy and sometimes violent. The Canadians were quieter. There was a civility in Canadian politics that Ronald knew did not exist in politics

7

south of the border. The Canadians sought compromise with one another. It was a fine difference in personality, a difference few Americans detected. The shared language made them feel at home, but certainly it did not cloud the fact for the Canadians that differences did exist. The United States was a product of revolution; Upper Canada was settled by many who had fled that revolution. Americans, Ronald thought, were more aggressive, while Canadians seemed to wait for events to take a natural course.

Ronald looked upward and squinted his eyes to read the Roman numerals on the grandfather clock that stood in the corner. It was almost midnight and he moved to leave.

"Oh, stay for one more round!" Henry Thompson urged. He was the owner of the local apothecary and lived only a few doors from the inn.

"It's a long ride back to Lochiel," Ronald said, shaking his head.

Old Mary was standing by one of the long oak tables with another round of whiskey. Her white apron was stained and her wiry gray hair frizzed about her round weathered face.

"It's a bad time to be leaving, Mr. Macleod! A bad time indeed! It's near to midnight, and you know what happens at midnight in this town! The ghosts of the soldiers killed by the Americans ride through the streets." She glanced toward the Americans in the corner, but they paid her no heed as they continued to drink and talk. "Best to wait 'til the witching hour has passed," she advised.

Ronald sat back down, a bemused smile on his face. "One more round, then," he agreed. "But just because I'd enjoy another drink, not because I believe in ghosts."

"Daughter at home?" Thompson asked. "I suppose you feel you ought to get back to her."

"No, she's down in Queenston for the weekend. She's visiting her cousins."

"Then you've got no excuse to leave. And even less excuse to ride back to Lochiel. You can stay at my place, and go home in the morning."

Ronald slapped the table. "Good idea! I didn't relish the

ride.'' He glanced up at Mary, who had remained near the table. ''Ghosts or no ghosts,'' he added.

''Oh, there are ghosts. At night you can hear them walking, you know . . . up and down the stairs. This inn is haunted.''

''But the ghosts don't trouble you?'' Ronald asked with good humor.

''No, not me! I understand them.''

The scraping sound of chairs on the wooden floor caused Ronald to look up. The Americans were standing, preparing to leave. They were telling dirty stories and slapping one another on the back.

''Loud and wild,'' Mary hissed. ''It's more peaceful when they pull out.''

''But you always serve them,'' Ronald observed.

''They pay cash, gold mostly. Business is business. You can't let a war that happened near fifty years ago interfere with commerce. If you're going to hold a grudge, you might as well make a profit.'' She leaned down. ''I charge them more for whiskey,'' she confessed.

''Are they staying here?''

Mary shook her head. ''No, at the hotel on the edge of town.''

Ronald finished his whiskey and set his glass down. Mary refilled it immediately.

Nell, one of Mary's girls, came over to the table.

''I'd like to be going now,'' she whispered in Mary's ear.

''Oh, you shouldn't go now. The witching hour is not yet over.''

Nell smiled and laughed. ''Oh, I don't believe in your ghosts.''

''Well, then you shouldn't be walking alone at night.''

''It's not far—only two blocks down the street, you know. I'll be quite safe.''

Mary nodded and Nell wrapped her shawl around her bare shoulders.

''Take care,'' Mary warned. ''And if you hear footsteps, walk fast.''

9

"Ghosts don't run?" Nell asked teasingly, as she arched a dark eyebrow.

"No," Mary answered authoritatively. "They move slowly in the mists."

"You'll scare her half to death," Ronald put in.

"Not me," Nell countered. "I've walked in fogs in London town, and if I wasn't afraid there, I won't be here."

She hurried away and out the front door of the inn.

"Why doesn't she live here?" Ronald asked.

Mary shrugged. "Says she'd rather be alone. She has a room over the greengrocer's."

Ronald accepted the information without comment. He returned to his whiskey and joined in the song that the others had begun to sing.

Craigflower Farm was a pleasant, cultivated estate on Vancouver Island. It belonged to the Hudson's Bay Company and had been established in 1853. In that year, Kenneth McKenzie had been appointed overseer for the new company farm. He had arrived in the colony along with carpenters, blacksmiths, and laborers aboard the British ship, *The Norman Morison.*

The first building erected was a huge farmhouse with a great stone fireplace. Soon to follow were a carpenter's shop, a blacksmith's, a sawmill, a flour mill, a brick kiln and a slaughterhouse. Fresh produce from the farm was shipped down the river gorge to Fort Victoria which was some ten miles away, thus helping to make the area self-sufficient.

Craigflower Farm was a microcosm of the entire colony on Vancouver Island—a colony far closer to the Washington Territory than it was to the wild, unsettled, and hardly explored mainland called New Caledonia. The farm was as isolated as the Colony itself—an island within an island. The farm was located half way between the docks at Esquimalt and the small village of Victoria. As a result, the manager of the farm often played host to high ranking British Naval officers and colonists alike. They wiled away their evenings in front of the great stone fireplace discussing India, China,

10

South America and the Caribbean. But tonight, the first of May, the visitors talked of war.

In March 1854, war had broken out. England and her allies fought against Imperial Russia. The Crimean War, as it was called, was of great interest to the inhabitants of Vancouver Island. The island was a British colony, but nearby Alaska belonged to the Russians. Although the residents of the small colony did not learn of the war's outbreak until three months after the fact, they were quick to understand the possible dangers. Sir James Douglas, Governor of the Colony and Chief Factor of the Hudson's Bay Post, had even gone so far as to suggest an attack on Alaska.

The idea of the attack was not considered for long, but attacks on Russian warships and military outposts were initiated, and in the first summer of the war, a combined Franco-British attack was made on the Russian fortress of Petropavlovsk on the coast of the Kamchatka Peninsula. The sortie resulted in a dismal defeat for the British, and since there were no hospital facilities in the Colony of Vancouver, the wounded had to be taken to San Francisco. In February 1855, the new commander of the Pacific Station, Rear Admiral Bruce, wrote to Governor Douglas and asked that hospital facilities be built. Douglas promptly responded by building facilities for 100 patients at Esquimalt, which, as a result, became a major British port. Now, it appeared that another attack on Kamchatka was imminent.

Cory MacLean, one of the visitors to the farmhouse, sprawled in his chair. It was a crisp, cool evening outside, even though it was the first of May, and the warmth from the stone fireplace made the room exceptionally comfortable. Then too, Cory had consumed four glasses of rum and was feeling entirely at ease with the world.

He had come from New Caledonia, as the mainland was called, that very afternoon with a rich load of furs. After weeks there, he had sought out the most pleasant circumstances imaginable; an evening at Craigflower Farm. Much to his delight—but somewhat to the frustration of his friend and companion, Blaise Baron—Cory had found Governor Douglas and four high-ranking British officers also as guests

11

of the farm's proprietor, Captain Edward Edwards Langford, who was generous with all his guests and who had no small reputation for his lavish dinners and parties.

Cory delighted in the stories told by the British officers, and they in turn delighted in his tales of life in the wilderness. Blaise, on the other hand, disliked the British officers and was uncomfortable among them. But apart from his stated dislike of the British, Blaise Baron was the ideal partner, Cory thought. Blaise Baron was articulate and intelligent; he was skilled and had a fine mind for business. He was a man of wit and charm—most of the time. But he was closed to discussions of his past, a past that Cory assumed had something to do with the British.

"We're going to make another sortie against the Kamchatka Peninsula," Commander Arlen announced dryly. He held his pipe firmly and stared intently into the fire.

"And it won't be like the last one," Lieutenant Jameson bragged. "This time we'll give the Russians a thrashing, I can tell you."

"I still feel the Colony is in danger of attack," Governor Douglas reiterated.

Lieutenant Commander Rake laughed. "There are a lot of British warships between this colony and the Russians."

Douglas didn't answer. He intended to set up a colonial militia—more for protection from the Indians than the Russians, but a militia nonetheless. Douglas was a man who planned for the future. The Hudson's Bay Company had only three years left on its trading license in the area, and Douglas wanted not only a militia but a legislative assembly in place before the leases expired. An increasing number of settlers were taking up lumbering, coal mining, and fishing. The time was coming for a formalization of the Colony's status . . . perhaps, Douglas dreamed, as a province.

"At least in this war the French and English are allies," Cory observed. He glanced at Blaise, who only sipped his drink quietly. Blaise Baron was French Canadian, and clearly considered the British his enemies. But then, Cory reminded himself, French Canadians lost little love for the

French as a nation. They were nationalists who usually pre-
ferred to go it alone.

"And the Turks are allies, too," commented the Lieutenant. He smiled and winked. "Now there's a port to have lib-
erty in! Give me Constantinople!"

"Or Shanghai," Lieutenant Commander Rake laughed.
"Ah, I adore Chinese women! They're so accommodating,
and seem to relish lovemaking so! I had a beauty in Shanghai, ah, she applied her rounded lips so well. . . ."

The men laughed. Victoria was hardly their favorite port.
Small wonder—there were practically no white women, and
the Indian women were notably uncooperative, save those
who had actually married settlers, and they were quite
proper.

"I suppose you find us boring," Governor Douglas said,
echoing Cory's thoughts.

"Isolated," Rake admitted. "But a real bit of British civilization, I must say! Yes, a real taste of home, in a way."

Captain Langford smiled. He and the directors of the
Hudson's Bay Company had their differences. The Company saw the 900-acre farm as a food-producing venture.
Langford saw himself as a bit of the country gentleman, and
he thrived on the compliments of his visiting countrymen.
"We try to do our best," he said, "though times are trying."

"Are you headed back to New Caledonia for more furs?"
the Lieutenant asked Cory.

"Not for a while," Cory answered. "I have plenty of
money. I think I deserve a rest."

"Too bad you want a rest," Commander Arlen put in. "I
was going to suggest that you come with us up to the Kamchatka Coast to have a look at the war for yourself. And the
Alaska territory, too. You speak Russian, and I may need a
Russian intepreter"—he laughed and winked—"to accept
their surrender, you know. I could justify your shipping on
for the voyage."

Cory beamed at Commander Arlen. "Are you serious?"

"I don't joke," he replied, draining his glass of rum.
"God knows how this will all turn out. When we've beaten

13

the Russians we might end up with Alaska. Langford tells me you and Baron lived up in Sitka for awhile and that you used to do a lot of trading with the Russians. He says you're a master of the language. Damnable tongue, if you ask me!''

"Do we want Alaska?'' Douglas asked. "I can't imagine why.''

"I admit it has no prospects,'' Arlen responded. "Damn useless place. Rather like a large icehouse.''

"The British usually only want what the Americans have their eyes on,'' Blaise said, somewhat sarcastically.

"Well, lucky for us the Americans don't want it,'' Arlen answered quickly.

"I'd really like to come with you,'' Cory put in. He glanced at his friend.

Blaise smiled. "Don't let me stop you. You know I'm headed East to bring wagon trains into the Oregon Territory.''

Cory nodded. He had known Blaise was considering returning to his old profession for a year or two. He had not known until this moment that Blaise had actually made up his mind. But then, that was a part of their friendship: unpredictability.

Cory MacLean had been born in the west. His parents, Ian and Bonnie MacLean, had settled in the Saskatchewan region. He had traveled all over the west and become a trader in Victoria, making frequent trips to the wild, unsettled mainland. At thirty-six, Cory was still an adventurer. He hadn't found a wife and he was unwilling to settle down for too long. In that respect, he and Blaise Baron were alike, though Blaise traveled farther afield for longer periods of time.

Blaise Baron was two years younger than Cory. They had met nearly eight years ago and discovered that they shared many interests. But Blaise seemed torn between two existences. He would go off to ply his trade of scout or wagon master in the United States, only to return to British North America to work traps with many of his French Canadian compatriots. He was torn between a nation he rejected and one he could not quite accept.

14

"Well, then it's settled," Commander Arlen announced.

"When do we leave?" Cory asked enthusiastically. He had always wanted to go to sea; it was a new adventure and he thrived on all things new and different.

"In two days," Arlen informed him. "Can you be ready so soon?"

Cory shrugged. "What I have is what you see."

"That's not entirely true," Governor Douglas interrupted. "He's really quite wealthy—he has a farm nearby."

"Furs?" Arlen asked, a flicker of interest in his eyes.

"And gold," Douglas replied on Cory's behalf. "He and Mr. Baron profited substantially some years ago in California."

Blaise shifted in his chair uneasily. He hated having his affairs discussed with the British. Knowledge brought curiosity; curiosity brought questions.

"And you still pursue the life of a nomad? I'm surprised you haven't settled down to enjoy your money, Mr. Baron."

Blaise shrugged. "It's all invested," he said vaguely. "Money is not always useful. I'm a dedicated wanderer."

"And bachelor," Cory added.

"I think you're both dedicated bachelors," Douglas added.

"What possible choice do they have?" Arlen asked good-naturedly. They all laughed. The subject of women in the Colony was a never-ending source of black humor among the settlers and seamen.

Blaise stood up and stretched. "It's been a long day," he said.

"If you're retiring, it's the fourth door on the left at the top of the stairs," Captain Langford informed him.

Blaise nodded. "It's been pleasant. I thank you for your hospitality." At least the second statement was honest. For Blaise Baron, no evening spent with British officers could possibly be pleasant.

15

CHAPTER II

May 7, 1855

The Reverend Aloysius McGrath lived with his only son Ernest in a small, neat house on a shady street behind the church. It was a modest dwelling that befitted a man of the cloth.

Aloysius McGrath's wife, Fanny, had died in 1841 when Ernest was fourteen years old. At that time, Aloysius hired the widow Mrs. Charmaine Conklin as housekeeper. Mrs. Conklin, a respected townswoman, came early each morning and left shortly after the supper dishes were done at seven each night. Mrs. Conklin's abilities were more than adequate, but while her morals were above reproach it was common knowledge that her tongue wagged a bit too much and too often. Thus, it was Aloysius' rule that nothing of a personal nature was ever discussed in her presence.

Ernest McGrath was a tall young man, an inch over six feet, with broad shoulders. But in spite of his naturally strong build, his muscles were not well toned. Unlike the other young men who lived in the community, Ernest had not led an outdoor life of hard work. After an academic life of study and prayer, he graduated from divinity school in Chicago and was ordained in the ministry at the age of twenty-five. Ernest then returned to Niagara-on-the-Lake to help his father and to await his acceptance as a missionary. But, as Dr. Simon Templeton Hobart had pointed out, a missionary must have a wife. Therefore, Ernest now found himself with the task of selecting a suitable woman to court. But the truth was, he deeply resented the fact that he had to marry in order to become a missionary and he dreaded the very idea of marriage. But his father was adamant.

"The problem," his father declared, "is not a lack of suitable, interested females; it is the selection of the best possible candidate."

It was true. Owing to his public persona and his vocation as preacher, Ernest was beseiged by women. He did not consider himself to be unattractive. His hair was thick, dark, and a trifle unruly. He had a serious expression. His eyes, which he considered his best feature, were great dark pools that shimmered with righteous indignation and burned into the hearts of parishioners who strayed too far from the dictums of the faith by visiting the local taverns.

Ernest McGrath had the perfect voice for his vocation. It was deep and moving. He could bring tears to the eyes of every female in the church when he softly told the parables, and he could invoke the fear of God in sinners when when he spoke of hell's fires and eternal damnation. Further, he could wrench a man's last dollar from his pocket when he talked of the needs of the poor and of the work to be done among the heathen savages, those lesser beings whom Ernest McGrath considered his personal responsibility.

Ernest could not remember just when he had first known that he had to be a missionary. It had been his dream since childhood; it was his dream now. But his antipathy toward the idea of marriage had caused him to delay; instead of getting on with what was necessary, he avoided the task of selecting a suitable female.

Now, it seemed, his state of indecision was to end. His father, Aloysius, had decided to take matters into his own hands.

"The time has come," Aloysius had declared at breakfast. "I have made a list of potential candidates from among the women of the congregation. We will discuss the matter this evening."

Mrs. Conklin, far from disinterested in the subject, had turned, her eyes and ears open. But one withering look from Aloysius had seemed to send her attention back to the dishes in the sink, although both men knew her ears were not closed.

After dinner, Ernest sat on the edge of the settee in the parlor. His legs were spread apart and his long arms dangled between them, his hands clasped together. He knew he possessed charismatic qualities. I am handsome, he reminded himself. I am compelling. I am the most eligible of bachelors. Many of the young women fairly swoon in my pres-

18

ence. But his thoughts did not cease his discomfort at the topic to be discussed; he found swooning women irritating.

And he reminded himself once again that women presented a constant threat to every man's morals. Eve had collaborated with the snake and because of that women were condemned to endure the pain of childbirth through the ages. "I will greatly multiply your pain in childbearing; in pain you shall bring forth children, yet your desire shall be for your husband and he shall rule over you." Ernest repeated the words from the Book of Genesis. Yes, women did desire—they were all wanton and desirous. My wife, Ernest vowed, must be aware of the Commandments; she must be obedient and I must direct her and rule over her.

In the hall beyond the parlor, Ernest could hear his father bidding the curious Mrs. Conklin good evening. Naturally, the discussion of the selection of his wife could not be held while she was in the house and, good woman that she was, her disappointment at not being allowed to partake in the discussion had been evident all day.

Aloysius McGrath was a strict man. He had emigrated from Paisley, Scotland, in 1820. He held old-fashioned, old-country views, and he believed in arranged marriages. Indeed, so great was his exasperation with Ernest in this matter that he felt Ernest should have nothing to say at all.

"I could stay later," Mrs. Conklin offered. "The kitchen floor could stand a wash."

"It will wait," Aloysius said in his extra-kind tone. " I wouldn't dream of allowing you to labor after hours. Good night."

Ernest heard the front door close. In a moment, his father entered the parlor. He walked directly to his desk, where he opened his special locked drawer and withdrew a sheaf of papers. Aloysius sat down opposite a disgruntled and somewhat apprehensive Ernest.

"I've been giving the question of your forthcoming marriage my undivided attention," he announced, "and toward that end, I have made a list of the qualities and characteristics a candidate for the position must possess."

"I've been thinking myself . . ." Ernest interrupted.

"Not with the same objective wisdom as I have. You can hardly be expected to look on this matter clearly."

Ernest fell into silence. His father's communication with him was always formal and high-handed. It was as if they were two strangers, rather than father and son. But his father's wish had always been Ernest's command, for Ernest feared his father, with good reason.

"First, the woman must be a virgin. And she must be a member of the congregation in good standing. We are seeking a devout, pious woman."

"Of course," Ernest muttered.

"Given those qualities, she must also be strong. Strong of will and strong of body in order to endure the hardships of the trip West and of the frontier. She ought to have good teeth."

"Good teeth?" Ernest questioned.

"Son, women are not different from horses. Good teeth are a sign of good health. Show me a woman with good teeth, and I'll show you a woman who can bear her pregnancies without complaint. You need a woman who can drop her children from her womb with the ease that a tree drops seed pods."

Ernest's face reddened and he simultaneously shuddered. The thought of birth nauseated him.

"Naturally, I want you to marry a woman of good Scots heritage. She must be thrifty and able to save. What we are looking for is a woman who is tight with the purse and generous of spirit."

"Missionaries don't make much."

"And that is the reason why she must be thrifty. Next, it would be helpful if she came from a family of some means. Over the long run, it would mean more donations for the church, and doubtless some added funds for your work."

Aloysius McGrath cleared his throat. "Then there is the question of appearance. Given the other qualities, appearance is the least important. But if possible, one would want to produce strong, healthy, good-looking children for the Lord. I know we've never discussed such matters before, but I daresay it's easier to couple, for the purpose of producing children, if the woman in question is not too hard to look at."

20

Ernest's face went a deep crimson and he coughed nervously. He sometimes dreamed of women—evil, naked women, women who . . . he shivered again. The very thought of his night terrors made him miserable . . . how could he marry!

"Not, of course, that you are to sleep with your wife unless you are attempting to impregnate her. We only condone a closeness of male and female flesh when procreation is intended. It's a filthy, tempting business. It's much too easy to enjoy it. But a man must have sons."

Ernest nodded his head. But the thought made him sick and angry; he did not wish to give any woman his seed.

Ernest's mind strayed to his youth . . . when his dreams had begun. In those days he had slept in the same bed with his parents, nestled between them. Was he twelve, or thirteen? Ernest could not quite remember. He only remembered awakening to find his appendage hard and straight as a stick. It had spewed forth a liquid and he had screamed out, thinking he had some strange disease.

His cry awakened his father and mother and when the lamp was lit and his father saw him, his father grew wild with rage and marched Ernest into the kitchen where he beat him soundly across the back with his belt and gave him the solemn order that he should not touch himself in that place nor allow anyone else to touch him. After that night, Ernest was not allowed in his parents' bed. Instead, he was made to sleep alone on a makeshift cot in front of the hearth, wrapped in heavy blankets. "You are too old to sleep in contact with female flesh," his father had proclaimed. Ernest had not understood then, but of course he understood now.

Aloysius McGrath frowned at his son. "You do understand how to procreate, don't you?"

Ernest felt defeated. His father's look was withering.

"Well, I suppose you're old enough to know. I can only trust that your faith is strong enough to keep you from exercising your knowledge until you actually desire a son."

"I'm certain that it is," Ernest stumbled. At times, he wondered how he could be so charismatic and strong with others and so intimidated by his father.

"You take your instrument of procreation—the append-

21

age—and you insert it into the passageway between the, ah . . . legs of your wife. It will enlarge itself at the proper time and give forth seed and the seed will make your wife swell with child if it is so ordained. On occasion, such a coupling will not impregnate the woman. In such cases it is all right to repeat the process nightly until the woman is impregnated. But coupling is to be engaged in only when a child is desired."

Ernest stared at his father, unable to speak or even move.

"It's a thoroughly disgusting business. Best done in the dark and with as little touching as possible. The object is to train yourself to experience absolutely no enjoyment from the act whatsoever. It's best to commit yourself to prayer directly afterward."

Ernest nodded. He knew he would not enjoy it, nor even be tempted to enjoy it. It would be like his dreams—filled with pain and guilt.

"And now, to get back to the subject at hand. Let us discuss the candidates I have selected. First, Hester Pring."

"Hester Pring?" She was Mrs. Conklin's niece, a young woman of medium height and not unattractive until she opened her mouth. Her voice was high and nasal; she laughed a bit like a horse and she always blinked her eyelashes. Ernest frankly considered the latter action revealing of her lustfulness. He was certain Miss Pring was wanton.

"She fits all the qualifications, save the fact that she is not Scots. Last week I noted that she had a new bonnet, the third in three months. I suspect this indicates a certain lack of thriftiness, not to mention an overt desire to impress others."

"Next is Winifred Fraser, a good Scots woman from a fine family. From all outward appearances, she would seem ideal, save the fact that her teeth are not straight. Still, I have no doubt that she has the strength to pull a hand plow and set the land to production."

Ernest stared at the braided rug on the floor. Its colors ran into one another, much the way Winifred Fraser's words did. Winifred was a most solicitous female, a fondling creature who would no doubt devote herself to his every need, but who would never cease talking.

"Last, and I do consider her the best candidate from all perspectives, is Margot Macleod."

Ernest suddenly looked up. He was actually afraid to show any enthusiasm, though in fact, of all the women mentioned, Miss Macleod was the only one who seemed pliable enough to accept a husband as master—and Ernest intended his future wife to fully understand the words of the Lord.

"Her father's not a member of the church," Ernest noted, feeling that he ought to be the one to bring up what he was certain was the only impediment to Miss Macleod's selection.

"But her aunt, Mrs. Gordon, is, and so are several other members of her family. Miss Macleod has not missed a Sunday in church for over two years. She is quite, quite devout. I have seen the fire of faith in her eyes. She is reasonably attractive, but modest. She was reared at Lochiel, the finest farm in the Niagara, and she knows how to till the soil. Moreover, her mother died when she was quite young and she has always looked after her father, which means she can cook and sew. And her father and the rest of the clan are rich. But most of all I was most impressed when we demonstrated before that infamous den of evil, the town Inn. Miss Macleod carried her placard proudly and she stayed and prayed much longer than the others."

"She seems a good choice," Ernest cautiously admitted.

"Her only drawback—aside from the one you have mentioned—is the fact that she is young and, worse yet, educated. As you well know, I do not hold with the education of the female of our species. Still, I have considered this, and I have consulted with Dr. Simon Templeton Hobart, who has assured me that though he too has reservations about learned women, a learned woman can be quite useful as a missionary since she can better teach the savages from the scripture. As for her youth, one supposes it gives you some advantage. You can still counter her father's influence and train her properly. And I have noted that she has excellent teeth."

Ernest nodded. Margot Macleod was quiet, competent, and young. She always looked at him adoringly and he felt she would accept his word as law.

23

"I suggest you waste no time. I suggest that you send a note immediately asking for permission to call on Miss Macleod. Then I suggest you ride out to Lochiel—no later than Friday—and meet with Miss Macleod and her father so you might ask permission to court her. A proper courtship lasts at least one year, and then you can be married just before leaving for the West."

"What if her father rejects my request?"

"Then I suppose you shall have to visit Miss Pring or Miss Fraser."

The Reverend Aloysius McGrath stood up. "Our decision is made," he announced in an imperialistic tone.

Ernest nodded.

My Dear Miss Macleod,

I beg you to forgive the presumptuousness of this humble communication. I have seen you in Church each and every Sunday since my return from Chicago as an ordained Minister of the faith. We have, on occasion, spoken.

I have seen the joy of the faith in your eyes and I know you to be among the most faithful in our congregation. I trust you to be a woman capable of true forgiveness and I trust that you will forgive me should this note offend you. Though I have kept silent, I have admired you from afar and it is my deep respect and admiration that prompts me to correspond with you.

I humbly beg your personal permission to call at your home on Friday, May 11 to request your acquiesence and your good father's permission to call upon you regularly and to properly court you.

If you find me wanting, in any way, please forgive me for openly expressing my devout and honorable intentions. If you find me an acceptable suitor, I shall look forward to your return note, granting me permission to call.

Yours in the faith,
The Reverend Ernest Makem McGrath

Margot held the note to her breast and sighed. Ernest's note was the fulfillment of all her daydreams! Ernest McGrath, who would soon become another Marcus Whitman, not only knew she was alive, but had chosen to court her! Surely this meant that Ernest recognized how like the pious Narcissa she was! Surely he realized that she would make the ideal wife he would need in order to go West under the auspices of the United Missionary Society.

Margot sped down the winding staircase to the first floor of the house. "Papa! Papa!"

Ronald Macleod was forty-nine years old. He was the son of John Macleod, the grandson of Andrew Macleod, and the great-grandson of Janet Cameron Macleod and Mathew Macleod, the original builders of Lochiel. He managed Lochiel with a firm hand and was known for his good humor and generosity.

Lochiel, restored after being razed during the War of 1812, had seven bedrooms, a library, a huge kitchen, a dining room, and a large, spacious living room. The estate was on lush, rich farmland; the house sat majestically one-quarter mile off the main road. Lochiel was several miles outside of Niagara-on-the-Lake, formally called Newark but renamed after the War of 1812.

Ronald lived alone with Margot. His only sister, Peggy Gordon, lived nearby. His brother Lawrence, two years his senior, had moved to Toronto to rear his branch of the Macleod clan. Ronald's wife, Tara, had been one of the many victims of the typhus epidemic of 1847, and he had reared his two children, Margot and Kevin, alone, with some help from his married sister Peggy.

On Sunday afternoons, all the relatives would come to Lochiel bearing food for the weekly feast. Then, Lochiel was as it had once been: full of laughing children and old people telling family stories. But during the week, Lochiel was quiet. Kevin was away in Toronto, attending Upper Canada College, and Ronald and Margot shared the huge house alone—the house that Ronald always believed to be filled with the benevolent spirits of Mathew and Janet Macleod.

"Papa!" Margot's voice rang through the empty rooms.

"I'm in the parlor," Ronald called back. It was after eight o'clock, but night had not completely fallen and it was still light outside. The days were getting longer, and though this was a wet month, it was spring, and Ronald loved the spring almost as much as he loved the fall.

"You're out of breath, Margot," he said, and smiled at his daughter. He felt fortunate that his daughter was a good, intelligent, hard working young woman. He felt fortunate too that she was unusually attractive. He did not feel fortunate that she, along with her aunt Peggy, had 'gotten the religion,' and had, as a result, become unbearably pious. Not that he wasn't a God-fearing man—it was just that the Reverend McGrath and his son Ernest were a bit too much for Ronald to accept.

Ronald walked to the liquor cabinet and poured himself a drink. He could feel his daughter's disapproving eyes on his back. But she had already spoken her piece on the evils of alcohol, and he had spoken his rebuttal, rejecting her request that he give up drinking. Now there was a silent truce between them.

"Papa, something wonderful has happened."

Ronald turned and studied Margot's face. It was alive with enthusiasm. Her deep green eyes glowed.

"I like good news."

"Papa, the Reverend Ernest McGrath has written to me and requested permission to call. I think he wants to court me!"

The smile faded from Ronald's face.

"You're not happy?"

"Are you?"

"Oh, Papa, how can you ask? Ernest is wonderful! I've admired him for so long! Oh, Papa, Ernest has been chosen by the United Missionary Society to go West!"

"I heard that."

"But, of course, he cannot go without a wife! Oh, Papa, I think I love Ernest . . . I think I've always loved him."

Ronald arched an eyebrow. His daughter's taste was a mystery to him. How could a young girl so full of life be attracted to a man so full of tales of hell, fire, and damnation.

26

Ronald's own nickname for Ernest McGrath was, "Wrath McGrath."

"Well, can he?"

"Can he what?"

"Can Ernest court me?"

Ronald sighed. "Is that what you really want?"

"Of course! Every woman in the congregation wants Ernest McGrath! Of course I want him to court me! It's such an honor! Papa, don't you understand? Ernest has chosen me!"

Ronald studied his daughter. Courtship, he decided, was not after all a final commitment. Perhaps when Margot got to know Ernest her girlish crush would fade. Certainly, if he objected, Margot would become stubborn. Forbidden fruit always had more appeal, in any case. Then, too, Ronald did not believe in arranged marriages. The choice of a husband was Margot's alone. Even if he was not in favor of her selection, he considered it unwise to intervene.

"You know I don't hold with arranged marriages," Ronald said aloud. "If you're certain you want McGrath to court you, I won't object. Mind you, if I start getting lectures from either one of you . . ."

Margot looked at the glass of whiskey in her father's hand. It was true that he was not a heavy drinker. And unlike the children in Ernest's sermons, Margot had certainly never gone hungry because of her father's occasional glass of whiskey. Nor, she had to admit, had she ever seen her father drunk or in a drunken rage. He was a moderate man with what she considered to be a few bad habits. Nonetheless, Ernest would certainly not look on it that way.

"Papa, you know how Ernest feels about going to church and drinking. You hardly ever go to church and you do drink."

"When I want to worship our Maker, I go out and sit under one of our Maker's fine trees. Or, I take the canoe and go for a quiet paddle at eventide. That's when a man can best converse with God. And when I want a drink I have one, Ernest McGrath or no Ernest McGrath. After all, he's not courting *me*."

"Papa, could you just not drink when he's here? That's all I ask. He won't be here all that often, even if he is courting me. Please, Papa. Just that, just refrain when he's here.''

Ronald grumbled, but he gave in. He supposed that a good daughter who had been motherless since the age of ten deserved some consideration. After all, she had kept house and cooked for him. She was a good student and she was a loving, concerned child.

"All right, if it makes you happy. But only when he's here! And as part of this bargain, no more lectures from you, my daughter. And no more disparaging gazes from you, either. Hell, a man ought to be able to enjoy his whiskey without being made to feel guilty about it.''

"And could you watch your language, too?'' Margot asked timidly.

"Damn! I suppose so. But I make no secret of the fact that I hope you change your mind. There are plenty of fine strong men hereabouts, men who could make you happy.''

"Ernest makes me happy. Ernest is strong.''

"Ernest wouldn't last an hour pitching manure!''

"Ernest has another kind of strength.''

"I hope so. If you marry him and go West, he's going to need it.''

"That's the most exciting part. Oh, Papa, have you heard the story of Narcissa and Marcus Whitman?''

"Can't say I have.''

"Ernest and I are going to be another Narcissa and Marcus. We're going to bring the joy of the faith to the heathen Indians.''

"First, I'm not certain that Ernest's faith permits joy, and second, I'd have thought the Indians had enough afflictions already.''

"Papa!''

Ronald smiled. "No need to get all self-righteous.''

"Let me tell you about Narcissa . . .''

"If you must.'' Ronald finished his drink and poured another. He sensed that Narcissa's tale was going to be at least a three-drink story.

CHAPTER III

May 10, 1855

Blaise Baron looked out from Esquimalt on the Strait of Juan de Fuca, which separated Vancouver Island from the mainland. "A fine natural harbor," he commented. He liked the idea that the area retained its Indian name, "place of gradually shoaling waters."

There were four ships in port, three British and one French, their flags fluttering in the strong breeze.

Cory MacLean stood next to his friend. He had his pack tossed casually over one shoulder. "It was good of you to come and say good-bye," he smiled. "You're certain you don't want to come?"

Blaise laughed. "Not only don't I want to come, I'm not sure why you're going. I can't imagine spending three months on board a ship. It's just a little confining for a man of my nature."

"And you don't like the British."

Blaise nodded. "I have my reasons."

"In fact, you don't really like anyone who isn't French and from Lower Canada."

"I like you."

"I feel you've made an exception," Cory said, grinning.

"Well, you speak French. Anyway, when we met we weren't in British North America."

Cory shook his head. "You really must explain yourself sometime."

"You've been my friend for years. Let's not get into politics."

Cory nodded. He'd known Blaise Baron long enough to know when a topic of conversation had come to an end.

"So," Cory said, changing the subject, "you're really

going to go East to bring another wagon train West. Well, my friend, I wish you well. It's a hell of a trip.''

"I wouldn't say you're going on a pleasure voyage. I know you don't get seasick in a canoe, but a canoe is not exactly a seagoing vessel."

"I'm sure I'll get my sea legs soon enough."

"And then what are you going to do? Join the Royal Navy and assist Queen Victoria in colonizing the rest of the world?"

"No, I'll just come back here and take up my life where I left off—going back and forth between my farm and New Caledonia."

Blaise nodded. "Then I trust we'll see each other again in sixteen or eighteen months."

Commander Arlen strode toward them. He was smartly outfitted in his deep blue dress uniform.

"The longboat is ready, MacLean."

"Have a good trip." Cory embraced Blaise instinctively.

"You too," Blaise answered, smiling. He thrust his hands in his pockets. You had to be a little crazy to voluntarily walk off into a war, he thought to himself. Of course, Cory *was* a little crazy. That was one of the reasons they were friends, Blaise admitted.

He watched Cory climb into the longboat; the crew pushed it out into the water. He waved and Cory waved back.

"British destiny," he mumbled under his breath. The British thought it their destiny to rule the world and to impose their glorious culture on the conquered, from Ireland to Cathay. They always failed to understand that their victims already had their own cultures. To make matters worse, the British had no understanding of representative government where their colonies were concerned. Blaise was of the opinion that the British didn't know the meaning of justice. "Well, I understand British justice," he told himself. "Hell, I understand it." He knew that he was bitter, and that he always would be.

Blaise ambled off. Tomorrow he would take the steamer to Fort Steilacoom, near Seattle, and two days after that he would be on his way east. He liked Seattle. It was basically a small village built around a sawmill, but the scenery was spectacular, with the Olympic Mountains rising to the west and the Cascades rising in the east.

The Washington territory had once been part of the Oregon territory, but when Franklin Pierce took office as President of the United States in 1853, Washington became a separate territory. Pierce had appointed Major Isaac I. Stevens as governor.

Blaise had not been in the territory since that time, but he had heard disturbing stories about Stevens. Stevens, it was said, was out to eliminate the Indians.

Blaise Baron shook his head. He loved the United States for many reasons, but their Indian policy was not among them. Where the Indians were concerned, the Americans were even worse than the British were with everyone else. The Americans were intent on either changing the Indians completely or eliminating them. In all of his experience in the United States, he had never seen reasonable treaties adhered to. The Americans seemed unwilling to recognize that the Indians had their own ways and their own laws. And the British in North America were not much better, though they kept law and order without violence. Only the French really got on well with the Indians, and in Rupert's Land and New Caledonia nearly all the French who had come had married Indian women. They were blood brothers in many tribes; they came and went without difficulty.

In a few days, I'll see for myself what the new governor is like, Blaise thought to himself. And a few days after that, I'll talk with the chief of the Yakima. Certainly, if there was any truth at all to the rumor that there was going to be an Indian war in the territory, Blaise wanted to know about it. It wasn't at all desirable to bring a wagon train of new settlers into that kind of situation.

Ernest McGrath awkwardly sat astride his rented mare. The absurd man at the stable had not adjusted the stirrups properly, or so Ernest assumed. His legs, while in the stirrups, hung below the horse's belly and he seemed to remember that they ought to be higher and bent at the knee so he could hold on to the horse with his knees. He felt even more unsteady since he was obliged to keep one hand on his black, broad-brimmed hat due to a persistent wind off Lake Ontario.

Ernest clutched the reins with his free hand, attempting to guide the animal along the road. "Come on, Buttercup." He made a clicking noise, as he had heard others do. But in spite of verbal encouragement and gentle prodding with his heels, Buttercup walked along at a slow pace, stopping now and again to graze by the side of the road. Each time she stopped, Ernest nearly fell out of the saddle.

Finally, his patience exhausted, Ernest let go of his hat, firmly smacked the horse's rear, forcefully kicked her ribs and pulled her head up. Buttercup came to life suddenly and started to trot rapidly down the road. Ernest's hat blew away as his whole body bounced up and down, his legs flailing from the sides of the horse.

Responding to the pain of being battered with the rhythm of the horse's movements, Ernest gave Buttercup another swat with his hand and she paused abruptly, rearing and throwing Ernest forward and backward in almost the same instant. He clutched Buttercup's mane, and barely held on as she came down and broke into a full gallop. Ernest's heart missed a few beats as he clung to the animal for dear life.

For what seemed to Ernest an eternity, Buttercup flew down the road, and he could feel the horse's muscles ripple as she surged onward. He could see the road that led to Lochiel coming up fast, so he pulled back on the reins as hard as he could, and miraculously Buttercup responded and slowed down enough to turn up the road. Finding his voice, Ernest yelled, "Whoa Whoa!" and the horse slowed to a fast trot, but as soon as she saw the straight road leading to the Macleod house she bolted again.

Margot was standing on the front porch, while her father was sitting in his favorite old rocker placidly looking out over his domain.

"Here comes Ernest!" Margot announced with delight.

Ronald leaned forward. "Looks like he's being chased by the devil himself!"

"Oh, dear!" Margot wailed. Then she whispered, "Mercy!"

Buttercup veered off to the left and headed for a low fence gate that led to an open field. Ernest held on with all his strength and shouted, "Whoa Whoa!" but Buttercup paid him no heed.

"His horse is out of control," Ronald observed without passion, or even much concern.

Margot's hands flew to her mouth and she let out a small but ladylike scream.

Buttercup floated over the fence gate and Ernest rose in the air, momentarily suspended over the saddle, arms and legs flying free of his mount.

"Freshly manured field, nice and soft," Ronald announced, smirking.

Ronald Macleod could suppress neither his grin nor his laughter and mumbled, "Rather graceful, he is!" They watched the horse pull out from underneath Ernest's flailing figure, suspended in midair, and heard a distinct "plop" when Ernest hit the ground. The earth was too soft for Ernest to be seriously hurt. Buttercup continued on her way and stopped when she came to some sweet grass.

"What kind of damn fool can't ride a horse?" Ronald asked aloud.

But Margot was gone. She ran toward Ernest.

"Oh, dear, Reverend McGrath! Oh, mercy, are you all right?" Margot waded through the manure, trying not to sink into it.

Somewhat dazed, Ernest pulled himself up off the ground, partially aware that his hands and backside were covered with thick, damp, foul-smelling manure.

"I am quite unharmed," he called back. "Oh, do not attempt to come further, Miss Macleod. I shall be quite all right, in spite of the madness of that cursed animal! I can assure you I will speak to the stable hand about this! Fancy giving me an animal with such a vile nature!"

"Disgusting," Margot agreed. She stood where she was and waited for Ernest to reach her side. He took her hand and lifted it to his lips, pecking it ever so lightly.

"I'm dreadfully ashamed to arrive in such deplorable condition, and I've lost my hat as well. Do forgive me."

"Oh, dear Reverend McGrath, there is nothing to forgive. Please, follow me into the house where you can be cleaned up. I can offer you some refreshment, too, some nice tea and carrot cake, perhaps?"

"That sounds splendid," Ernest replied as he followed Margot toward the house. As he walked, he attempted to brush the manure away, all too aware of its pungent odor.

"Seems like you had a bit of an accident," Ronald Macleod said, desperately trying not to burst out laughing.

"Yes, sir. That horse is one of the devil's own creatures. Quite wild and uncontrollable."

Ronald's eyes traveled to the field where the horse stood placidly. She was certainly not wild, she was old Buttercup from the stable in town. Little children rode her without difficulty.

"Let her have her fill of sweet grass," Ronald suggested.

Ernest climbed the steps and held out his hand. "I'm pleased to meet you, Mr. Macleod. We don't see you often in church."

"My sister and daughter attend every Sunday. They pray sufficiently long hours to pull me right into heaven behind them," Ronald answered cheerfully.

Ernest frowned, unsure of how to respond.

"Papa . . ."

Ronald recognized Margot's pleading tone as a request to change the subject. He turned and slapped Ernest on the back. "Come along, I'll show you where you can clean up. Best I get you a fresh pair of pants, lad, or you're going to have your tea smelling like the wrong end of the barn."

Ernest flushed. "Thank you," he muttered.

"I'll go and prepare the tea tray," Margot said happily.

When Ronald and Ernest returned, even Margot had to smile. Ernest was wearing her father's old pants. They were several inches too short for Ernest's long legs, and combined with his best Sunday meeting jacket they gave him the appearance of an ungainly rag doll.

Margot set the tea tray down on the table. "Here we are," she said brightly. "Please try the cake—I made it myself."

"You are too kind, Miss Macleod. And thank you, sir. I shall see to it that these, ah . . . clothes are returned to you at the earliest opportunity."

"No need to worry—got lots of them. Only use them to shovel the dung out in the fields."

"Oh," Ernest replied, wondering why a man with so much money would do such work himself. He turned and watched as Margot poured the tea. It was difficult to understand how such a finely bred religious woman as Margot Macleod could have such an outspoken, earthy, and doubtless hard-drinking father. The wonders of heaven are numerous, he decided.

Margot, all grace and ladylike charm, handed him the tea cup and a piece of cake.

Ernest sipped his tea, then, placing the cup on the table, leaned forward. "You received my note and I received your gracious response." He looked benevolently at her, rather the same expression he affected when baptizing a newly born infant. Then he turned and leaned sideways to face Ronald, who sat in a great overstuffed chair looking relaxed and somehow unnervingly amused.

"As you no doubt already know, sir, I have come to ask your permission to officially court your daughter. My intentions are, I assure you, entirely honorable. Miss Margot has my deepest respect and admiration."

"Mine, too," Ronald answered dryly. He reached in his pocket and took out his pipe. Then he rose from the chair and walked to the table and picked up a box of matches, striking one with a flourish. Damn handy invention, he thought. The world was changing. When he was growing up, they were still lighting fires with flint and pipes with tinder boxes. He sucked in and expelled the smoke. Margot had made him promise not to drink, but she had failed to mention smoking, which also displeased the dear Reverend. Ronald waited, but Ernest said nothing to rebuke him. God knew the aroma of the sweet tobacco at least helped to kill the smell of manure, which Ernest still reeked of in spite of washing.

Ronald returned to his chair. "My daughter has indicated to me that she is willing to have you as a suitor. And as it is she you want to court, I feel the decision is hers, not mine. Therefore, for the record, I do give my permission."

"Thank you, sir," Ernest said solemnly.

"With one reservation," Ronald added.

"Sir?"

"Well, I hear tell you intend to become a missionary and follow the Oregon Trail to the West—take up the work of the Whitmans . . . was that their name, Whitman?"

"Yes, Papa. Narcissa and Marcus Whitman."

"Well, I don't know much about them, save what Margot has told me, but I do know something about the frontier. You know, when I was growing up—just a lad—this was a frontier. My father, like his father before him, took me out into the wilds to learn how to survive. Now I can tell you, son, the trip West isn't the same as a trip to Montreal or even Boston. There aren't any real roads and no coaches. In fact, from what I know, I'd say there wasn't much of anything save a lot of trees, high mountains, and snow in the winter that can come right up over a man's head. Now it doesn't seem to me that that's the kind of country for a man who can't even stay on top of a sleepy old mare."

Ernest blushed a deep red. "Sir, the mare must have eaten something that made her . . . unpredictable. I admit I haven't ridden much, but I do intend to avail myself of lessons. I will learn all that is necessary. But it is my faith that matters, I am certain. It is my intention, no matter what the struggle, to bring that faith to the heathens. I know it is most necessary."

Margot looked indulgent and dreamy. "Oh, that's so noble. I know you can do it; I know you can overcome all the problems."

"Well, son, I expect that, before you take my daughter West, you will learn to ride and learn how to live off the land. I think you need some good, sound training. Faith may lead you, son, but God helps those who help themselves."

36

"I promise I shall learn, sir."

Ronald nodded silently. Margot's eyes were gleaming with a strange ethereal glow. It was absolutely no use, he thought. She was far too smitten to see what kind of man Ernest McGrath was. But Margot did know how to survive. She was well brought up and when she and Kevin were younger, he had taken them up North and they had fished and camped; they had even lived with the Indians for a time. Margot could shoot as straight as he, she knew how to ride, to ice fish, and she knew what plants could be used for medicinal purposes. He trusted that her religion had not caused her to forget the lessons of her childhood.

Then too, Ronald always remembered what his great-aunt Helena used to say: "Children have to make their own mistakes. You can't save them from themselves."

"Well, so be it," Ronald said resolutely. "Court away." He got up out of his chair. "I've got work to do," he announced.

"Thank you, Papa."

"Thank you, sir."

Ronald turned and left the room with a wave. "Got to go out to the barn," he called from the hall as he put on his jacket. There was a nice bottle of whiskey stashed in the barn. Ronald wasn't normally a solitary drinker, but given a little time to spend with Ernest, he would surely become one. He wondered what on earth the two of them would talk about when he was gone. As he was opening the front door, Ronald heard Ernest's voice as the young man solemnly began to read from the family Bible that sat on the table. That, regrettably, seemed to answer his question. Lord, Ernest McGrath the suitor was reading from *Revelation!* The man didn't even have enough sense to read the *Song of Solomon.* Ronald smiled, remembering how he used to read Solomon's love song to his wife.

Blaise Baron had arrived at Fort Steilacoom earlier in the day and had immediately requested a meeting with Governor Stevens. It was the sixteenth of May and Blaise intended to spend little time in Fort Steilacoom. The trip east was arduous and lonely; he was anxious to begin so that he could spend time with Indian friends and still reach Fort Boise before the first snows blanketed the prairies.

As Blaise sat opposite Isaac Stevens, he decided the man was even more threatening than he was described to be by his numerous detractors. Blaise was not a person to be put off by a man's physical appearance, but Governor Stevens' looks seemed to reflect his reputed personality.

Stevens was a short, squat man with unseemly long arms and a oversized head which seemed to roll on his almost non-existent neck. Those who knew Stevens had told Blaise something of the governor's past. Stevens' father was known to have been a bitter cripple, and his mother, an extremely ill woman, who had to be physically restrained from committing suicide.

Blaise tried to take Stevens' background into account, as well as the man's deformed body, before making too harsh a judgment. He knew that Stevens had worked long hours in a New England mill when he was only twelve, and that he had a compulsion to excel. He had graduated first in his class from West Point; he had supported Franklin Pierce for President and he had been rewarded for his political efforts with the governorship of the newly created Washington Territory.

But as Blaise sat in the presence of the man, negative images began to emerge, ones that shadowed the stories of his accomplishments.

Isaac Stevens filled the chair he was in, half sitting, half lying, his legs far apart. Stevens was arrogant, and he drank to excess. His tiny eyes were already blurry, even though they had just finished dinner.

"We need more settlers," he slurred. "Plenty of room— God's country, this is . . . beautiful!"

At least that was a statement Blaise could agree with.

"I've heard there's Indian trouble," Blaise said, without elaboration.

"My children, the Indians . . . yes, they're little children, innocent and in need of guidance—guidance right to

38

death's gates!" The governor sneered. "The only decent Indian is dead and buried."

Stevens paused to spit into his ashtray. "This won't be their territory for long. Got to make way for the railroads, the miners, and the settlers. God-damned Indians don't know what to do with the land. It just sits there, they ain't got the sense to build anything on it, or work it, or use it. They're parasites, they just live off it."

Blaise held his tongue and didn't say a word about the Indians, about their deep religious feelings and how those feelings were related to the land. He knew of the Indians' strong spiritual beliefs about the land and their stewardship of it. Land was not personally owned. It was given to every man and to all men by the Great Spirit.

"What are your plans?" Blaise asked.

"Got treaties with them, getting the rest to sign on the dotted line. Hell, you know there's gold up the Coleville River. Got to make way for the folks that will be coming." Stevens laughed. "I told the Indians they didn't have to leave their lands till the U.S. Senate ratifies the treaties. . . . Told them it would take years. But if the little red sons o' bitches don't clear out, I'll send in troops to wipe 'em out."

Blaise nodded and sipped his own whiskey. He always found it interesting how a bigoted white man assumed that all other white men agreed with him.

"Gonna put them all on reservations. The smart ones will survive, the dumb ones will die. Hell, there'll be a lot less Indians! No, you got nothing to worry about, not one damn thing. Look, it's gonna be over a year . . . eighteen months before you have to travel through Yakima territory. By that time, most of the damn savages will be dead and gone."

"I'll be bringing more missionaries," Blaise told him.

"Oh, just what we need, some bible beaters! Well, what the hell, they go in and dress the dumb bastards up, teach 'em to read, and then the bastards make fine house servants 'til they pop off from some disease. Then the Indians get all riled up 'cause they say the missionaries caused the diseases and they hack 'em all up and the papers back East write a

39

whole lot of horror stories and the government sends us more troops and nobody cares what we do! I'm not a religious man, but damn, missionaries do have their function!''

"How about the Catholic priests living with the Yakima?"

Stevens shrugged and his oversized head seemed to wobble on his shoulders. He got up and walked to the table where the whiskey bottle was. He poured himself a full tumbler. "More?" he invited.

"A little," Blaise answered. He allowed Stevens to pour a couple of shots into the glass. "Whoa!" he said. "I've got a long day on the trail tomorrow."

"Well, I'd be careful. We ain't got 'em under control yet, and a lone man traveling in that country has to watch his step."

"I always watch my step," Blaise replied.

"Yeah, Frenchie, you look like a man who knows where not to walk. But even a careful man can step in shit sometimes."

"Stepping in it is one thing, wallowing in it is another." Blaise smiled. He knew Stevens was far too drunk to take his comment personally.

"Where you going to winter?"

"Fort Boise," Blaise answered without hesitation.

Stevens made a face. "Ain't much there."

"There isn't much between here and the Mississippi," Blaise replied. He drained his glass. "Think I'd better be going to bed. Tomorrow's going to be a long day."

"Want an Indian?" Stevens offered, his facial expression unchanging. "I always keep a couple around—you can have either sex, depending on your taste."

"Thanks, but no thanks," Blaise answered, shaking his head.

"Just as well. They probably all got French disease anyway."

"I prefer to think of it as English disease."

Stevens roared, "I suppose you would!"

Blaise tried to smile. Talking with this bizarre little man was like playing poker—you either kept a straight face, or you gave a misleading smile.

"You can bed down upstairs. Been a pleasure talking with you. Ain't many educated men around here."

"No, there aren't," Blaise agreed. "I thank you for your hospitality."

"No need. Out here all us white folks have to stick together."

Blaise nodded and headed upstairs. As he left, he heard the governor pour himself another tumbler of whiskey.

He opened the door to the bedroom and tossed his pack on the floor. He patted the bed and turned down the handmade patchwork quilt that covered it. Blaise ran his hand over the quilt. Each square had been carefully cut, and the tiny perfect stitching indicated long hours of work. Vaguely, Blaise wondered who had sewn the quilt and decorated the room. The bedroom had a curiously female atmosphere. Was there a lost love? A daughter? Isaac Stevens gave every outward appearance of being thoroughly disgusting; Blaise could not picture him with the kind of genteel woman who must have made the quilt, papered the walls, and planted the flowers that bloomed in pots along the windowsill. He undressed and lay down beneath the crisp white sheets. He tried to put thoughts of the governor out of his mind and concentrate on the comfort of the feather mattress beneath him. This, he reminded himself, would be the last bed he slept in for a while.

But try as he might, Blaise could not easily turn his thoughts away from Stevens. He opened his eyes and stared into the blackness. Stevens was a killer. He didn't believe the Indians to be human; he would simply try to eliminate them. But the territory was immense, and the Indians knew it. There weren't enough troops to protect the area at the present time. An Indian war could go on for two or three years unabated.

In a few days, he would assess the problem from the Indian point of view. Advance information was important. Blaise Baron prided himself on always being prepared, but he knew full well that preparation required information. So far, he was not happy with what he had learned. War or no war, he was committed to bringing in settlers.

CHAPTER IV

May 27, 1855

The manicured green lawn in front of the church was filled with the congregation which had just emerged, full of chatter, from the Sunday morning service.

"There she is, over there by the willow tree." Mrs. Conklin, the McGraths' housekeeper, nudged her niece, Miss Hester Pring, and pointed surreptitiously.

Hester blinked and instinctively tucked a stray hair under her new and most fashionable bonnet. "I don't see anything special about her," she said sarcastically. "Just a dull little girl—I don't know what he sees in her!"

"And she can read, too," Mrs. Conklin said ominously. "Lord knows what kind of filthy books she's read. Poor young Reverend McGrath, he's been tempted by the devil. Imagine his father, letting his son court a—a hussy. I can't tell you how disappointed I am that he overlooked you."

Hester lifted her head proudly. "I'm not really certain I'd want him to court me."

"Well, let me tell you, young Ernest will get more than he's bargaining for if he actually marries that one. Her father is rich, but heaven knows how they made their money. I always say, there can be no good in a family with money. And gossip! Ever since I was a little girl, I've been hearing tales about that family. Her great-aunt Jenna MacLean had a baby out of wedlock! Or at least that's what they say . . . that Josh MacLean was born out of wedlock! You know him, he comes to church sometimes. The old geezer, being born out of wedlock, I don't know how he dares come to church!"

"Disgusting," Hester said in her high-pitched voice.

"Well, let me tell you, that girl has bad blood. Wild, the whole family is wild. I just don't know what the Reverend

Aloysius McGrath is thinking of, allowing young Ernest to court her.''

"I was the one who taught the Sunday School," Hester muttered, "but she's going West to be a missionary,"

"Never mind, dear. Perhaps they'll all come to their senses.''

Across the lawn, under the willow tree, Margot stood placidly waiting for Ernest, who had promised to meet her so they might go for a walk through the town. She was aware of the envious eyes upon her, but her mind was fastened only on the thought of marrying Ernest and going West with him.

"Have you been waiting long?" Ernest asked as he came over, having finally broken away from two elderly women with whom he had been speaking.

"No, and I know you have responsibilities.''

Ernest took her arm and they began walking.

"What day would it be most convenient for me to call on you?''

"Saturdays," Margot answered. "On Sundays my family comes and there are rather a lot of people about.''

"Then Saturdays it will be," Ernest agreed. "How do you feel about the possibility of going West?''

"I feel it is my destiny, Ernest.''

"It's my calling, I know it. Margot, the poor heathen Indians need the faith.''

"I know. And Ernest, I want to teach the little children. Do you think I can do that?''

"I think you can. I think it would be wonderful.''

Margot felt his strong arm on hers. "Do you like children?''

"I love them," he replied, trying to sound sincere. In actual fact, he found them something of a bother and nothing unnerved him more than a bawling child during the service when he was preaching. And the thought of having his own children terrified him. But, until his father had insisted, he had been terrified at the thought of marriage, too. So, for the moment he put the subject aside.

He searched his mind for another topic of conversation.

44

In truth, he hadn't the slightest idea what to talk about. "I enjoyed your cake," he said finally.

"Thank you." Margot paused in front of the General Store and looked in the window. She was pleased at her reflection and at the sight of Ernest McGrath clinging to her arm. I am the envy of every woman in the congregation, she thought.

"What are you looking at?"

Margot sighed. "Everything . . . and nothing. I'm thinking of what a happy life we could have, of the adventure of traveling West and following in the footsteps of Narcissa and Marcus. Oh, Ernest, I'm sure you're just like him."

"Like Marcus Whitman?" Ernest looked at his own reflection. "I suppose I am, rather." He felt he looked like the painting of Marcus, the one done by Paul Kane.

"Do you think I can be like Narcissa?"

Ernest looked at her. "I hope so."

Margot smiled. Ernest was so good-looking, his eyes were so dark. He must have very deep thoughts, she decided. If only he weren't quite so shy. She wanted to ask how many children they should have, what their lives would be like; she wanted to know how much Ernest had admired her from afar.

"I'm deeply happy, Ernest. Happy that you are courting me."

Ernest turned and looked down at her. "You do have a lovely smile and I admire your temperament and virtue," he replied. "Yes, Margot, if our courtship goes as it should, we shall go forth and save souls together."

"Together," Margot answered.

They walked on and came within a block of the Inn. Ernest came to an abrupt halt.

"What's the matter? Should we turn back?"

Ernest shook his head. "Let's cross the road. I can't bear to pass the Inn, the stench of whiskey in unbearable!"

Margot looked at Ernest's face. His features had hardened and his eyes glowed. "It is disgusting that it's open on Sunday, the Lord's Day."

45

"It's disgusting that it's open at all. That woman Mary and the sinful women she employs should all be run out of town!" His voice rose as if he were preaching from the pulpit.

Margot felt Ernest's hand tighten on her arm. His fingers dug in and she winced. "You're hurting me, Ernest."

He let go immediately, "Oh, I'm sorry. I just get so angry when I think of all that sin and evil. They should all be pilloried!"

Margot opened her mouth to reply, but suddenly Ernest marched off toward the Inn. He took long, purposeful steps, and though his arms hung at his sides, his fists were clinched.

"Ernest!" She followed quickly behind him. "Ernest, where are you going?"

Margot stopped and watched, wide-eyed, as Ernest strode through the doors of the Inn. "Dear heaven," she said under her breath. She lifted her long skirts and followed him through the open door. She came to a halt outside the drinking room.

"Sinners!" she heard Ernest bellow from within. Then came the resounding crash of a table being overturned. Margot bit her lip and peeked into the drinking room. "Oh, dear," she breathed. Ernest had overturned a table and stood towering over two elderly men and Mary, who, hands on hips, glowered at him.

"Sinners!" Ernest shouted. "This is the Lord's Day! And the Lord thy God is vengeful!" Ernest siezed a chair and broke it over the table. Splinters of wood flew in all directions, and Mary shrieked and ran from the room.

"There is no place to hide from the Lord!" Ernest yelled triumphantly.

The two elderly drinkers scrambled to their feet and ran away just as Mary had.

"We'll close this house of infamy!" Ernest proclaimed to the empty room.

"Ernest?" Margot said timidly.

He turned and looked at her. "Come, Margot. This is no place for a lady!" He walked to her side and guided her out the door. "It must be closed," he muttered. "Their souls must be saved!"

Margot let out her breath. "Perhaps you shouldn't have done that . . . broken the chair, I mean."

"A man must do what he must do," Ernest uttered solemnly. "Margot, sinners must be punished and then brought to the Lord. "

Margot frowned slightly. Ernest, she decided, had a fair temper.

The combined British and French fleets sailed up the coast of Alaska. The Russian villages were peaceful and quiet; no action was taken against them. It would have been a useless tactic, Commander Arlen explained. There were no Russian warships in Alaskan waters, and the Russians didn't use their small Alaskan settlements as a base the way the British and French used Esquimalt.

When it left the Alaskan coast, the fleet headed out across the ocean past the chain of islands called the Aleutians. They were barren and craggy, jutting up out of the water like stones in a giant pond. Some of them, Cory was told, were volcanic, and several of the islands even gave off what appeared to be warm steam, which combined with the cold air and water to cover the ocean for miles with an eerie mist.

They reached the coast of the Kamchatka Peninsula early in June. Kamchatka was on the edge of Siberia in the easternmost region of Imperial Russia. The terrain as viewed from the sea was startling, the mountain ranges majestic and somber. Unlike the mountains of New Caledonia, visible across the Strait of Georgia from Vancouver Island, the mountains of the Kamchatka Peninsula were not wooded but were stark and cold, surrounded by a swirling fog which seemed to guard the shores and ward off visitors.

"Incredible," Cory commented as he studied the coast from where he stood on the deck. He smiled to himself. His ancestors had begun in Scotland and traveled across the sea to the New World. His parents had traveled across that new world by land. Now, having left the western side of North

47

America, he had come to the far eastern edge of the Eurasian continent, more than halfway back to Scotland.

"We'll be able to see the Russian fortress of Petropavlovsk soon," Commander Arlen told him.

Cory nodded. The fleet was large, over twenty ships. "Looking at it, it's hard to believe there's any habitation."

"There isn't much," Arlen replied. He lifted his glass. "Ah, there. . . . There it is, you can just see it through the fog." He handed Cory the glass and sounded the gong for battle stations.

"Best to be prepared," he said. "Even if we do have the element of surprise."

"A wasteland," Cory commented.

Arlen nodded. "The fortress was built in the 1740s, but the Russians have never properly settled the area. They say it's unstable land—over a hundred volcanoes, and the earth shakes often."

"There are volcanoes in New Caledonia and in the Washington territory. The ground shakes there, too."

"But not like here," Arlen insisted.

"It looks deserted," Cory said, peering through the glass. "There isn't even a flag flying."

Arlen took the glass. "You're right."

"Are we going to move in closer?"

"It could be a trap. They may be trying to lure us within range of their guns."

Cory frowned. "Perhaps we could take a smaller boat ashore."

"That's risky, very risky. I shouldn't want to have them taking prisoners."

"There isn't even smoke from fires."

Arlen bit his lip. "We'll move a bit closer, fire a volley or two and see if there's return fire."

The ships went closer on signal and Cory, unable to tear himself away, leaned over the rail of the vessel, his eyes searching the deserted shore and the ghostly Russian fort that rose out of the cold, damp fog, ominous and intriguing.

Within half an hour, the big guns of the fleet fired at the high stone walls of the fort. There was no answering fire—

48

only the returning echoes of the British and French cannons as the sounds of their volleys reverberated off the sheer cliffs of the peninsula.

"No return fire," Cory said, feeling vindicated. "I really think it is deserted."

"Even I have trouble believing that the Russians would let us get this close without returning fire," Arlen allowed.

Cory found himself overcome with curiosity to see the Russian fort; he wanted to set foot on this far outpost of the Russian empire. "I'll go ashore," he suddenly said. "I'm a civilian, you'll lose no men."

"And if you are taken prisoner?"

Cory shrugged. "I don't think there's anyone there."

"You're a guest on this voyage. You're not even in the military. I can't take the risk."

Cory was insistent. "I'm volunteering. If I go ashore, we could find out more about the fortifications." He smiled. "Surely you have to report to the Admiralty."

"And if the report reads that I lost one of the most important men in the colony of Vancouver, I won't look too competent."

Cory laughed. "Arlen, I've wandered over half of North America! I've been in Indian uprisings, I've been marooned in the Rockies in the winter, I've lived off the land for most of my life. Good lord, man, you brought me on this trip because I speak Russian and because I'm an adventurer. Let me be what I am."

"I'll need a letter absolving me of responsibility."

"I'll write it."

"You understand that you won't be able to stay ashore long."

Cory nodded.

"All right. You'll have two hours. If you're not back in two hours, we'll have to leave."

"Agreed."

Cory pulled the oars of the small boat through the gray surf of the natural harbor adjacent to the fort. He climbed out of the boat and waded through the ice cold water, dragging the rowboat and beaching it. The silence was eerie; the sky and sea were cold and gray. The stone fort loomed before him in the fog.

Cory walked toward it and found that its gates swung open. It was not unlike other forts, save the fact that it was stone like the mountains surrounding it. Inside, there was no green grass, only the hard ground where Cory could see the rutted marks left by wagons. When it rained, or when the winter snows melted, the place must have been a river of mud, he thought.

He strolled to a building that looked as if it might be a barracks. Cautiously, he opened the great wooden door and walked in. The hearth was cold, the rooms empty. Clearly the Russians had left some time ago. There was no trace of recent habitation, no sound or evidence of defending troops.

He climbed the rickety ladder to the second floor and poked his head through the opening.

"Don't move!"

Cory all but lost his balance on the ladder as he whipped around to meet the long end of a musket, its barrel only inches from his head.

The Yakima Valley in the Washington territory was lush and fertile. It was entirely rimmed by mountains, and was irrigated by the streams that flowed from them when the winter snows melted. Part of the valley was heavily wooded, part was rich grassland. It was June 15, and the days were growing longer and the temperature warmer.

For nearly two weeks, Blaise Baron had enjoyed the hospitality of the Yakima chief, Kamiakan. He had learned more than he had bargained for from Kamiakan, from Chief Leschi of the Nisqually Tribe, who was also a guest in the village, and from an old friend, Father Jacques Pelletier, a French Canadian Catholic priest.

Tonight was the last night of Blaise's stay with the Yakima, and so he sat by the fire with Father Pelletier, Kamiakan, and Leschi. The conversation sounded much like those that had preceded it during the two weeks: a summing-up of complaints, and expressions of concern over the war clouds that were forecast by the leaders of Indian tribes from Puget Sound to the American Rockies.

"By treaty they have restricted the Yakima to this valley," Kamiakan said solemnly. "We once regarded all the land as ours, all that lies beneath the stars of the heavens. We were happy to share the land—apart from our sacred burial grounds, which belong not to us, but to the spirits." He shook his head sadly. "But we are no match for their guns. . . . So when we were offered this valley, we took it. There is food, the land is good. We thought we could live here in peace. But now they say they are going to bring white people into this area, too. We said, this is forbidden by the treaty you made us sign. This valley is ours and ours alone."

"I have sent letters to the governor," Father Pelletier added. "I have warned him that the Indian agent, Bolon, is an ignorant, bigoted, insulting man. Bolon threatened to bring troops here even though this valley is by treaty given to the Yakima. And I am not alone. Three other priests have also written, but there is no response. Ah, my friend, the Yakima and the others will lose patience. There is no holding back the young warriors of the tribe. Bolon cares nothing for the survival of the people."

Blaise shook his head. "And you have received no reply from the governor."

"None."

"It is so with the Nisqually people as well," Leschi intoned.

"I have no cause to disbelieve you," Blaise replied. Indeed, Leschi, chief of the Nisqually, was known for his honesty. He was a large, powerful man who was extraordinarily intelligent and who had a great deal of compassion, even for his foes.

"There is room for settlers," Leschi maintained. "If they do not try to settle on treaty land, if they respect our burial grounds, and if they live in peace, we welcome them. Even missionaries, if they bring wisdom and respect the Great Spirit. But those who come do not simply till the land. Instead, they bring armies and guns, whiskey and disorder.

51

They do not want to share the land or restrict themselves to any part of it. They demand it all. They talk of railways and mines."

"I am bringing settlers," Blaise reiterated.

"And they are welcome, but not on this treaty land of the Yakima."

Blaise nodded. "The wagon train must pass through this territory."

Kamiakan stared into the dancing flames of the fire. He seldom looked at those to whom he spoke. It was impolite to stare into the eyes of another, to try to read the soul through its windows. "To pass through, is not to settle. You will have peace on your journey insofar as I can guarantee that peace. But if things worsen, I can guarantee nothing. The young are impatient with injustice."

"I understand," Blaise told him. This part of the trip, he now believed, would be extremely hazardous, because having met the governor he had no cause to hope that the situation would not worsen.

"What manner of man is this governor?" Father Pelletier asked. "He does not keep his promises, not even those committed to paper and ratified by his own government."

"He is a man like his agent, Bolon," Blaise replied. "But he might sacrifice his agent to prevent a war."

"If he is like Bolon, then there will be another agent who is equally bad," Leschi observed.

"I agree. You must use great caution dealing with Governor Stevens. I believe he would take any excuse to eliminate as many of your people as possible. In fact, he all but told me that he would. He is not a man who disguises his evil intentions."

"What you say means there is no hope for us except war," Leschi concluded.

"But war will achieve his goal, not yours," Blaise stressed. "Still, I cannot lie to Leschi or Kamiakan. I cannot tell you that the governor of this territory is a just man when he is not."

"There is no hope," Kamiakan said bitterly.

"There is always hope," Blaise told him. "One can hope

the American government will replace him with a more just man. There is hope you and Leschi and the other great chiefs can control the warriors of your tribes until that replacement takes place.''

"And if we can't, we will be committed to defending our honor. The Yakima, the Nisqually, the Walla Walla, the Moxmox, and the Peopeo will rise as one nation.''

"I hope it will not come to that.'' Blaise was sincere. "I will talk with all the settlers I bring, and I will write to Washington myself in hopes of ridding the territory of Governor Stevens.''

"And will they read and understand?'' Leschi asked.

Blaise turned his head and looked at Leschi's profile. His face was stone hard, his expression burdened with sadness.

"That is a matter for the Great Spirit,'' he answered. '' I am not a man of influence among the leaders in Washington. I can relay the truth and warn of the dangers ahead.''

Leschi nodded. "It is all any man can do.''

Cory caught himself on the floor of the opening. "I won't move,'' he said, almost smiling. It was hard not to smile. At the other end of the musket stood a very attractive young woman with long blond hair and large, round, blue eyes. He could easily have grabbed the barrel of the gun and whipped it away from her, causing her to fall to the floor, but instead he stood still.

"Could I get off this ladder?''

She looked at him quizzically. She had spoken to him in English, but perhaps she only knew a little English.

"Can I come up?'' he asked in Russian.

She nodded and took a step backward, still pointing the musket at him.

Cory pulled himself through the opening and stood up straight, noting that now the musket was unpleasantly pointed directly at the lower part of his body. It might have made him nervous save for the fact that it was a very old-fashioned musket and he seriously doubted the young woman holding it could even fire it.

53

"You Englishman?" she asked in a heavy Russian accent.

"Da," Cory replied. It was too complicated to explain that he was from a British colony in North America.

"You speak Russian. Why?"

Her face was tense—beautiful, but tense. Her voice sounded angry and she looked a little frightened.

"I've traded with the Russians in Sitka, lived with them for over a year," he replied honestly.

"Sitka?"

"In North America, on the coast of Alaska. There are Russians there."

"North America." She repeated the words in Russian. "Do you speak English?"

"Not so good," she answered, frowning.

Cory looked around. "Are you alone?"

"That's not your concern," she snapped.

Cory shrugged. Obviously she was alone, but what the hell was a beautiful woman doing in a deserted Russian fort on the other end of nowhere?

"Ships, there are ships in the harbor. English?"

Cory nodded.

"I want to go to England," she said flatly.

"The ships are not going to England. They're going back to the west coast of North America."

"I want to go to the west coast of North America, then."

Cory laughed. At least she had an adaptable itinerary.

"Do not laugh at me!" She angrily jabbed him with the end of the musket. "I am nobility. You do not laugh at Anya Ivanovna Morozova!"

"Nobility?" Cory raised an eyebrow. She was dressed in men's clothes. This was not exactly how he imagined a member of the Imperial Russian family to look.

"Are you a princess?" he asked, trying not to laugh.

"Not yet, you dolt. That is why I am here. My father is an officer, my father gave me to a stupid fat count to marry. I will not marry him. He is too old, too stupid, and too fat! I want to go to North America!"

"That's the British Navy out there. I can't take you to North America."

"You will. Everyone is gone from here. They all left two days ago. I hid. I do not go to marry fat count. I will starve if I stay here. The fools took everything."

"I'm sure your father will come back for you."

"When he discovers I am not with them. That is why you will take me to America."

Cory fought a smile. When he had rowed ashore, this was one situation he had not bargained for. "Miss, in case you are unaware of the facts, there's a war between Russia and England."

"I know that."

"We don't take women as prisoners of war."

"I am not your prisoner. You are mine!"

"I still can't take you to North America. And if I did, what the hell would you do there?"

"I would live in exile until my father comes to his senses."

"And then what?"

"Then he would send a ship for me and I would return to Russia and marry a man I love. One who is not old and stupid."

"But no one will know where you've gone."

"I send message."

"From North America?"

"By ship."

"It could take two years to arrive." Cory shook his head.

"It will take my father two years to come to his senses."

"Ah, look, I don't know how to explain this, my Russian isn't that good . . . but North America is a wilderness. How would you live?"

"I have money. I have gold, I have jewels."

"Where?"

"That too is not your concern. Do not question Anya."

"But you ask me questions."

"You are a peasant."

At that, Cory did laugh. "There are no peasants in North America," he answered.

"Then who does the work?"

"Everybody."

"There are peasants everywhere," she answered. "You are lying to me."

Cory eyed her and thought, I could easily take the gun away from her. But if I did, I would deprive Arlen of dealing with this rather interesting situation.

"All right," he answered. "But first I have to look around here, make some notes."

"You are a spy!"

"Not exactly."

"I do not want you to make notes."

"Sorry, I can't go back to the ship without them. If I do, neither of us goes to North America," he lied.

She looked skeptical, but after a moment nodded. "I do not care," she finally said. "Make notes. Then you take me to North America."

Cory took out his paper and pen. He retreated down the ladder under Anya's watchful eyes and proceeded to note the dimensions of the garrison, the thickness of the walls, the number of possible gun implacements, and other vital information.

"Done," he said after a time.

"Good. We go."

Cory led Anya to the rowboat. He pushed it into the surf and invited her to get in.

"Carry me! Anya does not get her feet wet!"

"How can you keep the gun on me if I'm carrying you?"

Anya scowled. "If you try anything, I'll bite you!"

"Oh, well, I wouldn't want that." He picked her up and carried her to the boat, dumping her in none too gently.

"Dolt! Peasant dolt!"

"You know, you don't have the world's most pleasant personality," he said, rowing out into the gentle breakers.

"Personality?"

"Manner—you don't have any manners."

"I am very well bred, superbly educated, and quite beautiful. Who are you to tell me I have no manners?"

Cory laughed and shook his head. Arlen was going to

love this. Delivering Anya to him was a sort of colonial's revenge. Not only was she ill-mannered, she was haughty.

"At least you're not modest," he replied, smiling.

"I have nothing to be modest about."

As they climbed the ladder, Commander Arlen looked down on them curiously.

"And what is this?" he asked, as they clambered onto the deck and stood opposite him.

"This is Miss Anya Ivanovna Morozova. She is alone at the fort and she wants to go to North America. As you can see, she has a gun and I found myself quite helpless."

Arlen's facial expression didn't even change. Well, Cory thought, you had to hand it to the British. No matter how unlikely the situation, they never flinched.

"I sense there's more to the story than that," Arlen said.

"Oh, quite a lot more. And by the way, here are the notes on the fort. Miss Morozova was kind enough to allow me time to make them."

"Good. Now tell me about her."

"I can talk," Anya said imperiously. She looked at the gold braid on Commander Arlen's uniform. "You are not a peasant," she smiled. "You are a true English gentleman."

Arlen smiled and bowed. "At your service, Madam."

"I want diplomatic asylum. I request it."

Arlen frowned slightly. "May I ask why?"

"A family matter. I have money. I want to go to America."

To Cory's surprise, Arlen nodded.

"And I see no reason not to accept your request. In fact, I shall ask Mr. MacLean to look after you, since he speaks Russian. You will be delivered to the port near Fort Victoria within four weeks. In the meantime, you will be assigned a cabin."

"You are most gracious," Anya returned. "You may kiss my hand."

Arlen bowed and took her hand, kissing it graciously. "My dear, it is a pleasure."

Mischievously, he turned to Cory, hardly able to cover his own smirk. "Your responsibility, Mr. MacLean."

CHAPTER V

July 15, 1855

The hot summer sun reflected off the lake and the humidity in the air caused a hazy fog to settle over the land. Ernest McGrath carried a large basket and Margot walked by his side, lifting her skirts slightly to avoid the dust on the ground as the two of them followed the secluded pathway to the sandy shore of Lake Ontario.

"It's a lovely day for a picnic," Margot enthused.

"A bit hot in the sun." Ernest ran his finger around his high collar. He felt sticky and uncomfortable.

When they reached the sandy beach, Margot spread out a large blanket. "You can put the basket down, Ernest." She smiled warmly at him from beneath her broad-brimmed bonnet.

Ernest eyed her and tried to smile back. She was, he had to admit, astoundingly beautiful. Much too beautiful; the kind of woman who could tempt men. But, he reminded himself, she was prudent. After all, she was the woman his father had chosen for him.

Ernest had been dreading this day. He had been courting Margot since May, but his courtship always took the form of afternoon calls at her home. It was true that her father always found a reason to be absent except during dinner, but he knew that Ronald Macleod was around and about; he never really considered himself to be alone with Margot. But now he was alone with her. And after two and a half months of calling on her, he would certainly be expected to formally propose marriage and even to kiss her. Unconsciously, Ernest looked at her full lips. He steeled himself for the task ahead. In spite of her virtue, Margot would expect him to behave in a certain way and he deemed it wise to do the best he could to fulfill her expectations. There would be time enough after they were married for him to teach her how to behave toward him.

Usually he read the Bible to her and sometimes he read religious poetry. But today he had no Bible with him, and no poetry either. He would be forced to make conversation, something he also dreaded. He sighed. It would have been easier with Hester Pring, first because she was unattractive and second because she never stopped talking long enough to allow him to say anything. He considered his lack of ability to converse with Margot a strange contradiction in his personality. He had no difficulty whatsoever talking to the congregation for hours, but left alone with Margot Macleod, he was tongue-tied in minutes.

"Ernest, do sit down and rest."

Her eyes beckoned him, and awkwardly Ernest sat down, folding his long legs under himself.

"I love the sound of the gentle waves against the shore," Margot said, looking at the surf as it lapped on the sand.

"It's not like the ocean," Ernest replied.

"I've never seen the ocean, but I've seen Lake Superior. It's much more turbulent than Lake Ontario. My father says it's more like the ocean."

"Lake Ontario is like Lake Michigan," Ernest commented thoughtfully.

"Oh, Ernest, tell me about it. Tell me about Chicago and what it's like."

Ernest stared out at the lake. "I don't like to talk about Chicago," he said flatly. Ernest's mind left the present and he conjured up vague images of Chicago. He visibly trembled.

"What's the matter, Ernest?"

"Nothing." He didn't feel like delivering a sermon at the moment. In any case, he could not discuss Chicago without becoming angry. It was a terrible, evil community. During his year of training there he had felt he was in hell itself. The streets were lined with bars . . . loose, immoral women, dreadful, wanton women came right up to a man in the street and offered to . . .

Margot reached over and gently touched his hand. "Ernest, why did you choose to court me?"

Ernest looked at her steadily. "Because you are devout, attractive, and pleasant. Because you would make a good—" the words stuck in his throat "—companion," he finally finished with difficulty.

Margot glowed. Ernest was so good-looking! And his thoughts were so deep. All the other girls in the congregation adored him. But it was she who had him, and far from being annoyed at their stony glances during church service, she relished them. The others were jealous of her.

"Margot?" Ernest surmised this might be the proper moment to get his proposal over with.

"Yes, Ernest?" She looked at him with her large green eyes.

"Margot, I've been calling on you for the last two and one half months. I would like to go to your father and ask for your hand in marriage. Of course, we wouldn't be married until next spring."

"Oh, Ernest. . . ." Margot moved a little closer and Ernest felt himself flush again. This was the moment. He felt vaguely as if he were another person, as if some force outside his own body were propelling him. He reached out and put his hands on her shoulders, then leaned across and pecked her on the lips.

But Margot slipped her arms around his neck and kissed him back full on the mouth. Suddenly she was closer, and Ernest could feel her breasts pressing against his chest.

He suddenly jolted away from her, "Margot, you must stop!" He dropped to his knees and began praying aloud in the same tone he would have used before the congregation. His eyes were tightly closed against the sight of her. When he finished his prayer, he was somewhat calmed. He opened his eyes and looked at her.

Margot had struggled to her feet and was looking at him with wide, innocent green eyes, "Oh, Ernest . . . Ernest, I want to be the mother of your children. I want to be with you always . . . please, go and speak to my father, I do accept your proposal!"

61

Ernest could feel his face bright red. He nodded dumbly.

"Are you all right?" Her face was filled with concern.

"I had to pray," he explained. "I felt the spirit come over me."

She smiled at him benevolently. "I understand. But you do look flushed."

Again he nodded, then mumbled, "The heat, it's just the heat."

"We could move to the shade there." She pointed off toward a grove of trees."

"Let's." Ernest scrambled to his feet and seized the picnic basket. He fairly fled to the shade of the tree, then leaned against it, nursing his silent anger.

Margot spread out the blanket on the sparse grass. "Is it better here?"

"Yes, Margot, but I must speak with you."

"Of course, Ernest."

He sat down when she did. "Margot, I have the greatest admiration and respect for you. You are young and innocent. You do not understand how easily a man can be tempted by the devil."

"Oh, Ernest, I know you are above temptation."

"I am above giving in to it, but no man is above being tempted."

Margot smiled. "You have such strength."

"Margot, you musn't tempt me by . . . by kissing me that way. I want you to become my wife. We must, ah . . . only be close when it is desirable to procreate. That is, after we are properly married. I know you did not intend to tempt me, you are much too innocent to realize . . . that. . . ."

Margot studied his face. Oh, he did desire her! She had felt it in his kiss. And after they were married they would make such beautiful love together! But of course, Ernest was right. They must wait, she must wait to be taken by him in beautiful and honorable Christian love.

"I understand, Ernest." She patted his hand. "I can wait and I have faith in you."

Ernest patted her hand in return.

"And when we kiss, I think it advisable that we don't embrace."

Margot nodded. Great heaven, she thought. I must be a very tempting woman indeed.

"I offer my sincere apologies for the fact that our journey was delayed. One cannot predict the seas," Commander Arlen said as he held Anya's hand for what to Cory seemed a somewhat extended period. To say that Arlen had been solicitous of Anya Ivanovna Morozova would have been something of an understatement. He gave up his cabin to her, he gave her clothes purchased in the Orient that he supposedly was taking to his wife, and he dined with her every evening, with Cory in attendance to translate. Aside from these dinners, Anya had spent most of the trip either in her cabin alone or walking with Arlen on deck, asking questions and attempting to improve her English.

Anya doted on Commander Arlen. She was pleasant in every way to him, obviously considering him to be a man who equaled her God-given station in life. But with Cory, Anya was cold and distant. She referred to him as a 'peasant' less often, but it was clear that she still thought of him that way.

"I apologize for having to leave you in such a poor and remote possession of the British Empire," Arlen added. "But you will find life calm here. There exists a certain charming, although limited, society."

"I shall manage," Anya cooed, her large blue eyes seeming to devour Captain Arlen.

"And where do you suggest I take our honored guest?" Cory said somewhat sarcastically.

"Well, to Craigflower Farm, for a start. She can be entertained there until she's able to find accommodations of her own."

Cory nodded. It was as good a suggestion as any. He looked at Anya. She was certainly going to cause trouble. First, there were hardly any women near the farm, second, there were no unattached women, and third, even he had to admit that she looked close to ravishing in the long brocaded

63

gown she was wearing. But ravishing or no, her miserable personality would probably put off the most wanton mountain man. And her conceit was unbearable.

"We should be going," he said with resignation. He watched glumly as two crew members took Anya's trunk to a carriage. The trunk too was a gift from Arlen. It was filled with the English-style gowns he had commissioned the dressmakers of Shanghai to make for his wife.

"You have been hospitable indeed," Anya said, smiling at Arlen. "I shall remember your kindness forever."

"What did she say?" Arlen asked.

"She said you've been hospitable and she'll remember you."

"Tell her I shall visit whenever we put into port," Arlen announced.

Cory looked at him, standing there on the dock in the middle of nowhere, dressed from head to toe in his dress uniform, ludicrously out of place. Cory turned to Anya and translated, but it was only in the translation that he realized that Arlen had long-term plans. Probably he hoped to make her his mistress. This, after all, was a port Arlen didn't have a woman in.

"I should be charmed to receive you."

"What did she say?" Arlen was grinning like some animal coming in for the kill.

"She said, fine."

"Take good care of her, Cory," Arlen said, slapping him on the back.

"You're mad," Cory said between his teeth.

Arlen laughed. "A delightful lady," he replied lecherously. "I do believe you're jealous, old man."

"Not likely," Cory bluffed. No. She might look inviting, but she was shrewish and full of conceit.

"I certainly am looking forward to my next trip to this port," Arlen grinned.

Cory scowled. For all he knew, they were already lovers. He certainly didn't know what either of them did at night. After all, he was not sharing quarters with Arlen. "You're a charming bastard," he mumbled.

"Terribly," Arlen replied. "Well, you should be on your way," he said, finally.

"Follow me," Cory said to Anya.

She gave Arlen one last dazzling smile and followed Cory to the carriage. She stood still while he opened the door, and climbed in, looking vaguely annoyed that no one was there to assist her. Cory climbed in behind her and sat down opposite. She ignored him and looked out the window.

The driver jolted off down the dusty lane. They bumped along for half an hour before Anya said a word.

"There's nothing here," she said, still looking out the window. "Nothing but trees."

"Lumber's a growing industry. I told you this was a wilderness."

"Are there no people?"

"There are people in Victoria and at the farm. Listen, Kamchatka was not exactly overpopulated."

"It is the most barren, miserable outpost of Imperial Russia."

Cory smiled. At least for once she didn't disagree with him. "Well, this is the most distant, isolated outpost of the British Empire."

"Why do you stay here, then? Why do you live here?"

"I like it."

"You probably have no choice."

Cory scowled again. "I have a choice. I'm a reasonably rich man. I can go where I want."

She looked up at him quizzically. "Rich? You did not tell me you were rich. You don't dress as if you were rich, you don't look as rich as Commander Arlen. You did not offer me a trunk-load of furs."

Cory stared out of the carriage window, feeling considerable anger. "You claim to have jewels and money, but you weren't dressed that way when I found you. Look, men in this territory have money from trading, from finding gold. But they don't necessarily show it. Arlen is an officer in the British Navy. He just has gold braid on his uniform. He's probably not rich."

Anya frowned. "Not rich?"

So, Cory thought, that was her concern. "Not rich," he confirmed.

"But he gave me beautiful gowns," she protested. "He is a true gentleman."

He wanted to tell her she was naive, but he didn't know the word in Russian. "He just wants to go to bed with you," he finally managed, deciding to be blunt with her, and frankly hoping to shock her.

"But all men want to go to bed with me." She answered him with what Cory thought was her typical display of modesty.

"I don't," he lied emphatically. And sadly he admitted to himself that it was a lie. The truth was, he hadn't slept with a white woman since he and Blaise had been in San Francisco. *I'd have to be dead not to find her body desirable*, he thought.

"You are not telling the truth," Anya said boldly. "I know I am beautiful. But it is of very little concern to me. I certainly would not give myself to you."

"How about to Arlen?" Cory replied somewhat meanly.

"Nor to him. I shall marry a rich man."

Cory mumbled, "Wasn't the man your father wanted you to marry rich?"

"Very. But he was old and fat. I want to marry a handsome, young, rich man."

"Naturally." Cory shook his head. At least one could not fault her for lack of honesty.

"We're coming to the farm," he noted.

Anya looked out the window. "Ah, a house! Oh, a nice dacha! I am looking forward to a bath."

Cory folded his arms over his stomach. He found himself thinking of her in the bathtub. Long wet blond hair, falling over lovely white bare shoulders. He allowed his mind to linger on his fantasy.

"Do you live here?"

"No, a few miles from here. I have my own house and farm."

"You live alone?"

"Most of the time. A lot of the time I'm gone."

"Gone where?"

"Gone for furs . . . across to the mainland, or up north. Then I live with the Indians."

"Who lives in your house?"

"It is looked after by the people here . . . it stays empty."

She nodded as if saving the information for later. Then, just as the carriage ground to a halt before the large farm-house, she leaned over to him. "When will you go away again?"

"Soon," Cory answered.

"And how long will you be gone?"

"Months—maybe six or nine."

"Oh." She leaned back and actually smiled at him.

Captain Langford greeted Anya with much enthusiasm, though Langford's wife seemed to look on her somewhat skeptically.

"You'll stay for dinner," Langford pressed Cory. "Help us to get to know our guest."

Cory thought of his house. It was closed up and would take a full day to re-open. It was already four in the after-noon. "I'd be delighted," he smiled. "And for the night too, if possible. The house has been closed for some months."

"Of course!"

Captain Langford turned to his wife. "I imagine our guest would like to bathe and rest before dinner."

Mrs. Langford nodded. She was a plump little woman with a proper British attitude toward all things. "This way," she said. She led Anya away, and Cory watched as the two women retreated up the stairs.

Langford walked to the liquor cabinet. "And you?"

Cory smiled. "I'll have a drink first."

"Thought you might. I say, that is an astoundingly attrac-tive woman."

"She's quite arrogant," Cory told him.

Langford laughed. "But beautiful."

Cory held out his hand to accept the offered whiskey. "She does speak some English."

"Well, we have the school. She can go with the children until she masters the language. My heaven, that woman will attract a lot of suitors in this territory."

"I suppose so," Cory said casually.

"I must say, old man, you don't seem so terribly interested."

"She's conceited. She wants to marry a rich, handsome man."

"I'd say you qualify. I mean, I don't specialize in seeing what females see in a man, but my wife always says you are one of the most handsome men in the territory. And I know you are one of the richest."

Cory smiled. That description more often went to his sometimes-partner, Blaise Baron, who had the added attraction of being somewhat mysterious as well.

"I'm not the type to settle down. In any case, I'll be leaving soon for New Caledonia."

"Good lord, man, you just got back from an adventure at sea. Don't you ever rest?"

"Sometimes. That's why I built the house and farm. . . . It gives me something to come back to. But I'm feeling a little itchy."

Captain Langford nodded.

Cory drained his glass. "I'll go upstairs now and get cleaned up."

Langford smiled. "Have you clean clothes?"

Cory nodded. "In my bag." He hoisted it over his shoulder.

Dinner at Craigflower Farm that night was the usual triumph, a six-course meal beginning with prawn appetizers and ending with Mrs. Langford's famous flan. It was served on a white linen tablecloth, on English bone china, and with the finest silver. All the officers who were entertained at the farm always said that the meals and their presentation rivaled the dining in the finest homes of London. In fact, Cory reflected, there was a certain spirit of class in the little colony that uplifted all its residents. The genteel population was few in number, but they lived elegantly and always considered themselves to be the very finest representation of British civilization. The food was grown locally, except of course for the fine teas which were imported by British ships sailing East out of the Indian Ocean. Fine china, silver, and European paintings were likewise imported, even though there was a local furniture maker and a potter of some talent.

"What a splendid meal," Anya praised. "I have not eaten in such elegance since I left the palace in Saint Petersburg!"

"We try, my dear," Mrs. Langford answered.

Anya sighed deeply as she finished the remainder of her flan. "It must be terribly difficult to be so far from civilization."

"Well, we get lots of goods from San Francisco, and the British ships always bring exotic spices and all kinds of wonderful things."

"Still, it must be difficult."

"We British always manage, and"—she lowered her voice to a whisper—"when we don't, we're masters of subterfuge."

Anya tilted her head and turned to Cory for help. He did his best to translate.

"You know," continued Mrs. Langford, "my sister's husband is in the foreign service and they're on the Gold Coast—in darkest Africa. Well, they have plenty of servants, but the climate is simply appalling and the ants simply get into everything. She wrote me once about a tea party at the Governor General's mansion. The little sandwiches were simply crawling with ants, but everyone ate them anyway—form, you know. You can't just lift up a sandwich at the Governor General's house and complain that it is full of ants. It simply wouldn't do at all! Yes, form is terribly important to maintaining one's position."

Anya listened, but clearly she didn't understand.

"I'm not sure I can translate that story," Cory finally said.

Mrs. Langford smiled sweetly. "No matter."

"Lucky us. We only have bears in the outhouse!" Captain Langford roared. He was drinking his sixth whiskey.

Mrs. Langford gave him a withering look and he straightened up in his chair, properly chastised.

"What are your plans, my dear?"

Anya seemed to understand. "Mr. MacLean is going on a trip. He has been kind enough to offer me his house while he is gone." Anya spoke in halting phrases. She smiled devastatingly at Cory, and he looked at her in amazement.

"Oh, Cory, how wonderful of you! That's a splendid idea."

"Very generous, old man," Langford exclaimed. He winked at Cory. "Something to come home to?"

Cory flushed. How the hell could she say something like that? And now what was he to say? "We haven't worked out the details," he stuttered. He looked across the table at Anya. She looked back warmly and fluttered her dark eyelashes.

"Mr. MacLean is so kind."

"He's a most eligible young man," Mrs. Langford observed. "Health, wealth, and he's not married."

Cory felt like crawling under the table. The Langfords seemed to be deepening his dilemma by the second.

"What a pity, I had hoped you'd stay with us for a time." Captain Langford lamented.

"We go tomorrow," Anya smiled. "But, of course, I will need to hire servants."

"Of course," Cory said dully, his head swimming.

"I can send over one of the Indian women. She's very well trained."

"Oh, you are too kind."

"Everyone is too kind," Cory mumbled.

"I think this calls for another drink! Now we'll have a new neighbor." Their host poured some more wine. "I hope you like this. It was given to me by Commander Arlen."

"Very good," Anya nodded.

Cory looked up and met her blue eyes. She met his gaze unflinchingly.

"Tell us about Russia," Mrs. Langford asked. "In spite of the war, it's always sounded so romantic to me."

Cory drained his glass and didn't object when Langford repeatedly refilled it. The conversation droned on. After what seemed an eternity, they adjourned to the parlor.

"I feel the need for fresh air," Cory announced. It was both the truth and an excuse. "Please, Miss Morozova, let me show you the garden."

Anya smiled and took his arm. Cory guided her out the door and away from the house until they were safely out of earshot of the Langfords. His head was pounding from the wine, his stomach churned with suppressed anger. In his entire life, he had never met such a conceited, arrogant, self-possessed young woman! How dare she announce she was moving into his house! And how dare she do so in such a way that he couldn't object? How dare she assume! How dare she have the effrontery to think about entertaining Arlen in his house!

Anya paused in front of the flower bed. "The garden is lovely. Nothing grows in Kamchatka. I haven't seen flowers since I left—"

"Saint Petersburg!" Cory interrupted angrily. He grabbed her by the shoulders. "How could you? I didn't invite you to live in my house. How could you say such a thing!"

Suddenly, great tears welled in her huge blue eyes. "You are hurting me," she said, in a truly wounded tone.

Cory dropped his arms immediately. The tears were running down her face and he felt ashamed.

"I'm sorry," he said softly. "But you made me angry."

"Do you not think I am frightened in a strange place with strange people? I do not want to live with other people. What difference does it make if I stay in your house? You will not be there!" She was sobbing now and her shoulders shook.

Cory bit his lip. She was young and, doubtless if she were normal, she was frightened. Perhaps, he reconsidered, all her arrogance was show, and he had to admit that what she said made perfect sense. What difference did it make if she lived in the house? He wouldn't be there anyway.

Cory nodded. "All right. You can live there."

Anya smiled. "I will look after it," she said haltingly.

71

Cory took his handkerchief out of his pocket and wiped the tears off her cheeks. She blinked at him with eyes that had a childlike innocence.

"You are really quite nice," Anya allowed.

"For a peasant," Cory answered. Then he remembered Arlen. "But you are not to entertain Commander Arlen in my house."

Anya looked down at the ground. She didn't answer, but she nodded.

"We'll go tomorrow. I'll show you around."

"Thank you."

It was an improvement, he thought. At least she had said "thank you" for something.

CHAPTER VI

April 6, 1856

". . . and God bless Queen Victoria!" Ernest McGrath intoned as he finished his sermon.

The faithful congregation responded in unison. "God save the Queen!"

"And we thank God that the Crimean War has ended, even though we still bear hardships," Ernest put in for good measure.

The war, which had begun in March 1854, had ended two months ago, but its effects were still being felt in the little province of Canada West.

The war had resulted largely because of power conflicts between Imperial Russia and Great Britain, but it had certainly not been fought without religious significance. The Russians had apparently demanded the right to exercise control over the Orthodox subjects of the Ottoman sultan, and the dispute had grown between the French and the Russians over the privileges of Russian Orthodox and Roman Catholic monks in the holy places of Palestine. Britain had supported the Turks. The battles were fierce, and the names Sevastopol and Balaklava became known around the world, even in the remote province of Canada West. The newspapers in Toronto and even in the Niagara region duly reported the events, albeit some time after the fact. News came from the continent by ship, then by telegraph from the eastern United States.

Britain's North American colonies were affected by the far-off war in unexpected ways. Britain focused her energies on the Far East, which for economic reasons was more important than were the struggling agricultural communities of Canada East and Canada West, both of which now offered less because of their dwindling fur trade. Britain was becoming more industrialized; the agricultural colonies had little to offer.

In the little community of Niagara-on-the-Lake, there were fewer imported items from Britain. Many staples had to be purchased in the United States, in spite of the fact that the purchasing power of the British Crown had dropped drastically.

As if the effects of the war were not bad enough, British North America had been further affected by the repeal of the Corn Laws in Britain. This meant that corn or corn flour could not be exported to England in exchange for needed currency. Moreover, the British Parliament repealed special trade status for the colonies, leaving the timber and agricultural products produced by the hard-working farmers of Canada West to compete on the world market. Family after family in the Niagara were abandoning their farms and heading West. The lure of gold still beckoned, and it was now believed that there might well be gold in all the great rivers of the Pacific Northwest.

But Ernest McGrath did not concern himself with the closure of mills, nor the high rate of unemployment. Ernest was frustrated because he could not purchase, even in the United States, the bottled Jordan River water with which to baptize the newly born and the newly converted. It was a hardship the congregation endured, but only with the promise that when the precious water again became available, those baptized with the waters of the Niagara River would be re-baptized with the water of the holy River Jordan.

On this Sunday morning, as on others, Ernest preached about the westward movement. He spoke about greed, and about the need to bring religion to the poor Godless savages as well as to the many settlers that were now moving West.

"They all need the strength of salvation!" he had declared. "Those who seek gold are a wild lot, deprived of the teachings of the faith, lost to the way of the faith, drowning in greed and the evils of whiskey!"

Ernest wiped his brow. Preaching was a draining task. He smiled down on his intended, Margot Macleod. She looked up at him with her luminous green eyes, eyes filled with love and devotion.

"Go forth and keep thy faith!" Ernest called out as the congregation began to leave the church. Margot, who had been sitting in the front pew, hesitated for a moment. Ernest was so shy when they were together, but so powerful when he spoke! It will all be different when we're married, she thought. Then he won't be so shy, and besides, it is only because he desires me so much. Poor dear Ernest. Margot delighted in his attraction to her.

Ernest nodded at her. She knew he had to go and greet the congregation now, but afterwards, unlike other Sundays, Ernest would come to dinner.

Margot hurried home. She stepped into the vestibule and took off her shawl, hanging it on the rack near the front door. "Papa!" she called out, "I'm home from church!"

"In the kitchen!" Ronald Macleod called back.

Margot took off her bonnet and pushed a stray hair off her forehead. Her long black hair was done up in a great bun. She rarely let it hang loose; Ernest wouldn't have liked it. "The Moslems may be heathens," he once told her, "but they are correct in their belief that a woman's hair should be kept hidden. Flowing tresses give a man far too much temptation—that's why Saint Paul, in all his wisdom, ordained that the lesser of the species should always cover their heads while in a house of worship. And all proper women should wear hats on the street as well. Hair is far too suggestive to be allowed to hang loose."

This Sunday was unlike other Sundays, when relatives from miles around brought food for the weekly feast. This was the Sunday before Margot's wedding, and since everyone was to attend the wedding, they did not attend Sunday dinner. Kevin would be home from Toronto, but he could not come until Monday because the riverboat didn't run on Sundays. Kevin, unlike Margot, was not taken with religion, but with politics instead. It was an endeavor that Ronald Macleod approved of. "One day we will be one nation instead of a collection of British colonies," Ronald often declared. "And being involved with politics and having an education will be important—more important than it is now."

Margot was well aware of her father's dedication to learning. She was literate and well-read, having been taught by special tutors, and her family owned more books than any family in the Niagara. Most of the young men of the area were educated; at least, most had been to school long enough to know how to read. But few of the women were truly literate. They attended school, but they learned the skills that would make them good wives. They mastered cooking, nursing, and sewing.

"A woman who can read may well be tempted by the ideas put forward in many books. A woman's brain is not meant to be strained," Ernest often told her. "Still, Margot, you are pious. I know you will not be tempted to understand what you read. And your ability to read can be put to use when we are married and living with the heathen Indians. You can teach the young ones from the Bible, thus assisting me in the ministry." Margot was flattered that Ernest trusted her so, and she was even more flattered that, like Narcissa, her heroine, she would be able to help her husband in his ministry.

"Papa!" Margot stood in the doorway of the large airy kitchen. Ronald Macleod was sitting at the table, a glass of whiskey in front of him, his feet resting on another chair.

"Ah, my God-fearing daughter has returned." He smiled up at her mischievously. "And how was the wrath of McGrath this fine Sunday morning?"

"Papa," Margot sighed, "you know Ernest is coming later, he'll smell the whiskey on your breath. What will he think? What kind of father-in-law will he think he's getting next Saturday? It's a sin to drink, especially on Sunday."

"It's my day of relaxation. A little whiskey helps a man to relax."

"Ernest says it's the devil's brew. Ernest says it addles the mind and corrupts the soul, leading a man away from the righteous path of Christ."

Ronald laughed. "I like my whiskey now and again, girl. I like it, my father liked it, and his father before him. We all managed not to become addled, and I may say we managed quite well.''

"I do wish you were more of a Christian. . . . The faith is beautiful.''

"I am a Christian. . . . A hard-working, God-fearing Christian who likes his whiskey now and again, and who doesn't think drinking will keep him out of heaven.''

"It might. Heaven is for the righteous. It's a beautiful, wonderful place. Ernest makes it real for me. Sometimes I can hardly wait to die so I can go to heaven.''

"I can wait, I'll tell you.''

"Papa!''

"I take it back. The Lord is punishing me. I'm about to acquire, 'Wrath McGrath' as a son-in-law, and I have a daughter who thinks, acts, and talks like one of the holy angels. Heaven save me!'' He laughed again and gulped down the whiskey.

Margot swung the kitchen door back and took her spotless white apron off the hook. She put it on, tying it in the back.

"Well, you won't have to put up with us for long. We're being married next Saturday, on Sunday Ernest will preach his last sermon, and by Monday afternoon we'll be on our way West.''

"To plague the Indians, roping them into the faith like cattle into a pen.''

"Papa, I just don't understand you, you're so sacrilegious!''

"Just old fashioned. God knows, with the likes of 'Wrath McGrath' preaching hereabouts, it'll soon be that a good decent man won't be able to get drink on Sunday.''

"Oh, Papa.''

"You ought to try a bit. Loosen you up. I never should have let you spend so much time in church. It's not good for you, all that hellfire and damnation.''

"Ernest says ladies never drink.''

"You great-aunt Jenna MacLean, who, bless her soul, died at the age of eighty-five back in 1849, could put a glass away with the best of them. And let me tell you, she was a lady! And out in the family plot—out there under the great

Celtic Cross, lies my great-grandmother, Janet Cameron Macleod. She, my little archangel, died with a brandy glass in her hand—an empty one. I was a young one then, but I remember that night—it was at a gathering of the clan, it was—and I remember the funeral when people came from hundreds of miles away to pay tribute to her. It wasn't the brandy that killed her, and she was a good woman, a real lady.''

"And a Catholic," Margot whispered.

"Yes, poor woman. She hadn't seen the divine light of salvation as you have.''

"You're making fun of me, Papa.''

"Only a little. I'm happy that you're a good girl. It's every father's dream to have a respectable daughter, especially if she's been reared without a mother. I count myself a fortunate man. It's just that I don't want you to be too good. I want you to enjoy life.''

"I do enjoy life. And Papa, I do love Ernest.''

"If you say so.''

"Papa, you promised not to drink when Ernest is here. And for heaven's sake, please don't discuss great-aunt Jenna, or your great-grandmother. What kind of women will he think we have in this family?''

"High-spirited, full-blooded, and bright. Of course, I doubt that's what Ernest is looking for in a wife.''

"Ernest believes education is a temptation for most women.''

"Nonsense! He doesn't want the competition!''

"That's a terrible thing to say, and it's not true. Ernest wants me to help him in his missionary work.''

"Well, my dear, it's you who are marrying him, not me. Possibly, you haven't inherited a single characteristic of any of the good women in this family. If that is so, you and Ernest should be divinely happy.''

"We will be.''

Ronald pushed back his chair and poured himself another drink. "As I am condemned to a pious afternoon with my future son-in-law, I'm sure you won't mind if I have another drink.''

"And you must never, never tell Ernest that your great-grandmother was Catholic. He'd die, he probably wouldn't even marry me."

"My dearest daughter, at one time most of Scotland was Catholic or High Church Anglican, and then we had bestowed upon us the glorious likes of John Knox—a man I'm certain your Ernest McGrath is trying to emulate. And what did Knox create? He left heirs who created an environment so strict that it drove Bobby Burns to write good dirty poetry—and I'm certain that Burns could only have written such earthy verses while surrounded with the purity and piety of the faith. I think he wrote so every Scots would be reminded—assuming they recovered from their Knoxian afflictions—that we were once an earthy lot."

"Not all of Mr. Burns' poems are earthy."

"More than you think, though my heart tells me it will be a while before the *Muse of the Caledonia* sees the light of the printed page again . . . in its original form."

Margot tossed her head back. "Perhaps no one cares to read such things." She walked to the icebox and began taking out the bowls of prepared food. It was Sunday afternoon fare: cold meats, baked beans, carrots, and home-baked butter tarts. One did not cook on Sunday; one ate foods prepared the night before.

"I could sing you a few verses . . . how about the original verses of *Jon Anderson, my Jo Jon?*"

"I've heard you sing it before."

"It's a very appropriate song for a woman about to be wed."

"I don't think so. Ernest doesn't think about things like that."

Ronald burst into sardonic laughter, coughing on his whiskey. "Then I have no grandchildren to look forward to?"

"Procreation is quite different. It's all right to couple when you are planning to have children."

"So sayeth the Lord when he speaks in the voice of Wrath McGrath!"

Margot put down the baked beans and stared at her father

79

pleadingly. "Please, Papa. We're different, you and I. I've found the faith, and I'm happy. Please stop teasing me, especially about Ernest."

"You should be spoken with before your wedding night, especially as you are marrying the world's most upright man."

Ronald smiled at his own pun, even though he knew that Margot didn't understand.

"Aunt Peggy has already spoken with me."

"And what did she tell you?"

"I can't discuss that with you!"

"Why not? I'm your father! I was in the room when you were born. I watched you pop right out of your mother's womb, naked as a jaybird."

"Please." Margot's face was flushed.

"Good God! You're blushing! And with your own father!"

"Aunt Peggy has told me everything. I have no need to know more."

"Well, at least you've had the benefit of growing up on a farm. I don't suppose you can possibly be as ignorant as those city-bred women in Toronto, the ones who've never seen a mare mounted and who think that babies are found under some cabbage leaf."

"It's not the same with people as it is with horses," Margot replied.

"Ah, I see you are still ignorant. Well, I'm here to tell you that it is sometimes like that with people, though it can be gentler and much more enjoyable."

"For those who have the faith, the act of procreation is an ethereal experience. Ernest says so."

"Ernest says . . . I hope Ernest does as he says."

"I don't want to discuss this anymore. I'm going to my room to change my dress. Ernest will be here within the hour. Please, Papa, please behave."

Ronald shook his head in amazement. "So sayeth the daughter unto the father. Somehow, I always thought it was supposed to be the other way around." He smiled and winked at her. "I'll try . . . I suppose I can manage for another week."

Margot bit her lip, but then she leaned over and kissed her father on the forehead. "Thank you," she whispered, before she left the room.

Ronald leaned back and took another sip of whiskey. "Damn!" he mumbled. Why couldn't he reach Margot? Every time he tried to talk to her, he succeeded only in good-natured ribbing. But it was serious; indeed, at this point there seemed nothing he could do. He had hoped Margot would outgrow her infatuation with Ernest, but it hadn't happened. He had hoped she would outgrow her naive faith, and that hadn't happened, either. She was soon to be nineteen, and sooner yet to be married. And beneath all of Ronald's teasing, and beyond his concern that Margot was merely naive and infatuated, lay a real fear and dislike of Ernest McGrath. The man, Ronald Macleod thought, is strange. His eyes glow with hell, fire, and damnation. He doesn't stop by asking people to believe in his faith; he demands that they believe and adhere. Ronald suspected that Ernest had a vile temper, too, one that could explode at any time.

Ronald shook his head. There was a futility in mentioning his feelings of ill ease to Margot. She was, in spite of his teasing, a Macleod woman to the core. She was just plain stubborn!

The sky above Fort Boise was blue-black as the first light of dawn illuminated the eastern sky with a streak of brightness; the moon still shone and stars were still bright overhead. A cold breeze swept across the plain and the rolling hills that rose in the distance.

Blaise inhaled. This was his favorite time of day. He loved the eerie silence of the plains, the images of the weaving shadows as the tall grasses bent to the wind.

Fort Boise's walls were dark against the lightening sky, the heavy gates closed, the flag fluttering in the air. Like many other forts, Boise was now surrounded by a small, thriving community. There were tradespeople and saloons,

81

a general store and a mill. On the other side of the fort, friendly Indians camped, and some Indian woman—half-breeds and those estranged from the tribe—opened the flaps of their teepees to wanton soldiers, mountain men, and all others willing to pay for a night's pleasure.

Blaise had wintered at Fort Boise. Now, after his last night there, he paused before leaving the teepee in which he had slept. A naked Indian woman still slumbered there, her light brown breasts, dark nipples, and smooth soft body hidden under a homespun blanket. He didn't know her name, but he had come often to her tent during his winter stay, deeming her the cleanest and most attractive of those available.

She was silent when he made love to her and he was unsure whether or not she enjoyed it, even though she always seemed glad to see him. Perhaps, he thought, he was gentler then the others who came to her. Perhaps it was only that he spoke her language.

He fastened his gun belt and put on his hat. Again, he looked at the woman who slept, half thinking that he should wake her and say good-bye. Blaise reached into his pocket and withdrew a gold coin. He leaned over and put it near her. He had already paid her; this was his parting gift. A wave of sadness passed through him. He often availed himself of prostitutes, but when he left them he always felt more lonely because the relationship was fleeting, without substance.

Blaise rejected the idea of waking her. Instead, he mounted his horse and rode off toward the widening streak of light in the eastern sky. He glanced back once, and still felt his sadness. I might have married, he thought, if things had been different.

Blaise Baron was a handsome man. He was unusually tall for a Frenchman, and his mother had always claimed he owed his height to her Irish grandfather. But apart from his height—and his sense of humor—Blaise bore no other Irish characteristics. He had his mother's wavy light brown hair and soft expressive brown eyes. He had his father's square jaw, a physical characteristic that gave him a look of strength and decisiveness. And, when he chose, Blaise Baron had a ready smile and a flirtatious wink.

Blaise Baron was also a man with a past, and those who traveled with him often referred to him as a loner, although it was not a description that Blaise would have used himself. Rather, he would have said that he had the appearance of a loner and that when he led wagons to the West, his position necessitated that stance. On wagon trains, terrible tensions developed among the settlers—a kind of wagon fever. Over the rough months of the journey, fights broke out, marriages were shattered, men were killed. A leader of such a venture could have no real friends because a leader's decisions had to be impartial; they had to favor the welfare of the whole, rather than satisfy the needs of the few.

No, he thought, he was not a loner, but he did suffer loneliness—loneliness bred by his past and fed by the fact that while he could survive in most places, he belonged nowhere.

Blaise, his father had once observed, was born to the struggle for French Canadian nationalism, and his youthful rebellion against the British in Lower Canada had resulted in his permanent exile. He could not return to his beloved Quebec.

Blaise Baron was born in the year 1821 in Montreal. His father, Richard Baron, was a highly political man, a member of the Assembly and an arch supporter of Louis Joseph Papineau, who was destined to become the leader of the so-called 'French Party.'

Blaise grew up with politics, and the issue that eventually caused his exile began to develop in the very year of his birth; it simmered till it reached the boiling point sixteen years later and spilled over into bloody violence.

In 1822, when Blaise was an infant of one year, the British House of Commons in London proposed a bill to bring about the union of Upper and Lower Canada. They wanted to create one Legislative Assembly for the new United Province. The bill featured two highly objectionable proposals. One concerned the amount of property a man would have to own in order to vote. The property requirements would have effectively disenfranchised most French Canadians. The second provision stated that within fifteen years of the proposed union, the only language of the government would be English. The total effect of the bill would have been to smother and gradually kill French Canadian nationalism and the French culture in North America.

The introduction of the bill resulted in a storm of protest in Lower Canada, and in the face of overwhelming objections the proposed union was shelved. Next, a financial scandal rocked the province. Some 100,000 pounds was found missing from the treasury, and the Assembly held the British government representative responsible. Louis Papineau, a leader in the Assembly and one of those who had led the fight against the Act of Union, attacked the British government representative so vehemently that the Assembly was officially dissolved for a time.

Those events were followed by investigations, reports, more investigations, and still more reports. Then, in 1831, the British, seemingly in a more conciliatory mood, offered Papineau a seat on the Executive Council. But Papineau and Blaise's father were not to be bought off. Both wanted reform rather than positions in government. They fought for an elected Legislative Assembly based on the model of the United States Senate. Such a democratic concept was obviously contrary to the British government's idea of how colonial administrations should work.

In 1832, when Blaise was only eleven, British troops fired on a crowd of protesters in Montreal. Three French Canadians were killed, and this incident fueled the fire of resentment against the British.

The following year, a month before Blaise's twelfth birthday, his mother, Lillie, died of cholera. But Lillie was not alone. Cholera was brought to Lower Canada by shiploads of diseased British immigrants, and its spread gave the French new reasons for hate.

Blaise could remember sitting on Louis Papineau's knee and listening to him talk. He remembered being at political meetings and listening as Papineau guided members of the Assembly in drawing up and adopting the Ninety-Two Resolutions, which included a long list of grievances and criticisms of the British colonial policies. The thrust of the resolutions was clear—the British had allowed a minority of British settlers in the colony to control the large French majority. In the elections which followed, Papineau and Blaise's father were swept to victory.

In 1837, when Blaise was sixteen years old, the British Colonial Office took a new hard line. It drafted Ten Resolutions for Lower Canada. The British Resolutions rejected the demands for a democratically elected Legislative Assembly—both the Assembly and the demands of the reformers were bypassed.

Papineau, Richard Baron, and their followers began to speak of rebellion; they said there was no hope of attaining reform by constitutional means.

For all of his sixteen years, Blaise Baron had been steeped in politics. He was well-read and well-educated; his family was monied. The Americans had inspired the French Revolution, and now the French Canadians too burned with the fire begun by the American Revolution. With the Boston Tea Party firmly in mind, sixteen-year-old Blaise Baron helped to organize *l'Association des Fils de la Liberté*. There were mass meetings, fiery speeches, outbursts in the press.

On October 23, 1837, Blaise Baron attended a rally on Rue St. Charles in Montreal. The mass rally passed resolutions that went beyond the demands of Papineau—resolutions that satisfied the young, those who were unwilling to wait, those who knew they had waited too long. But there were counter groups. The members of the English Constitutional Party clashed with French Canadian *fils*, and Blaise saw his childhood friend, André Vachon, killed.

Les Fils de la Liberté seized positions in and around Montreal, and British troops and militia were dispatched from Upper Canada. Papineau left Montreal, hoping to avoid violence, but the British believed he was trying to begin a revolt in the countryside and issued warrants for his arrest. Armed patriots, including Blaise and Richard Baron,

85

obstructed the British troops; Blaise's father was killed in the skirmish.

On November 23, 1837, fighting broke out on Rue St. Denis between the British troops and the patriots. More fighting broke out on Rue St. Charles and at St. Eustache, north of Montreal. The patriots were brutally crushed.

Blaise Baron killed two British soldiers. He pulled the trigger thinking of his father and of his mother. He never regretted fighting for what he believed in, but he became a wanted man.

Blaise escaped in a nightmare run which landed him, three weeks later, across the U.S. border. Blaise Baron was an exile, and his family's home and fortune were confiscated by the British.

Young, penniless, and orphaned, Blaise headed west across the United States. He worked on farms, he lived off the land, and finally he came to Independence, Missouri, where he hired on a wagon train heading even further west into the Oregon Territory. Two years later, he returned and worked as a scout on another train. In 1847, when he was twenty-six, he followed the trail to California. He panned for gold in Virginia City and met Cory MacLean; the two found gold, and formed a partnership. Then he headed into the Northwest with Cory, and they stayed for a time with French trappers near the Hudson's Bay Post. Then, again, he returned east to guide another train west. It became a pattern, and Cory, who was like him in many ways, became his close friend.

A few weeks short of thirty-five, Blaise Baron was considered one of the best wagon masters available. He spoke French and English fluently. He spoke seven native tongues as well, and he knew the trail and the weather conditions. His muscles were well-honed, and he was in his physical prime.

Blaise paused and sipped some water from his canteen. The sun was ablaze now over the golden hills, and the barren beauty of Idaho impressed him anew. He smiled, wondering what this wagon train of passengers would be like.

* * *

The long table in the Macleod dining room was covered with a white linen cloth and set with the family's fine bone china and sterling silver. In the middle of the table, Margot had placed a bouquet of yellow flowers.

Ronald Macleod sat in his customary position at the head of the table; Margot sat on his left, Ernest McGrath on his right.

"That was a delicious meal," Ernest announced, untucking his napkin and placing his fork on the table.

"Thank you, Ernest."

"I must say, it's a real comfort to be marrying a woman you know can cook." Ernest nodded toward Ronald. "She sets a fine table. A man in my position needs a woman who can set a fine table."

Ronald suppressed himself. In his mind's eye, he imagined Ernest and Margot in the bush wilderness of the West, a white linen tablecloth set out on a log, the makeshift table set with china and silver. Ernest seemed to have absolutely no idea of what he was heading into. He seemed to envision himself as the greatest preacher in the West, a man who would have power and position.

"I doubt the Indians will care how well she sets a table," Ronald finally said as he wolfed down the last of his baked beans.

"I was hardly thinking of the miserable, heathen savages, sir. I was thinking of the pillars of the new communities that are being built."

"Of course," Ronald muttered.

"I've inspected all the items Margot has packed. There are three trunks in all—rather a lot, but I think we'll need everything."

"And no doubt more," Ronald replied.

"Well, there are steamers from San Francisco and ships from the Orient. It's not that far from civilization."

"It's a wilderness," Ronald said, lifting his eyebrow.

"Well, you're the one who's always talking about your great-grandmother, how, when she came here, this was a wilderness," Margot put in.

"True enough," Ronald agreed. Silently he considered

the fact that Janet Cameron Macleod had been married to Mathew Macleod, and that Mathew certainly did not count on God to clear the trees and plant the crops.

"Great-aunt Jenna's son, Ian—Uncle Josh's brother— went out West way back in 1815," Margot reminded her father.

"1812," Ronald corrected. "Married one of the Selkirk settlers and just kept going. Never heard from them again. Hell, we got relatives all over."

"Papa, please don't swear, especially on Sunday."

Ernest was looking at his plate. Ronald sighed. His own daugher was twice as straight-laced as old Aunt Helena had ever been.

But perhaps experience would change her for the better. It was a long, hard trip out west, even if one did travel through the United States. It would make or break Ernest, and along the way Margot might outgrow her primness. Still, Margot's attitudes troubled him less than his strong feelings about Ernest's character. It was the look in Ernest's eyes, the banality of his conversation, the tremble of his hands. Ronald always had the feeling that Ernest was on his best behavior, and that he was holding himself in somehow, afraid to be the hell, fire, and damnation preacher he was. Ronald suspected that Ernest's religious beliefs were little more than a covering for his tyrannical ideas. But, he conceded, a man could change, and perhaps the Westward journey would change Ernest, too.

"How's business at the mill?" Margot asked, changing the subject away from their coming trip. The mill belonged to the MacAndrews', who were also cousins.

"Shut down for now," Ronald told her. "The economy is bad, and things aren't looking up. There's a lot of unemployment."

"It's the fault of the British," Ernest put in. "We can only get imported goods now from the United States."

"Where our money isn't worth half what it should be," Ronald added.

"It would be easier if we were part of the United States," Ernest argued.

Ronald shook his head. "The hell it would! What we need is to be independent of both Britain and the United States! Hell, the more dependent we get on America, the worse things will get. They've been trying to annex us for years."

"I can't say that I fully agree. . . ."

Ronald scowled at Ernest.

"Papa, let's not discuss politics. When Kevin gets home you can discuss politics with him. I'm so excited about our trip! It'll be such a wonderful way to spend our honeymoon."

Ronald shrugged. He didn't really want to discuss politics with Ernest in any case.

"Have you relatives in the United States?" Ernest asked.

"Got some relatives down in Vidalia, on the Mississippi. Trace MacLean, for one. He's Josh's other son—you know, there's Colin, who lives down in Queenston, and there's Trace, Colin's twin. Both born in 1812. Well, in 1843, their uncle died—lived down on a plantation. Left the whole thing to Trace and Colin. Colin didn't want to go, but Trace went. Only thing we ever heard was that he married some Irish girl and had a couple of sons."

"He married a Papist?" Ernest looked across at Margot.

"I said she was Irish. I don't know what her religion was."

"Where exactly is Vidalia?" Ernest asked.

"Upriver from New Orleans."

Ernest shook his head knowingly. "New Orleans is a wicked city. I've heard it's the most wicked city in the whole United States, except for San Francisco."

"Wicked?" Ronald questioned.

"Probably because it was settled by the French," Ernest proclaimed. "The French are not only Papists, but they're wicked and immoral. Dreadful people, simply dreadful!"

"They founded this country," Ronald said flatly, sounding more than a trifle annoyed. "Half this country is French!"

"The wicked half," Ernest replied tersely.

Margot shot her father a warning look. Ronald sipped

some tea. He knew his daughter didn't want him to mention just how many of the Macleods were married to men and women of French heritage. And God knew, the Catholic side of the family was off conversational limits altogether. He gulped down the remainder of his tea, wishing it were whiskey. He hoped his future grandchildren would have more sense than their father. Still, Ronald admitted to himself, Ernest was expressing a view held by many of the good people of Canada West who sympathized with the Ulstermen of the Orange Order. Orange influence was being felt more and more in Canada West, and they were all vehemently anti-Catholic and thus anti–Irish-Catholic and anti-French.

"I don't think your attitude is truly Christian," Ronald uttered, wanting to make his personal views completely clear.

"If they came to the faith, they would be forgiven their worship of graven images."

"Doubtless," Ronald muttered. Ernest was not to be rebuked easily. Ronald wished Kevin were here to carry on this argument. Kevin was young and still enjoyed debate; Ronald was at the age where he simply had decided what was right and what was wrong. He tired of the endless debate over religion; this debate, like a disease, infected the whole community with prejudice. Above all, Ronald wished that the dinner table were full, so that he did not have to bear the brunt of conversation with Ernest.

"So," Ronald said, again wanting to change the subject and turn to safer, less controversial ground, "are you all packed and ready for your voyage?" It was an absurd question; he knew full well they were.

"I shall love traveling in a covered wagon," Margot said dreamily.

"You'll have a sore bottom, I'll tell you."

"Papa!" Margot exclaimed in a shocked tone.

"It's a matter of fact, but excuse me for mentioning a part of your anatomy."

"Papa!"

Ernest cleared his throat. "Margot is quite prepared to

make sacrifices to help bring salvation to the heathens. She is a noble, virtuous woman, unafraid of hardships."

Margot beamed as she basked in the warmth of Ernest's praise and kind look. He reached across the table and patted her hand.

Margot stood up and began to clear the table. "Are you sure you'll be able to get on without me, Papa?"

"You have to have your own life. But the house is too big for me. I'm thinking of asking your Aunt Peggy and her family to move to Lochiel. Be nice to have all the rooms filled for a change."

"What will happen when Kevin gets married?"

"He's young. I think I have a few years to worry about that. He might not want to live here, in any case."

"You just want him to go on and become a lawyer and go into politics."

"I wouldn't mind that at all," Ronald admitted. He stood up and stretched. "Shall we retire to the parlor?"

Ernest jumped to his feet. "As you wish, sir."

"Would you two like to be alone?"

"We'll soon be alone all the time," Ernest replied.

Ronald studied him. Ernest sounded wary of being alone with Margot; it wasn't the tone a man about to be married should be using.

But Ernest recovered quickly from whatever thoughts were running through his mind. "You should be proud of your daughter, sir. It's not every woman who would do what she's about to do. It's not every woman who would give up a life of relative comfort to dedicate herself to bringing Christianity to the deprived heathens."

"How fortunate they are," Ronald mumbled, not bothering to hide his tone of sarcasm.

CHAPTER VII

April 11, 1856

Cory MacLean guided his horse down the road toward his farm. Perhaps, he thought, he should have sent some sort of message on ahead to Anya to let her know he was returning. He had been gone nine months—three months longer than intended.

But it had been a fruitful adventure. He had returned to the Hudson's Bay Post with a rich load of furs and with gold. It was the gold that had delayed him. The strike had been made only weeks before he ambled onto the scene, but Cory was quick to join in and he had stopped long enough to stake his claim, vowing to return within months to work it. He smiled to himself. The news of the gold strike in New Caledonia would filter out of the hills, and within a short period of time boatloads of men would arrive, veterans of the California gold rush, newcomers seeking their fortunes, adverturers and mountain men. The sleepy, genteel little colony would be changing, Cory thought.

He rode up the path leading to his farmhouse and dismounted, tying his horse to the hitching post. A breeze rustled through the low trees in front of the house; flowers bloomed in carefully cultivated beds. The farmhouse looked lived in and cared for. Cory walked up to the front door and knocked, although it seemed strange to him to knock at one's own house.

Anya herself opened the door. Cory smiled. She looked quite different than when he had last seen her. Gone were the ornate taffeta gown, the jewels, and the elaborate hairdo. She stood before him in a plain ruffled gingham dress, her long blond hair pulled back and tied behind her head with a blue ribbon. But her eyes were the same—large and magnificent.

93

"Mr. MacLean!" She looked truly surprised.

Cory smiled. "I did tell you I'd come back."

"But I did not expect you!"

"I should have sent a message ahead," he half apologized. He noted that her English seemed much improved.

Cory dumped his pack on the floor. "May I come into my house?"

"But of course." Anya moved ahead of him, and Cory followed her into the sitting room. He looked around, and found that things had vastly changed. He had always maintained the house well, but he had kept its furnishings plain. Anya had put bouquets of fresh flowers on the tables, and the furniture was covered with brightly colored material. There was a warmth and charm that had not been there before.

He looked around, relieved to see that his liquor cabinet was still in place and that it was at least as well stocked as when he had left. He walked over and poured himself a drink.

"Looks nice," he said, gesturing to the room about him.

"Less spartan," Anya agreed.

Cory sank into a chair. She was even more beautiful than he remembered; he wondered if she was still as arrogant, or if nine months in the little colony had changed her.

"How are you getting on?" he asked casually.

"I am well. I have learned the language, I have some friends." Anya too sat down.

Cory nodded. "Homesick?"

She looked steadily at the floor, avoiding his eyes. "Sometimes, yes."

"I'm sure it could be arranged for you to go home."

"I don't want to go home. I have no home!"

She said it almost vehemently, and Cory shrugged.

She still did not look at him. "Now I suppose I will have to leave here."

"You don't have to. I don't think I'll be here for too long."

"You're going away again?" She sounded a little distressed.

Cory nodded. "But not for as long. I've got a claim I want to work before winter sets in."

"A claim?"

"Gold," Cory answered. "There's gold up the Fraser River."

She looked up brightly. At least she hasn't lost interest in money, he thought. "Gold." She said the word almost reverently.

"Look, I'm going to be here for a few weeks. Does that bother you?"

"You will not sleep in the same room with me," she said. It was half a question, half an announcement.

"I have my own room," he replied. "Your virtue will be protected."

Anya nodded. "Then I do not mind if you stay."

"How nice of you," Cory grinned. After all, it was his house. No, he thought, she has not changed all that much.

"I have mulatto girl as chaperone," Anya announced. "I pay her to help me in the house."

"Well, I didn't really expect that you would be working."

Anya frowned. "I work, but I do not do the floors. I work because there are not enough books to read."

Cory glanced up at the shelf. Actually, he had quite a good library. Vaguely he wondered if in her obvious boredom she had worked through all his books.

"Have you read all those?"

Anya nodded. "And Captain Arlen is bringing me more on his next trip. I've been going to school, but it's still easier for me to read English than to speak."

Cory scowled. "Was Arlen here?"

"No, I saw him at Craigflower Farm."

Cory felt a surge of irritation toward Arlen. He had felt it before, and he wasn't quite sure why he felt it so strongly. He wanted to ask if she and Arlen were lovers, but he withheld the question.

"Well, if you're not going home, what are you going to do? You can stay here for a time, but what are your plans?"

"I'm going to build a theater and become an actress."

95

Cory looked at her in surprise. "What?"

"I'm building the theater in Victoria." She pointed up to his bookshelf. "We'll do Shakespeare."

Cory burst out laughing. *The Taming of the Shrew,* no doubt—a role in which Anya would be typecast.

Anya looked icily at him. "You're laughing at me!"

"A theater in Victoria? You, an actress?"

"I have acted before. I'm making an investment. People will pay to see theater. You will not laugh anymore!"

Cory nodded. He thought of all the people who would be coming to seek gold. Well, maybe she did have something—maybe people would pay to see drama. At least, she had plans for something. And who was he to question the value of Shakespeare? As a boy, his mother had taught him to read using a tattered volume of the Bible and another of Shakespeare's plays. She had made him commit whole roles to memory.

"Sorry," he said. "Here, I brought you something." He reached in his pocket and handed her a large gold nugget.

Anya took it and turned it over in her hand. "Ah, gold," she smiled at him.

"Somehow, I thought you might like that." He grinned at her again. She was a real gold digger, but she was so damn honest about it.

"What do you want for this?" she asked suspiciously.

"I don't want anything. It's a gift."

"I can't take it. Men don't give without wanting." She handed it back to him.

Cory was surprised and he immediately thought of Arlen. He had most certainly made port here several times in the nine months Cory had been gone. Perhaps they were not lovers, or perhaps she had learned from Arlen a little more about men.

"I don't want anything," Cory reiterated. "Take it as a contribution to your theater, then."

Anya took it back. She turned the large nugget over and over in her fingers. "Gold from the ground," she whispered. "If you want to make a contribution to theater, I will accept."

Anya stood up. "Rosa!" she called out.

Within a minute, Rosa appeared, and Cory couldn't help but stare blatantly at the young woman, his eyes feasting on her obvious charms. She was a mulatto girl, perhaps eighteen or nineteen. There were a number of mulattos in the colony, mixed-blood peoples who were often part Negro, part white, or part Indian. Rosa was clearly all three. She had high Indian cheekbones, golden dusky skin, a rounded sensuous mouth, and mops of curly black hair. She was, to say the very least, an earthy temptress whose voluptuous body proportions were all too visible beneath her cotton dress.

"You will prepare dinner for Mr. MacLean and myself," Anya said imperiously.

Rosa met Cory's look and smiled at him seductively. Certainly Anya did not miss the exchange of glances. "You may go now," she said coldly.

Rosa nodded and disappeared. Cory followed her with his eyes and thought to himself, there is, after all, some joy in homecoming.

The woman's long red tresses fell nearly to the small of her bare back. Her pink-tipped breasts were heavy and full, and her rounded hips moved seductively as she danced in front of him, pushing herself ever closer till he was forced to reach out for her and pull her close to him.

He held her buttocks roughly, feeling the pliable flesh between his fingers even as her breasts were flattened against his chest. He moved his hands, they burned like fire with the feel of her hot flesh. . .

Ernest felt a seering pain across the small of his back and he jolted awake with a shriek. "Devil! Devil! Devil!" he cried out. "Women are devils!" He jolted upright in bed, shaking like a leaf and drenched in his own perspiration. He dropped his hand from his limp member and stared at the white fluid on the bed. "Devil!" he whispered, still shaking. He drew up the sheet and clung to it fearfully, and waited, praying that his scream had not awakened his father. He listened intently and only began to relax slightly when he

97

was certain that his father was still snoring peacefully in the room next door. Ernest let out his breath and sunk down in his bed, too terrified to close his eyes again least his dreaded nightmare return.

Tears filled his eyes and he looked at the ceiling of his room. What could he do about dreams? Never, never in his waking thoughts did he conjure up such evil images. . . . But at night—not often, but sometimes—he suffered intensely lustful dreams.

"It's the she-devil trying to tempt me," he muttered. Without lighting the lamp, he poured himself some water from the pitcher that was on the nightstand and, with his hand still shaking, he sipped it. "It's the reality of my coming marriage," he said into the darkness. "Oh, God, give me strength! Tomorrow is my wedding day." He set the glass down and rolled over on his side. "Temptation, get thee behind me!" Ernest muttered, over and over, till finally sleep overcame him.

A brisk wind blew off Lake Ontario. The sky was blue overhead, but puffy clouds on the horizon threatened a spring rain by evening. Still, the weather was unseasonably warm for April and it appeared as if summer would come early to the Niagara frontier.

Within the white clapboard church, each and every pew was filled with guests. On one side of the aisle, Mrs. Conklin sat with her niece, Hester Pring, and sniffed into her handkerchief, doing her best to fulfill the role that might have been played by Ernest's mother were she alive. "What a happy day," she declared flatly, dabbing at her eyes. "Such a fine young man."

Next to her, Miss Pring looked straight ahead. At this moment, she hated Margot Macleod and felt nothing less for her than the loathing that grew out of her own jealousy.

On the other side of the aisle, old Susanna MacAndrew sat leaning forward, her hat tilted slightly to one side. She was seventy-six, the oldest person present, and Jenna MacLean's only surviving daughter. Old Susanna had journeyed all the way from Kingston for the wedding. She sat next to her fifty-year-old son, Andrew MacAndrew, and his wife, Ulna, who was German and still hardly understood a word of English. Andrew MacAndrew's three children filled the rest of the seats in the row.

Behind old Susanna sat Peggy Macleod Gordon with her family. She was Ronald's older sister. In the next row were the MacAndrews of Niagara and behind them the Murray clan, related to the Macleods through the Frasers, one of whom had married Helena MacLeod, the oldest daughter of Mathew and Janet, the founders of the family. In back of the Murrays and Frasers were the Knights, the O'Brians, the McKenzies, the MacPhersons, the Spencers, the Filmores, and four other families related by marriage to Clan Macleod.

On the opposite side of the church, behind Mrs. Conklin, were all the MacLeans with their relatives. Colin MacLean, son of Josh and Colleen, sat with his wife, Estelle, and their five children.

Old Susanna squinted toward the front of the church. She was both myopic and deaf. "When are they going to start?" she demanded loudly. "No event in this family ever starts on time except for funerals!" Susanna always spoke in a near shout, unable as she was to hear herself speak.

A twitter rippled through the church and her son patted her on the knee, hoping to quiet her, but old Susanna was not to be silenced. "Aren't we going to have pipes?" she asked loudly. "Can't have a wedding without pipes!"

Peggy turned around to see if anyone was assembling in the rear of the church.

"What's a wedding without pipes?" old Susanna continued to grumble, much to the amusement of most of the guests, but obviously to the shock of Mrs. Conklin and a few other members of the congregation.

"I do wish that woman would be quiet," Mrs. Conklin whispered loudly to Hester Pring.

"She'll ruin the wedding," Hester let out with her nervous horsey laugh.

No sooner had Hester finished her statement than Miss Winifred Fraser came out of the vestry. She was dressed in a long gray dress and wore a large, ungainly bonnet with a huge blue bow. She looked neither to the left nor to the right but proceeded to the piano, where she sat down and began immediately to play a rousing hymn.

"I like pipes better!" old Susanna proclaimed. "Can't hear that thing!"

The Reverend Aloysius McGrath walked out of the vestry. He stood before his congregation and the invited wedding guests, looking out on them benevolently.

"Who's he?" crusty old Susanna asked skeptically.

"The preacher," her son whispered loudly in her ear, "and the father of the groom."

"Humph! Looks like a chicken hawk!"

Kevin Macleod, dressed in his Macleod kilt, came through the vestry door followed by Ernest McGrath who was dressed in a dark funeral suit.

"That the groom?" Susanna queried. Having just arrived from Kingston, and not having visited the Niagara for five years, she had not met Ernest McGrath.

"Yes," her son replied. His face was flushed, owing to his elderly mother's running commentary and incessant questions. She was embarrassingly frank. As age had overtaken her, Susanna MacAndrew, like her own aunt, Helena Fraser, had become outspoken in the extreme and didn't care what others thought of her. He smiled at the very thought of great-aunt Helena. She had cursed so at the American soldiers that they had burned Lochiel to the ground. The story forever circulated that old Winfield Scott would have shot her, but he couldn't see for the spit in his eye.

"Good thing he's got God on his side," old Susanna declared as she squinted to examine Ernest McGrath. "I doubt that boy could fell a tree. He'd have to depend on lightning!"

One of the children in the rear giggled, and Winifred Fraser glared down from her position behind the piano. Then, returning to the keyboard, she struck up a marching hymn. Almost in unison, the congregation craned their necks around. Walking down the aisle were Ronald Macleod, in his full dress kilt, and Margot, on his arm, wearing a long white dress with a diaphanous veil that covered her face and hair.

Margot carried a bouquet of wildflowers and a bible. She and her father walked slowly toward Kevin and Ernest. Her dress, which was in fact her mother's wedding dress, clung to her fine figure, although it was high collared and modest as morality demanded.

"Grown into a fine woman!" Susanna declared with pride. "She's got the green eyes of the Macleod women and the black hair of our mother."

Andrew MacAndrew braced himself for his mother's next comment, certain that it would have something to do with Margot's ability to reproduce. But, mercifully, silence reigned momentarily, punctuated only by the restless movement of the younger children.

The Reverend Aloysius McGrath cleared his throat. "Dearly beloved. . ." he began in a deep voice.

Margot stood stark still, aware of a hundred pairs of eyes riveted on her back. She felt as if they were boring straight through her. She stared at the floorboards and then studied the tips of her white satin slippers. They too were her mother's; someone said they had been imported from Paris.

I'm on display, she thought. They've all come to watch me being given by my father to Ernest. She reminded herself that the giving and the taking was the form of the ceremony, that she had chosen Ernest willingly. In this matter she judged herself more fortunate than many other women. Most had their husbands selected for them, and though her father was not enthusiastic about her marriage to Ernest, the important thing was that he hadn't tried to stop it, either. But why was she thinking these things now? A wedding should be a happy time! All of the guests were either family or friends, she reminded herself. Why then did she suddenly feel like a piece of merchandise in the window of the general store?

"Do you, Margot Janet Macleod, take this man, Ernest Makem McGrath, in lawful wedlock?"

Margot felt frozen. Ernest nudged her roughly in the ribs.

"I do," she replied, in a voice that she hardly recognized as her own.

"To love, honor, obey, and serve, until death do you part?"

"I do," Margot whispered. She felt a little faint, but forced her eyes wide open and stared straight ahead, looking beyond the Reverend Aloysius McGrath to the spot in front of the plain altar where a sunbeam fell on the uneven plank floor. It seemed warm in the church, and Margot was aware of feeling constrained by invisible bonds. She felt as if she couldn't breath or move. She had wanted a big wedding like this, but now that it was happening, she felt out of place, and it was as if the whole affair was happening to someone else.

Somewhere in the distance, or at least it seemed as if it were in the distance, Margot could hear Ernest taking his vows, except of course that Ernest did not have to promise to serve and obey. He promised only to provide.

"In the name of our Father and His only beloved Son, Jesus Christ, Our Lord, I now pronounce you man and wife."

Again Margot felt Ernest nudge her and she turned to him still feeling otherworldly and in a trance.

Ernest lifted her veil and pecked her on the lips. She felt as if she were a puppet on a string, with her limbs being manipulated by some unseen puppet master. Margot blinked up into Ernest's solemn face.

"Now you belong to me," Ernest whispered.

A sudden chill ran through Margot. Not in the entire time that Ernest McGrath had been courting her had the reality of actually belonging to Ernest occurred to her. She was no longer her father's daughter. She was Ernest McGrath's wife; his chattel.

Briefly, Margot wondered if Narcissa Prentiss Whitman had felt the same on her wedding day, but her thoughts were drowned out when Miss Winifred Fraser began to play the familiar marching hymn on the piano.

"Margot, are you all right?" Ernest whispered.

Margot nodded. She looked up into Ernest's face, and suddenly, Ernest McGrath seemed a total stranger.

* * *

Anya pulled the brush through her hair and looked at her image in the mirror.

So, Cory MacLean did not think she could become an actress! Well, if only he knew what an actress she was. She fought back angry tears, but sadly she admitted that she was angry with herself. "I have woven a web of lies," she whispered to herself. She bit her lip. If I had not lied, he'd have never taken me to Commander Arlen, she thought, and he in turn would certainly not have brought me here to freedom.

Anya opened the jewelry box on her dresser. The emeralds, rubies, and diamonds sparkled. "Baubles," she murmured. But they had served their purpose. She had to sell only two in order to begin the construction on the theater and to have sufficient money for food and to hire Rosa and the farmhand who worked Cory's neglected fields. She sighed, thinking how she had sewn the precious gems into her clothes, making it possible for her to escape with them. But the gems held no other value for her, save the fact that because she had stolen them, she could never return to Russia.

Anya closed her eyes and tried to remember her beloved parents who had died in St. Petersburg so many years ago. "I love you," she whispered.

Anya stood up and walked to the bed. She took off her robe and lay down. Perhaps she ought to have told Mr. MacLean her true story.

No, she decided. No matter what her life here, no matter how lonely, it was better than the life she would have had in Russia had she remained. It was at least warm here, and there were trees and flowers, high mountains, blue sky, people who were kind. Perhaps things will work out.

The image of her uncle's face came into her thoughts. His bearded visage haunted her and she could still see his mad eyes flash with lust and anger. When her parents had died, Anya, then a mere girl of thirteen, had been given to her uncle. He was a harsh, cruel man, and as unlike her real father as night from day. He was in the army and at first he had left her in St. Petersburg, but later he had taken her to live wherever he was stationed—even to the far outposts of Siberia.

As she grew older, her uncle's treatment of her turned

103

from cruelty to lust. He had begun when she was sixteen, shortly after he had returned from being away. It was a night Anya could never forget, a night that haunted her dreams and intruded on her consciousness.

He had called her into his study, and when she thought about it she could almost remember his breath, which reeked of garlic and vodka. He had ripped her clothing away and he had grasped her breasts, and he had mawled her roughly before raping her brutally.

From that night on, he demanded her in his bed. Often he tied her so she could not struggle against his vile appetites; always, he possessed her cruelly. It was a never-ending nightmare from which there seemed no escape. She was never left alone, she was never free of his unwanted caresses unless, for his own reasons, he tired of her and spent the night with one of the servant girls.

Then, seeking to make himself richer and to achieve more status, he promised to sell her in marriage to Count Vaslov, a fat sixty-year-old whose appetites were no less perverted than his own.

"He will both tie you and beat you," her uncle had threatened on the last night he had spent with her. "You should enjoy yourself with me now; your life will not be so pleasant with the Count!" Anya had known the marriage would take place as soon as they returned from the far outpost of Kamchatka.

Thus she had spent one last night in her drunken uncle's bed, and while he slept she stole away the family jewels and sewed them into men's clothing. In the early hours of the morning she had dressed warmly and gone to the mountains, where she had hidden in a cave without food for three days, until her uncle was forced to stop looking for her and to obey his orders to remove the troops under his command from the fort.

When she had seen the British ships in the harbor, Anya had emerged fearfully from hiding and returned to the fort, where she had encountered Cory MacLean.

But Anya had deemed it wise not to tell Cory or Captain Arlen that the jewels were stolen, or that if she was returned to her uncle he would have her killed. Nor, she thought, wiping a tear off her face, could she let Cory know that she was the victim of her uncle's lust. No man would marry a woman with such a past, she thought sadly.

"I shall have to get on by myself," she whispered aloud. "I shall have to go on letting Mr. MacLean believe me to be what I am not. I have chosen my own role, now I must act out my part."

Anya sat up. She had hoped to take a short nap, but her mind was too filled with past and present to rest. She walked to the window and looked out on the peaceful landscape.

Her eyes fell on Cory MacLean, who was standing near the shed. "Such a handsome man," she said. His sandy hair, his soft eyes, his obvious strength. But it was not only his looks. . . . He was a kind man, and though he laughed at her, it was in a good-natured kind of way.

"But I will not allow myself to want you," she promised herself. "You would not like me if you knew the truth—if you knew what my uncle did to me, if you knew I was a thief."

Anya stood and watched Cory, then she saw Rosa appear. Cory greeted the mulatto servant girl with a warm smile, and put his hand on her shoulder. Then together they walked to far side of the shed, out of Anya's view.

Anya felt the flush of jealousy sweep through her—surely Cory MacLean wouldn't carry on with a servant! But then she remembered the look of pure lust in Cory's eyes when he had first seen Rosa. "Men!" Anya stamped her foot and let the curtain drop. Mr. MacLean was no better than the others!

CHAPTER VIII

April 12, 1856

Ernest McGrath lay on the bed, his unruly hair falling across his forehead, his long hairy legs exposed beneath his red flannel nightshirt. His hands were folded across his belly, and he stared straight ahead.

He wished to flee this room, to hide somewhere and not to have to face another single second more of nagging apprehension. It was a horror! How could he spend night after night with Margot?

The night before his wedding, his nightmare had returned to him; as a result he had hardly slept at all. Instead he had lain awake and, for the first time, tried to design a plan to deal with Margot.

Virginal she might be, but she like all the others would certainly expect to couple on her wedding night. She would justify it by saying that she wanted children. "Well, I don't want them," Ernest muttered under his breath. "And I will not touch her!" After all, the missionary society deemed he should have a wife, but they certainly didn't say he had to unite with her physically.

Ernest tried to push the thought of coupling from his mind and concentrate on the wedding ceremony.

"The actual wedding ceremony is hard on every man," his father had told him at the ungodly reception that had followed. He had begun by commenting that Ernest didn't look well. And Ernest had replied that he was nervous and hadn't slept the night before.

"I would certainly be the last person not to admit that some of Margot's family are . . . well, not our kind. But nonetheless, I feel you've married a good, virtuous woman. In any event, you're taking her far away from her family.

You, Ernest, will be the total influence on her life. It is up to you to mold her into the proper image."

Ernest reflected on his father's little speech, made in a whisper and well out of earshot of the other guests, most of whom were consumed with listening to and watching old Susanna MacAndrew.

Susanna's crochety voice echoed in Ernest's mind. "An old harridan," he mumbled.

Susanna MacAndrew had walked right up to the punch bowl and filled her glass with cold apple drink. But when she tasted it, she had made a nasty face, gulped it down, and shouted, "It's not fermented!"

"Our Lord tells us that the taking of fermented beverages is an evil act," Aloysius McGrath had told her in an equally loud voice.

But Susanna had only squinted at him as if he were some small insect and shouted back, "Obviously, we don't have the same Lord! Mine has never said a word about fermented drink, and if He were going to speak to anyone it would definitely be me!"

Among the guests there had been one ripple of agreement and another of disagreement. Ernest had only noted the look of pure pleasure on Ronald Macleod's face. Margot, on the other hand, had looked flushed with embarrassment at her aunt's behavior.

Of course, nothing closed old Susanna's mouth. "First, no pipes!" she declared. "What kind of Scots gets married without pipes all the way to the wedding bed!" Then she had stamped her foot and announced, "Well, I've been in this house often enough to know where what I want is, and I intend to have some!" With that she had marched off to the cellar and returned with three bottles of blueberry brandy and four bottles of whiskey. Those among the guests who drank, drank heartily, and those who were abstainers, abstained. Margot, Ernest was pleased to note, abstained utterly and busied herself with mumbled apologies to members of the congregation.

But the day is over, Ernest thought. And now . . . now the test was about to begin. He tried to steel himself.

Margot peered out at him from the small dressing room adjacent to the bedroom. Why Ernest insisted on spending their wedding night in his father's house was beyond her. Perhaps it was a little more convenient, since they were to catch the lake steamer quite early in the morning.

She had brushed her long hair out until it hung loose and gleaming over her white nightdress. It was a modest nightdress with a high top, and it fell to her ankles.

"Ernest?" She hesitated on the threshold of the bedroom door.

"I'm waiting, Margot."

Margot walked into the room and stood at the foot of the bed. She felt cold all over, and though the memory of her marriage vows seemed to be directing her, her every instinct was to run away.

Ernest shifted uneasily, seemingly looking right past her as if she did not exist. He must feel as nervous as I, she thought. But somehow his lack of attention annoyed her. She wanted him to say she looked beautiful . . . she wanted him to hold her and make himself less of a stranger. She momentarily remembered his moment of passion on the shore when they had picnicked. But, of course, they were only just courting then, and he had had to exercise great self-control. But now there was no need for that. They were man and wife; Ernest could be as passionate as he wanted.

"Shall I come and lie next to you?"

"Yes."

Margot lay down and stretched herself out next to him, feeling the warmth of his body next to hers. But Ernest didn't move. He lay exactly as he had been, like a great long stone.

"You seem uneasy," Margot ventured.

"I have never lain with a woman . . ." His nightmare returned. No, dreams did not count. He could not control his dreams. But he certainly could control what did or did not happen when he was conscious.

"I should hope not!" Margot responded.

"It is a vile temptation."

Margot turned her head toward him. "Ernest, we're married. You need not be so uneasy . . . I certainly have never been with a man before, either.''

"Good heavens! The thought that you had never even occurred to me!''

"Ernest, kiss me.''

"Margot, I've been thinking. I've been thinking that although we will obviously require children, we certainly don't want them right away. The journey west is arduous, it would be ill-advised for us to . . . to couple.''

"Not couple?'' Margot felt overwhelmed. Was he serious? Didn't he find her attractive? Surely Narcissa Prentiss Whitman didn't have a husband who refused to couple with her. She was pregnant by the time she reached Fort Laramie.

"Ernest, I don't understand.''

"It is evil to couple with a woman unless you intend to impregnate her, and since I do not intend to impregnate you, we ought not to come together in conjunction on this night.''

"It's our wedding night!''

"Shh! My own father is in the room right down the hall. My God, Margot, do you want him to hear you? He'll think you are some kind of wanton animal with no self-control whatsoever!''

"Ernest, you are my lawful husband!'' Margot sat bolt upright in bed. "There is nothing evil about a man . . . a man making love to his wife!''

Ernest too sat up and turned to face her for the first time. "Margot, my dear Margot, you are a lovely virgin angel. I respect you and worship you. And I forgive you because you are so young and innocent, but you are tempted by the flesh. You must overcome temptation before you can know the joy of true salvation. It is a test, don't you see? It is a true test of our faith to lie together without coupling and without touching one another.'' Ernest's voice was trembling.

"For how long?'' Margot blurted out. The truth was, she had wanted to be pregnant like Narcissa before she reached Fort Laramie. How else could she and Ernest properly recreate the journey of Narcissa and Marcus?

"Until my prayers are answered. . . . Until I hear the

110

voice of the Lord telling me it is the time to couple with you."

Margot stared out across the strange room. Inside, she felt a growing anger born of exasperation. Ernest had so seldom kissed her properly and had hardly ever held her close. Now he wanted to spend night after night with her in bed and not even touch her?

"Ernest, I am your wife. I love you. At least, I think I love you."

Margot was aware that she wanted him to hold her tightly, to kiss her. She supposed she wanted him to make love to her, but she wasn't really sure what she wanted. "Ernest, hold me."

"Margot, I am shocked! You are behaving like a hussy! And look at you, your hair is loose and you look . . . you look desirous!"

Margot's eyes fell on Ernest's naked toes. They were long and pointed and there was a tuft of dark hair on the big toe. She allowed her eyes to travel up his legs, past his slightly knobby knees. Under his nightshirt, she could see there was a bulge; she stared at it, fascinated. He certainly did want her! Margot looked into Ernest's face and saw that it was bright red.

In a moment of utter brazenness, Margot reached out and grasped the bulge. Ernest jumped straight up and emitted a strange gurgling sound from deep inside his throat. He automatically lifted his hand and struck out at her, slapping her across the face. "Margot! Unhand me at once!" His voice was unnaturally high.

Margot let go instantly and lifted her hand to her face, which smarted from his slap. Tears welled in her eyes and she was aware that Ernest was shaking violently.

"What in heaven's name is wrong with you?" she sobbed.

"Shh! I told you to lower your voice. My father can probably hear every unseemly word you utter! I will not be tempted by the devil!"

Margot looked down at the covers. She felt betrayed and wounded, rejected and lonely. "I don't understand you, Er-

111

nest. I really don't. Do I displease you? Don't you love me?''

"I honor you. I want you to be innocent and virginal. I'm very fond of you, but love is . . . It has to grow."

"I do displease you. . . ." Tears flowed down her face.

"Only when you touch me . . . there. It's evil. No woman should be so presumptuous as to touch a man in that place. Only a harlot, a devil, would do such a thing!"

"I am not a devil or a harlot!"

"I realize you are merely ignorant. I forgive you."

"Ernest. . . ." Margot heard the pleading in her own voice. She closed her eyes to stop the tears from running down her face.

"Margot, I shall allow myself to kiss you good night." He leaned over and pecked her on the cheek. "Good night."

Without further hesitation, Ernest extinguished the lamp. After a moment, Margot lay down, turning over and rolling up into a ball on the far side of the bed. Margot, indeed. He spoke her name and he sounded distant and unattached. She longed to hear her father's voice. There was warmth in his voice, even when he was annoyed with her. She lay staring into the blackness, listening only to Ernest's heavy breathing on the other side of the bed. She wished she were a child again, playing in the fields of Lochiel instead of lying next to this mysterious and obstinate man of the faith.

"Ernest, I don't understand you at all," she said, not turning in the bed. "If you can't or won't make love to me on our wedding night, the very least you could do is show me some affection and consideration."

"You seem like a stranger," she heard him reply. "Yesterday, you were prim and proper, tonight you're brazen and wanton."

"I yearn to have you hold me, Ernest. I need love and affection. I lost my mother as a small child. . . . So did you. I need . . . no, I want your arms around me. Ernest, I don't see this night as a test. . . . I believe in God, I believe God intended us to love one another. It is no sin to take one's wife!"

"I shall decide what is sinful and what is not! It is not for

112

you to interpret the word of the Lord. I'm sorry, Margot. But I have made a vow not to possess you until the Lord speaks to me. I have prayed for, and received the strength to remain celibate until the Lord gives me a sign.''

Margot didn't answer. Instead she curled herself into an even tighter ball. The past year of her courtship flitted across her mind. She didn't know this man with whom she now shared a bed! But I am his wife, she reminded herself. The vows are sacred . . . I am committed by the law and by God. She closed her tear-filled eyes and hugged the feather pillow beneath her head. She prayed only for sleep to release her from her disappointment, confusion, and fear.

Ernest busied himself directing the two dock workers who loaded the trunks onto the steamer. Margot stood, satchel in hand, looking at her father. She felt tongue-tied and unable to move. On the one hand, her marriage vows commanded her to follow Ernest. But she knew now that she had made a horrible mistake, or at least she felt so at this moment. But it was her mistake . . . It was a mistake she had to live with because certainly her father had not wanted her to marry Ernest.

''Margot, are you all right?'' Ronald asked with concern. She nodded.

''Frankly, you don't look well.'' Ronald hesitated. Knowing Margot's propriety as he did, he didn't want to be too blunt. ''Did everything go well?'' he asked vaguely.

Margot looked down at the ground. ''Yes, I'm just tired.''

Ronald didn't reply. He supposed a woman might be tired after her wedding night—he certainly had been. But he recalled his wife's face in the morning. Tara had glowed, and between them had been the knowledge of their love for one another. It troubled Ronald that Margot didn't glow as a well-bedded woman should. In fact, she looked weary and unhappy, not how he expected a blushing bride to look.

''You're certain you want to leave?''

''It's too late now,'' Margot answered. She realized she had revealed too much as soon as she spoke the words. She

113

quickly covered herself, forcing a smile to her face. "Of course, Papa."

"It's time, Margot!" Ernest called from the end of the dock.

Margot looked up into her father's face. She threw her arms around him and tears began to run down her cheeks. "I love you, Papa! I really do!"

"And I love you!" He enfolded her in his arms and kissed her on the cheek.

"I'll miss you, Papa. I'll miss you and Kevin."

Ronald pressed his lips together and nodded. "I'll be here," he whispered "And I'll miss you, too."

Margot dropped her arms and Ronald let her go. She hurried down the dock toward Ernest; then she turned and waved. Her father waved back.

Margot followed Ernest to the deck of the steamer and stood by the railing as the boat hooted its horn and pulled away from the dock out into the glassy blue of the lake. Margot clung to the rail, waving now and again to her father, who soon became a speck on the dock.

She felt empty inside as she watched the hills grow more distant. "Lochiel," she said under her breath. She thought about all the family stories she had heard over the years. . . . She thought about her great-great-great-grandmother, Janet Cameron Macleod, who left Scotland in 1746 after the battle of Culloden. She wondered how she had felt, leaving her ancestral home. She wondered if Janet had felt the same loneliness and the same dejection. Margot sighed.

"We're leaving the past," Ernest proclaimed. And he admitted to himself that he felt almost happy for the first time in some while. He fervently prayed that he could properly mold Margot into a good, prudent wife who would not, in the future, demand that he couple with her. He felt confident that once she was away from her family, she would do his bidding and his bidding alone. In time, she would understand the evils of the flesh.

"I like my past," Margot said, tears again filling her eyes.

Ernest did not reply.

* * *

Cory lay on his bed in the half-light provided by the small flickering lamp. Its subdued light cast long shadows across his room. Rosa stood at the foot of his bed. She moved with the silence of a cat and with the grace of a dancer.

Cory smiled as she pulled her camisole up over her head, enabling him to take a lingering look at her well-shaped golden breasts. Her skin seemed to glisten and her sensuous pouty lips looked ready and willing to devour him.

She slipped off her skirts and bared her rounded hips, her mound with its tight black curls, her lovely legs—although, he thought, her thighs were a trifle too plump. She smiled at him and arched one eyebrow, silently asking if he were ready.

Cory held out his arms to her and she spread herself out over him, her breasts pressing against his chest, her dark hair hanging in his face. Cory breathed deeply. She was pure lust and her movements against him achieved their goal instantly. It had been too many months since he had had a woman, he decided. Small wonder she aroused him so easily.

She touched him and stroked him, then she made a noise of satisfaction at his length and dimensions. Cory reached for her breasts—her brown nipples were erect and he toyed with them, watching as they grew harder.

"You are a big man," she breathed, kissing and biting his neck. Cory seized her bare buttocks; he caressed them, even as she moved them suggestively and groaned with pleasure.

Rosa was an experienced whore. And, servant or not, she had bargained for her services even though it was quite clear that she liked him. Her almond-shaped golden eyes fastened on his face and she separated her legs, kneeling astride him.

"Touch me," she whispered.

Cory slipped his left hand from her buttocks around her hips and toyed with her. Her sensuous mouth opened slightly, her almond eyes closed, and she moved her hips in small circles. The tips of her breasts moved across his face, and Cory caught one in his mouth and sucked lightly, flicking his tongue at her nipple.

Rosa groaned again, a deep guttural sound, and Cory watched her as his teasing brought her to satisfaction. Her mouth opened wider, her breathing almost ceased, then she arched her back and tossed her head. Letting out a gasp, she collapsed against him.

He waited a moment, then he rolled her over onto her back and began anew, kissing her nipples, moving his hands over her smooth flesh until he came again to her mound. She twitched and embraced him; he pushed her legs apart and sunk into the moist depths of her, feeling her softly close about him. She nearly danced beneath him, writhing this way and that, almost humming as she moved, lost in her own sensations. Cory burst into her, shaking and falling into that abyss of pleasurable satisfaction. His eyes were closed tightly, and in his mind's eye he saw Anya beneath him rather than Rosa.

Cory let out his breath and collapsed beside the panting, damp body of Rosa. He stared at the ceiling of the room. Why had he thought of Anya, who no doubt was sleeping peacefully in her own room down the hall? Cory shook his head, trying to bring himself back to reality. It was an absurd thought. Anya showed no interest in him whatsoever, save that she seemed mildly interested in his money.

Rosa reached over and caressed him. Strangely, he did not rise again. She ceased trying and cuddled up beside him. When, he asked himself, had he not been able to satisfy a woman more than once? Reluctantly, he admitted it was because he was thinking of another woman.

"You don't like Rosa?"

"I like you," Cory replied.

"No, you don't," she pouted.

Cory didn't answer.

"You like Rosa's mistress."

"I like her, but not like this."

"That's not true. I see the way you look at her."

Cory frowned. How did he look at her? "I don't know what you mean," he answered, trying to sound unconcerned. "She's too, too cold."

116

Rosa shook her head. "She's not cold. She cries a lot, she's very lonely."

Cory turned and looked into Rosa's eyes. He had never found himself in bed with one woman and discussing another. "What do you mean she cries a lot?"

"I see her sometimes. She is lonely. I think she likes you."

"She likes my money."

"She has her own money. I have seen her jewels. No, I think she likes you."

Cory laughed. This was an absurd conversation. "Don't you?" he asked.

Rosa smiled. "I like you. You are gentle, you are nice and you pay me well. But I do not love you. I love Sir Fitz!"

Sir Fitz was the horse trainer at Craigflower Farm. He was a tall, strong mulatto from the Caribbean, probably from the same place as Rosa. They made a fine match. Sir Fitz was an amiable sort, called Sir Fitz because he had elegant manners and affected an imitation of the British so well.

"Doesn't he mind that you . . . ah . . ."

Rosa shook her head. "We are saving money to get married and have our own farm. Sir Fitz doesn't mind; he knows I can earn a lot. He doesn't mind as long as I don't do everything with the others."

"Everything?"

Rosa smiled lecherously. "Sir Fitz and I . . . we do different things."

Cory almost laughed.

"Would you be hurt if I asked you to leave me alone?"

Rosa shook her head. "Not if I get the same money."

"Oh, you will. I promise."

Rosa dressed more quickly than she had undressed, and, Cory noted, she looked happier. He sighed. "Must be losing my touch," he said out loud after she had closed the door, leaving him in the lamplight alone.

Cory got up and blew out the lamp. He returned to bed and lay in the darkness, thinking of Anya. "Damn!" he said aloud.

Cory hummed to himself and, with a gesture of supreme confidence, tossed the eggs in the pan into the air, catching them and returning them to the stovetop.

"What are you doing?" Anya asked, wide-eyed.

"It's the only way to make an omelet. You'll like it."

"Men in Russia do not cook. Where is Rosa?"

"I sent her away."

Anya didn't answer him. Not only had she seen Rosa leave late at night from his room, she had heard the noises she so easily recognized as the noises of two people making love. But of course, Rosa had seemed to enjoy it, while she herself had never known pleasure in a man's arms. Somehow that thought had made her even more angry, and more resentful. Love, she thought, ought to be enjoyed, and she felt she had the same right as Rosa to know such enjoyment. Fate had dealt her an unfair blow. The only man she had slept with had been brutal . . . She felt she might never know gentleness.

"You should not have sent her away. Now there is no one to cook," Anya finally said, shaking her head.

"I cook. Don't you cook?"

"Never. Peasants cook."

"Well, you said I was a peasant," he reminded her, cutting the omelet in half and putting the halves onto two plates. He handed one to Anya and took one for himself. He had already put out bread, jam, and coffee.

Anya looked at her plate suspiciously.

"Go on, try it." Cory sat down and took a mouthful. "Good, if I do say so myself."

Anya delicately took a little. She tasted it as if she expected poison. "Oh, it is good."

"When will the theater be completed?"

"In few weeks time . . . so they tell me." She looked up at him with her huge blue eyes. "Would you like to go into Victoria and look at it?"

Cory nodded. "Tell me, what is your first production going to be?"

"Romeo and Juliet. I would do Pushkin, but nobody understands Russian.''

"Ambitious. And whom do you intend to use for the other actors?''

"Oh, I will train them. But Commander Arlen said he would play Romeo. He knows the part.''

Cory choked, "I'll bet he does," he said sarcastically.

"But that's a long way off.''

Cory finished his omelet and drank some of the coffee. He looked across at Anya. She was beautiful. "Are you well?'' he asked her.

"Why?'' Her blue eyes flashed.

"Because Rosa said you were unhappy.''

Anya looked down at her plate.

Cory's face reddened. He reached across the table to take Anya's hand, but she snatched it away.

"I am not Rosa! Don't you touch me!''

Cory scowled. "I promise I won't," he mumbled.

"Men!'' she uttered.

"Are human," Cory countered. "I'd really like to know what makes you unhappy.''

"I am not unhappy! Rosa is incorrect. I am very happy! I am blissful!'' She burst into tears.

Cory stood up and came around the table. "So happy you can't help crying?'' he asked softly.

"Leave me alone!'' Anya stood up and ran from the kitchen. "And don't come near me! Don't you ever come near me!''

CHAPTER IX

May 25, 1856

Blaise Baron smiled to himself as he approached the outskirts of Independence. Today, May 25, 1856, was his thirty-fifth birthday and had he been able to choose a place to spend it, he could not have chosen a more appropriate locale except for his native Quebec.

Independence and its adjacent river ports on the Missouri were the eastern terminus for the wagon trains headed west. The dusty little town, full of livestock pens, ramshackle houses, raw frontier saloons, and warehouses, represented a new beginning for Blaise; it was here that he had begun his new life eighteen years ago. And, he thought sentimentally, this trip would probably be his last. The railroads would soon cross the entire continent; the rumbling wagons would disappear into history. The telegraph already reached to the Mississippi. Times were changing. One day the land between the river and the Pacific ocean would all be settled and towns would replace forts.

Earlier this morning, Blaise had come to the fork in the trail. He had turned his horse around and faced west momentarily to read the rotting wooden sign at the crossroads of the rutted wagon routes. One arrow pointed off across the plains and simply read, "Santa Fe Trail." The other, indicating a more northward direction, read, "Road to Oregon."

In 1838, when Blaise was nearly seventeen, he had chosen the road to Oregon, and that choice had led him to the majesty of the Pacific Northwest, and into a varied career.

Blaise wiped his mouth. It was dry from his long ride. He guided his horse down the dusty street toward the livery stable. On either side of the road were wooden houses and places of business. At the far end of the street, a large uneven sign advertised, 'The Missouri Saloon,' and across the street stood the less than impressive 'Independence Hotel.' Down the street was the 'Missouri Outfitters.'

Blaise left his horse at the stable and walked down the main street, keeping close to the buildings in order to avoid the piles of horse manure which sat in fly covered clumps on the road, giving off a heavy pungent odor in the hot sun.

A slight, humid breeze blew off the Missouri River—it was always humid here, and the humidity made the air seem even hotter than it was. Hell, Blaise thought, it was so humid that sometimes winter ice formed on the roads simply because of the moisture in the atmosphere. He smelled the aroma of frying catfish from the campground where would-be settlers spent their days waiting for their wagons to be ready.

Blaise pushed open the door of the saloon. The floor was covered with sawdust, the tables rough-hewn, with uneven legs. In one corner, two elderly men sprawled in chairs and silently drank whiskey. There were five or six men sitting around, all deeply absorbed in their drinking. It was only ten in the morning; larger groups didn't usually appear until late in the afternoon.

"Whiskey," Blaise ordered, leaning against the bar, one foot on its iron rail.

"Blaze Baron! Ain't seen you in a mule's age, Frenchie!" Old Henry, the barkeeper, smiled his toothless grin as he shoved a bottle of whiskey and glass across the surface of the bar.

Blaise smiled. All Americans pronounced his French name with the hard z sound, rather than with the more subtle French pronunciation.

"Well, where you been, Blaze?"

"The Northwest. I guess it's been two, two and a half years," Blaise admitted. He poured himself two fingers of whiskey.

"How you been keeping, Frenchie?"

"Good," Blaise answered. "Here, get yourself a glass and let me buy you a drink."

Henry produced another glass and wiped it on his stained

apron. "Don't mind if I do." He looked at the glass. "I usually drink out of the bottles."

"Wish me a happy birthday," Blaise suggested, raising his glass.

"Happy birthday," Henry responded, gulping down his drink. "Be taking a wagon train west?"

"A bunch of 'greenhorns.' Some missionaries and settlers. It's called the Oregon II. Any of them arrived yet?" Henry nodded. " 'Bout ten or twelve been in here. Don't know how many are them missionaries, but they're abstainers."

Blaise made a face. "They won't be by the time they're in Boise." He gave Boise its proper French pronounciation, and Henry laughed.

"Hey, Frenchie, you'll never lose your accent. We say Boysee."

Blaise took a gulp of whiskey and licked his lips. *"Les bois! Les Bois! Voyez le bois!* That, my friend is what a French U.S. Army Captain named Benjamin Louis Eulalie de Bonneville shouted when he stood on the ridge and saw that beautiful river lined with timber. First trees and good water the settlers saw after days and weeks in the hot sun on the treeless plains back in the 1830s. *Boise* is a French name. You are the one with an accent." Blaise smiled and winked.

Henry gulped another glass of whiskey. "You ain't changed a bit. You're a walking, talking book, Blaze Baron. Only educated cowpoke 'round. Rest of 'em got ten words in their vocabulary and eight of 'em are cuss words." Henry nodded appreciatively.

Blaise grinned. "Have another drink."

"Sure, don't mind if I do."

"Where are my greenhorns holed up?"

"Some at the hotel—hear tell the missionaries are there. Hear tell one of them is a real hellfire preacher. Says lustful women should be branded like cows and drinking men should have their pants beat off!" Henry laughed. "I guess the rest are down by the river living in their wagons."

Blaise made a face at Henry's description of the preacher. "Have they had any elections yet?"

It was the custom that those who participated in a trek west elected their own government for the journey. Usually, the families elected one person as leader. They were also obligated to draw up a sort of constitution and to make laws and rules for the trip, as well as a schedule for guard duty. A wagon train had to be highly organized for the venture to be successful; it had to operate with military precision. This, Blaise thought, was an excellent and democratic system. Of course, given the strains of the trip, the dangers, and the close quarters people lived in, disputes did develop. If the elected leader could not deal with them, he was forced to step in as arbitrator.

Henry shook his head. "Nope, think they're meeting tomorrow night. Heard a couple of fellows in here talking yesterday. Said they might elect the preacher, but they all refused to go west dry."

"Somehow the preacher doesn't sound like a compromising man to me." Blaise rather hoped there would be a military man aboard. They generally made the best leaders.

"Guess I better go off and get cleaned up and find the lot of them," Blaise said. "I'll be back later."

"Got a new woman here," Henry whispered. "Real nice if you got the money."

Blaise grinned. "I've got the money."

Henry raised his own half-filled glass. "Happy birthday," he repeated.

Cory MacLean sloshed the water in the pan and smiled. There was gold in the Fraser River; now the trick was to find the vein and to begin working it.

He stood up and stretched. He always enjoyed the mountain air and the sound of the wind in the tall pines. But soon, he thought, the hills would be alive with prospectors; towns would spring up from out of nowhere, the mountains would no longer be uninhabited.

He walked back to his campsite. "Time for a good breakfast," he said aloud, listening to his own voice. The fire he had made nearly an hour ago was reduced to a bed of red-hot coals and was ready to cook on. He put the coffee tin on to heat and he cracked the spruce grouse egg he had found earlier into the pan.

Memories filled his thoughts, memories of Anya and his house on Vancouver Island. He had left two days after his failed attempt to find out more about his house guest. Originally, he had intended to stay on his farm until late June, but he had left almost immediately following his argument with Anya in the kitchen. She haunted his every thought and he had felt a strong desire to go off alone in order to think.

Certainly he was alone now. There wasn't a quieter, more deserted place a man could go in order to work out his own state of mind. Cory felt attracted to Anya on the one hand, and frustrated with her imperious attitude on the other, and he was concerned with her unhappiness. But he felt unable to understand her, and so he rationalized the fact that his claim should be worked and used it as an excuse to flee the situation. So he had packed his gear and left, promising to be home before winter came to the mountains. In time, he hoped, Anya might change. She might be more willing to confide in him when he returned.

Anya had bid him goodby somewhat coolly, but her eyes spoke of different emotions and Cory felt confused by her as well as attracted. "Time to think," he said aloud. "The mountains give a man time to think and to consider things."

Cory wiped his brow. He felt warm for so early in the morning. He blinked into the fire, aware of a certain lightness in his head. Instinctively, he lifted his hand to his brow, then shrugged. If he had a fever, he couldn't tell.

Cory ate his breakfast, but not with his usual enthusiasm. Ordinarily, the mountain air and the hard early morning work gave him a splendid appetite, but now all he felt was mild nausea. He rinsed out his pans in the clear stream and drank some water. Then, somewhat listlessly, he returned to panning.

Midday, when the sun was burning down, Cory felt overcome with fatigue. He walked back to the campsite and crawled into his tent and stretched out. He fell asleep almost instantly, a deep dreamless sleep.

Some hours later, when twilight had fallen over the forest and the sun had dropped behind the mountains, Cory awoke

125

in sudden fear. He was shivering and shaking violently. His teeth chattered and his brow was extraordinarily warm. He drew his blanket around him and closed his eyes. "It'll pass," he told himself, not really believing it. "Got to ride it out." He was too far from civilization—miles from even the nearest Indian village. "I'll be all right tomorrow," he told himself. "Rest—I need to sleep more."

The Independence Hotel was the tallest building in town, rising three stories from the dusty dirt road. Unlike the buildings in Upper and Lower Canada, with their peaked roofs, the Independence Hotel and the other buildings in town were all flat roofed. The hotel's walls were made of clapboard and the building had an overhang in the front which helped shade the narrow walkway on the side of the street.

The lobby consisted of a wide corridor furnished only with a desk. To one side was the dining room outfitted with long family-sized tables, and on the other side was the hotel saloon, which offered competition to the Missouri Saloon across the street. There were, in fact, seven saloons in Independence, but in spite of the number, each was filled to capacity by nine every night, a state of affairs that both rankled and appalled the Reverend Ernest McGrath.

The individual rooms of the Independence Hotel were as sparsely furnished as the lobby. The room shared by Ernest and Margot had only an iron double bed, a small wooden table with a lamp, a crude wardrobe, and a small wooden dresser above which hung a tin mirror. On the dresser was a pitcher of water and an old porcelain bowl which served as a sink for washing. Underneath the bed was a yellowed chamber pot, and out behind the hotel was an enclosed shower stall for the benefit of the hotel's guests. Apart from that, a bath in a large wooden tub could be arranged.

It had taken Ernest and Margot about a month to get to Independence. Since their arrival, Ernest met with the other participants of the wagon train nightly. Much to Margot's unhappiness, he was caught up in campaigning to be elected leader, and each evening, following the meetings, he bragged to her about his abilities and told her how taken the settlers were with his preaching. Tonight, they were all meeting down by the river to set out the rules and regulations by which the train would be governed.

"You need not come, Margot, The meetings are for men. What is decided is of utterly no importance to women."

Margot had only nodded. She found herself with no desire to listen to Ernest preach, to see him be elected, or even to know what was going on. It was quite bad enough to have to listen to him afterward.

With each day that passed, his ego grew larger and his religion stricter. When he baptized infants, he held their heads under water so long that the poor babies emerged coughing and sputtering and terrified. When he married a couple, he instructed them endlessly on the evils of coupling and he counseled parents to beat the fear of God into their children lest their sons grow up lustful and their daughters wanton. And he urged all to cease drinking and ban foul liquor from the train. So intense had Ernest become that he frightened Margot. Her father had been right; in Ernest's religion there was no room for joy. But in spite of everything, Ernest had charisma. More than half the members of the train supported him, yeaing to the constant commands in his sermons like sheep.

Margot stared into the tin mirror over the dresser. Her image was slightly distorted, and she wondered if her face revealed her unhappiness. She seemed to go through each day by rote, doing whatever there was to do and attempting to bury her apprehension and fear of the future.

Not since their wedding night had she and Ernest spoken of coupling, and on the long journey to Independence he had faithfully kept his vow of celibacy and his promise not to unite with her until the Lord spoke to him.

Day by day, Margot felt more distant from him; day by day she admitted to herself that they had never been close in the first place. She felt angry, frustrated, and betrayed. Ernest always seemed to have time for others. He gave of himself to others, he offered advice, he preached nightly. Ernest, Margot decided with irritation, was busy promoting himself and trying to win new adherents to the faith, a faith that he was daily corrupting to suit his own purposes.

127

"He gives everything to others," she said to her image in the tin mirror. "He gives nothing to me!" But then, she admitted, she did not want anything from him anymore.

Margot inhaled deeply. She felt she could congratulate herself on one score; not since their wedding night had she spoken to Ernest about her feelings. Her pride was strong, and even now as she pulled the hairbrush through her long hair, she did so with a determination never to let Ernest know how much he had hurt her. When she cried, she cried alone. All she allowed Ernest to see was her will to survive. He was certainly not the man she thought she had married; he had the capacity to be vain and mean. And there were other facets to his personality that troubled her; his intensity, the way he sometimes looked at her, and even his tone of voice. There was something . . . something she simply couldn't define. But still, she reminded herself, she was his wife. Margot shook her head; part of her wanted to rebel, part of her demanded she adhere to her sacred marriage vows.

Margot set down the brush. "And I don't love him," she whispered.

She shook her head dejectedly. Her pride would not allow her to write her father about her problems, or to return home from her loveless marriage. Margot divided her thick black hair into two sections and tightly braided each. She had learned while traveling that braids helped keep her hair from getting dirty. When she completed the braiding, she crossed them on top of each other and pinned them up on top of her head; then she put on her bonnet.

Ernest had gone off to the election and they hadn't even had supper. For night after night, Margot had eaten alone in their room. "I don't care if it isn't proper," she declared to the mirror. "Tonight I'll eat in the restaurant. I'll not spend another night cooped up in this room."

Margot shook out her gingham dress and pulled it on. She slipped into her shoes and, satisfied that she looked as respectable as possible, went downstairs to the dining room where the waiter, a black man, showed her to one of the long tables. At the far end of the table, three men looked up as

128

she sat down. They grinned lecherously at her and doffed their hats. Margot acknowledged them with an icy stare.

She studied the tablecloth until the waiter brought her a huge pile of biscuits.

"Catfish or stew?" he drawled.

"Stew," Margot replied, "and some tea if you have it."

He nodded and disappeared. Margot looked about uneasily. She was the only woman in the room. She took a biscuit and buttered it, then nibbled at it delicately, all too aware of the men's eyes on her. Margot noted that their looks were looks of admiration, but she did not turn her head. Speaking to strangers, especially strange men, was simply not proper and could only invite improper advances on their part.

"Hey, Frenchie! How come you're not at the meeting?" One of the men at the far end of the table had called out. Margot turned slightly. A tall, very good-looking man had entered the dining room.

"It's up to them to choose a leader," he answered in what Margot recognized as a French Canadian accent. "I'm an employee. A simple wagon master."

"And the one who'll get those greenhorn bastards across the prairies and the Rockies!" the man shouted, and then his hand flew to his mouth and he looked sheepishly at Margot for having cursed.

"Sorry, ma'm," he stumbled.

Margot looked up and nodded. She turned quickly back to her crumbled biscuit.

Blaise Baron looked at her appraisingly, then he walked over and casually sat down. "You must be Polly Mae, and I must say you're prettier than I was expecting. Henry sent you over, didn't he? Well, I've got money, and I'll certainly enjoy a night in your bed."

There was laughter at the other end of the table. Margot flushed a deep red. "I don't know what you're talking about! I'm not Polly Mae, whomever she may be. I am Mrs. Ernest McGrath!"

There was more laughter, and it was Blaise's turn to be embarrassed.

"Good evening," he said, suppressing his smile. "I

thought you were someone else. . . . Henry said he'd . . . she's supposed to meet me here, ah . . . I'm sorry."

How could anyone mistake her for a . . . a prostitute! "You are bold, presumptuous, rude, and clearly immoral," she said haughtily.

Blaise smiled warmly. "And hungry." He signaled the waiter. "Mrs. McGrath. Oh, you're the preacher's wife."

Margot didn't answer. Her face was still flushed and she stared at her plate.

"Allow me to introduce myself. Blaise Baron, your wagon master."

Margot lifted her eyes and looked at him. "This is not a proper introduction," she said coolly. "As wagon master, I presume you should be speaking with my husband and not myself. He's gone to a meeting."

"I know," Blaise answered with a wink.

"Sir, I do not fraternize with strange men."

Blaise laughed. "I'm not strange, I'm really quite normal."

Margot blushed anew. His tone was insinuating and he seemed to be looking right through her clothing.

"Sir," she said in a reprimanding tone.

Again he smiled. "My dear lady, I do not desire to speak with your husband, unless of course he is elected leader of the train, and if he is we will talk in due course of time. I do desire to sit here and talk with you. Surely you know it is improper for a lady to be in the hotel restaurant unescorted."

"Improper or no, I have no intention of starving!" Margot answered angrily.

"Nor do I, Madam, And as we are about to spend many long months together on the same wagon train, and since I have introduced myself, it is quite proper that I sit with you and offer you the respectability of an escort."

"I don't need an escort."

"Of course you do, lest some other man take you for the woman I was expecting."

Margot stared at him. The waiter came and brought her tea.

"Whiskey?" he asked, looking at Blaise.

Blaise smiled mischievously, "No, tea for me, too."

There was laughter at the end of the table. "Blaise Baron drinking tea!" one of the men roared.

Blaise glanced down the table, a warning look in his eyes. The men fell silent almost at once.

Margot let out her breath. It was true that since he was the wagon master they would be seeing one another all the time. Especially if Ernest were elected leader.

"Perhaps you are right," she allowed. "Perhaps it would not be improper for you to join me."

"I've already joined you," he returned.

"You're French . . . from Lower Canada?" Margot queried. Somehow his accent made him seem like someone from home.

"Montreal," Blaise replied.

"I'm from Canada West," she offered.

In spite of the severity of her hair style, she had a remarkably beautiful face, Blaise noted. Luminous green eyes, high cheekbones, a full lovely mouth. She was much too pretty to be alone.

"English," he said evenly. "The enemy."

Margot arched an eyebrow. "Scots," she answered with some pride.

"I meant English-speaking," Blaise corrected. "Oh, there are many Scots in Montreal—wily old merchants who would deprive the French of their language and their rights. Scots or English, it hardly makes any difference."

"Monsieur!" Margot answered in French and continued to speak in French, "My family came to Lower Canada in 1746 and they fought on the same side as the French on the Plains of Abraham! It is true that many Scots are now Protestant and some are anti-Papist." Margot thought of Ernest and paused. Well, Ernest's views were not necessarily hers, although she had never thought of expressing her own views on the subject before. "None of us want to deprive you of anything!" she concluded.

Blaise's eyes twinkled. She had quite a temper, and her French was excellent. Her background reminded him of his friend Cory MacLean. His family too had sided with the French on the Plains of Abraham.

"And you are not anti-Papist?"

"My great-great-great-grandmother was a Scots Catholic," Margot whispered, unsure of why she was telling him the secret she had guarded from Ernest.

Blaise nodded. "I doubt your good husband, who is unquestionably anti-Catholic, would agree. But to you I apologize for assuming you were a bigot as are many of your countrymen. And allow me to compliment you on your French. It's excellent. And it's nice to speak a language the others can't understand, eh?" He motioned down toward the end of the table, conspiratorily.

Margot actually smiled. "Thank you," she replied. Then thoughtfully she added, "My husband and I do not always agree."

"No matter," Blaise answered. "We are not in British North America, we are in the United States. Here, our argument has no place. Here we can be friends." He was expressing a thought that occurred to him often, and which he found difficult to explain. He had encountered many English-speaking Canadians in the United States, and he had felt akin to them. It was as if they could share a feeling of kinship outside of the British colonies, but not in them. The only exception was Cory MacLean.

"How do you come to be leading a wagon train through the United States?" Margot asked.

She was approaching dangerous ground for him. Only once had he told his story, and he had no intention of breaking his rule again. Besides, the McGraths might not be the only people from Canada on the wagon train; the less they knew of his past, the better.

"I emigrated here some years ago," he said. "I presume you and your husband are the missionaries," he added, hoping to move away from the whole area of his own past.

Margot nodded. The waiter put down huge plates of stew.

"Oh, dear," Margot said, looking at the gigantic helping. "I can never eat all of this."

"They're used to feeding men who have come in off the trail. But you should try to eat it all." He looked at her figure appraisingly. "You could stand a few more pounds," he observed. "Put a little weight on your fine body. You'll lose it again on the trip."

Margot flushed again. He honestly looked as if he could see right through her dress! His soft eyes still rested on her. She was vaguely aware of both her embarrassment and her increased heartbeat.

"I've made you blush again," he said with a wink.

"Your comments are most improper," she whispered, stuttering. "I'm a married woman."

"On the contrary, I'm simply a very observant man."

"And very bold."

"And you are not as shocked as you act. In fact, you are flattered."

Margot's eyes opened wide. "Sir!"

"Could you pass the salt?" Blaise motioned toward the salt shaker on Margot's side of the table.

Margot passed the salt. He seemed unaffected by her rebuke. She decided not to say anything more. Silently, she began eating. The stew was rich and thick and delicious.

Blaise ate rapidly and drank all the tea the waiter had brought.

"Have you and your husband got your own wagon?" he asked after a few minutes.

"Yes, a prairie schooner. It's really quite nice. Ernest is seeing to the supplies."

"Keep them light," Blaise advised.

Margot smiled. "We don't have too much."

"I'll be giving the men some lists of supplies tomorrow," Blaise informed her. He stood up. "Finished?" he inquired.

"Yes. I don't think I can eat another thing."

Blaise shook his head and looked at her half-consumed plate of food. "They'll dump it back in the pot and give it to someone else," he smiled.

Margot looked at the food suspiciously. "Would they do that?"

"Yes—what is it you Scots say? 'Waste not, want not'? Now, come along. I'll see you back to your room."

"I can see myself back to my room," Margot replied stubbornly.

133

"Come along, don't argue."

There was a firmness in his voice and Margot stood up. "I doubt this is necessary."

Blaise shrugged and took her arm, leading her out of the dining room. He looked up to see a voluptuous older woman in the doorway. Her dress was low-cut, her hair piled high on her head, her lips painted bright red. He sighed and stopped.

"You must be Polly Mae?"

She smiled, "Mr. Baron?"

He nodded.

Margot dropped his arm and moved quickly through the doorway.

"Wait here for a moment, please."

"Sure," Polly replied, following Margot with her eyes.

"Please, Mr. Baron. I shouldn't want you to keep your— your friend waiting." Margot looked neither to the right nor to the left. She started up the stairs purposefully, only too aware that Mr. Baron followed.

"She won't mind," he said cheerfully. "Gets paid by the hour."

"'I really don't care to hear about your immoral arrangements."

Blaise laughed, "God, I love the English! And the Scots, too! Amour, my dear Mrs. McGrath. . . It's very nice."

"I seem to be safely here," Margot said, standing in front of the door of the room she shared with Ernest.

"Good, now I'll go enjoy my woman."

Margot's face burned deep red again. "You're a sinner!" she said, stomping her foot.

"*Oui*," Blaise answered. "Dinner with a lady, bed with a woman. It makes for a full evening."

"I am appalled!" But he had turned, leaving her by the unopened door. Margot watched as he strode down the hallway. "What a dreadful, immoral man!" she exclaimed under her breath. And arrogant! Margot opened the door and stormed inside. Then, with a flare of temper and suddenly filled with her own frustrations, she slammed the door. "Damn you, Ernest McGrath!" she said aloud.

CHAPTER X

May 26, 1856

It was pitch black inside the tent and Cory's head throbbed. His sleeping bag was wet with sweat. He was shivering again. He tried to think . . . he must have slept all day.

Somewhere in the distance a wolf bayed, and Cory strained to listen, but all he could hear was the occasional howl of the faraway wolf, the scampering of the raccoons as they searched for bits of food, and a slight rustling of the leaves as a breeze came up.

He tossed restlessly. Every part of his body ached. He fumbled for the lantern and his matches. Lifting his arm seemed harder than lifting a two-hundred-pound stone, but he managed to drag the lantern over and light it. He blinked in the sudden light and was aware of how hard it was to focus his eyes. He looked down at his bare arms. They were covered with red blotches. He groaned. "I've got spotted mountain fever," he said aloud, almost drunkenly.

Cory reached for the canteen and gulped down some water. Then, with his last ounce of strength, he blew out the lantern and fell back against his bed roll, panting.

He could die out here. The thought sent a chill through him. Panic was not his usual reaction to danger. He spent a great deal of time in the interior alone, but this was an unusual situation. Illness was a rare state in Cory's life. He closed his eyes and heard the distant rumbling of an approaching thunder storm. He tried to fight his thoughts of death and his fear of the fact that he was alone. He pulled the blanket closer around him, but his eyes snapped open at an ear-piercing roar of thunder overhead and the vigorous flapping of his tent walls.

Waving arms like shadows passed across the tent canvas in front of him and large raindrops started to plop heavily on the tent. Was he having another dream, or was a major storm breaking overhead? "Lucky the tent isn't too close to the river's edge or I could be washed away. . ." Deliriously, Cory heard himself mumbling.

He shook his head. "Damn fever!" It was interfering with his ability to think straight. He forced himself to concentrate on listening to the elements, on trying to judge the severity of the storm. The wind was now howling through the fir trees, and he heard the crackling of twigs and a low growling sound. There was a sudden sharp bolt of lightning, and Cory made himself sit up.

He saw shadows of the trees, and then one of the shadows seemed to be a large animal-like form coming close to the tent. It was certainly not a raccoon—too large—nor was it a deer—too heavy in the legs. Cory's heart began to race. With the next boom of thunder the lumbering form roared in wailing agony.

"Bear!" Cory stuttered. Electrical storms made them crazy. He sat frozen, then his hand felt around the tent and the first object it hit was the shovel handle. "Where's my rifle?" He blinked; his eyes were so out of focus. He closed his hand around the shovel handle; he was too weak to move, too blurry-eyed to shoot even if he could lay his hand on his rifle. His head spun, and the tent seemed to be moving.

Another bolt of lightning, and then thunder. The beast lashed out, its claws ripping the side of the tent. Cory hovered in its gigantic shadow, unable to swing the shovel. His arm felt dead.

The grizzly was up on its hind legs, twelve feet tall above him. Its huge mouth was open, its small dark eyes were filled with animal terror. It let out another sound—part grunt, part growl, part some kind of scream he had never heard a bear make before.

Cory didn't move a muscle; he couldn't see his gun, though he could feel his knife in its sheath. He was paralysed. The bear moved closer, slashing again at the tent flaps. In one split second of action, Cory swung the shovel at the slashing claw of his attacker. The blow missed the bear, but hit the center pole of the tent, which fell in on Cory. As the canvas closed about him, he felt himself being pushed backward by the collapsing tent. Cory heard the bear yowl with pain and then he blacked out.

Polly Mae seemed like an exceptionally girlish name for a woman who was most certainly over forty. What's more, Blaise thought as he watched her disrobe, it was a totally unsuitable name. Somehow he associated a name like Polly Mae with a wholesome farm girl, not with a woman of easy virtue plying her trade in a frontier town.

He noted that in spite of her age she was well preserved. She had told him that she was a dancer, and he assumed the daily exercise she received contributed to the preservation of her figure.

She had long legs and slim hips. Her breasts drooped without the support of her dancing costume, but they were full and firm for a woman past the prime of youth. Her hair was light brown—a little blonder on top from exposure to the sun. Her eyes were pale blue and her skin, which was tanned, would have been paler had she worn a bonnet. She was not the most beautiful woman Blaise Baron had ever been with, nor indeed was she the plainest. Women were in short supply, especially those who would bed a man for a few dollars. Most of the women on the frontier were like Mrs. McGrath, with whom he had just dined. They were straight-laced, and usually married. They frowned with self-righteousness on dance hall women, and they were aghast at the thought of white men who took Indian wives.

But west of Independence, white men outnumbered white women five hundred to one, and in the Pacific Northwest where Blaise had just come from, the figure was closer to two thousand to one. More often than not, Blaise slept with Indian women, as he had at Fort Boise. And in the matter of pure gratification, he noted that the Indian women were often more thoughtful and took the naturalness of sexual liaisons in their stride, whereas it was always something special for white women, who somehow always insisted on using the word 'love' so that their actions might be morally justified.

Alas, even the dance hall women who hired themselves out possessed a moral code. They wished to perform in the dark and they too demanded words of love, however meaningless. But worse than that, they talked constantly. On the other hand, the Indian women did not talk at all, and he missed some form of conversation both before and after fulfillment. Sometimes he wondered if there was a happy medium which he had not yet encountered; an intelligent woman with passion and compassion. Perhaps, he contemplated, if such women existed in the United States, it must be in the large cities of the East. There, he suspected, life was more sophisticated and private morality was not so much a matter of public knowledge.

Polly Mae let her final bit of clothing fall to the floor. She, at least, did not insist on turning out the light and this he attributed to the fact that she was a trifle older than her compatriots at the Missouri Saloon. He gazed at her white flesh, then dropped his eyes to her tuft of brown hair. Unexplicably, Mrs. McGrath came into his mind. He wondered what she would look like with her clothes off. He imagined milk white skin, pink nipples, jet black hair. The thought caused him to harden, and he beckoned Polly Mae to his side.

"Will you be here long?" Her voice had a slight southern drawl.

He reached out and pulled her willing body down beside him. The light caresses of his hand made her shiver, and goose pimples broke out on her arms.

"A week more," he answered abstractedly. He watched her nipples harden as he played with them, then he himself reached over and turned out the lamp. His mind, he discovered, could not discard the image of a nude Mrs. McGrath; darkness seemed more conducive to his fantasy. He fondled Polly Mae's breasts and kissed her nipples, and ran his hand along her thigh as he conjured up his own dream. Would Mrs. McGrath wiggle beneath him as Polly Mae did?

"Oh, you're so strong!" Polly Mae's slightly irritating voice intruded on his thoughts. "And so tall!"

"Sh!" he requested, exploring between her legs where the flesh was softer. He felt her hand wrap around him and pleasurably he imagined it to be the delicate white hand of Mrs. McGrath.

"My, you are strong!" Polly Mae gushed.

"Please, be quiet," he said, trying not to sound too harsh. He caressed her most sensitive areas, and she groaned.

Blaise kept stroking her, his mind now firmly on Mrs. McGrath whom he imagined beneath him. Her green eyes would be huge, her lovely lips would quiver with anticipation, her body would shake and tremble with pleasure as he lightly removed her clothing and explored her. . . . Suddenly, Blaise exploded into wild satisfaction and he heard Polly Mae gasp with delight.

"God! That was wonderful! Really wonderful!"

Blaise rolled off her and looked up into the darkness. He wondered what Mrs. McGrath's first name was.

When Cory opened his eyes, everything seemed hazy. He ascertained that he was in some form of shelter, but it was as if there were a great sea fog inside. He tried to move, but found his arms and legs were secured. He looked around again and realized that he was in a large hut, full of steam.

Cory thought he should call out; then he wondered if he could. He sniffed. He could smell the fire and see the steam. They must have built a fire beneath his bed and then covered it with something wet to create a hot box affect . . . yes, that was how the Indians treated fever. He was in a steam house.

Cory strained and lifted his neck. His legs were covered with some kind of poultices . . . he tried to wiggle his toes . . . but there was no sensation. That knowledge sent a shock of fear through him. He shrieked.

A moment after his cry, the hut door opened and the shaman entered. He was wearing the headdress of the Coyote; a mask which was utterly grotesque. Hand carved, it displayed a gaping open mouth and vicious teeth. It was painted brown and black and was covered with fur. The shaman lifted his arms and began to dance around Cory, rattling his rattles and chanting in low grunts to dispel the evil spirits.

Cory shook slightly. First he wondered if his legs were paralysed, then he wondered if he had gangrene. He saw himself as a cripple, or he might well die of infection. But in spite of his fear, he remained silent, waiting for the shaman to finish his ritual. As a man who traveled the mountains and lived among the Indians, he respected their ways. One did not interrupt a shaman, no matter what one's fears.

The shaman finished his prayers to the gods. Medicine and belief in the gods of the universe were one; there could be no treatment without spiritual cleansing. The shaman ventured closer to Cory.

"I am cured of my fever," Cory said in Salish, the language spoken by the Lillooet who inhabited the region. "Your medicine is strong."

The shaman grunted. "You were half-dead with fever when we found you, and mauled by a great bear . . . mad bear, filled with evil spirits from the skies."

The shaman pointed to the far corner of the hut where, on the end of a spear, rested the head of the grizzly, dried blood still clinging to the matted fur of its neck, lice crawling in and out of its gaping mouth.

"We kill," the shaman announced.

"I am in your debt," Cory replied, trying not to show his revulsion for the trophy.

"No. The mad bear killed a child in our village. We followed the bear and killed it, then we found you."

"I can't feel my legs," Cory said.

"I put salve on your legs to heal them. You will walk upright again."

Cory smiled. It was more than could be said for the bear.

"You will stay until you are well. I am Nkula, chief and shaman to the Lillooet."

"Thank you," Cory replied, understanding that the order was in fact an invitation.

"Why is a white skin so far from the great sea? Few venture beyond the Two Sisters."

Nkula referred to the great mountain peaks the English called the Lions. They guarded the harbor of the mainland. But they were not lions to the Indians; they were two sisters, about whom a tale of love was woven.

"I came to seek gold in the ground. Soon many will come to take gold from the ground."

Nkula nodded. "I have heard of men taking gold from ground. We had sacred gold."

Cory had heard of such tales. The Indians didn't know how to mine gold, but they often recovered it from river beds. When this happened, it was melted and molded into objects and became the sacred gold of the tribe. But these matters were not often discussed with outsiders. And then, too, Nkula had spoken of having had gold, indicating it no longer existed.

"You do not have it now?"

"Stolen," Nkula replied. "We sent a brave to recover it, but he has not returned"

"The gold I seek comes from the ground."

"The ground is under the sky. It belongs to all men who walk the earth."

"Many will come seeking it."

Nkula frowned as if he were carefully considering his next statement. "You speak our language well," he said.

"I have been among other Salish and Squamish. I have been all over the great mountains and beyond."

Nkula again nodded, but the frown of concern did not leave his face. "And the others who will come, do they speak our language and understand our ways? Do they respect the sacred grounds? They must not hunt for gold in the ground there."

"Some may respect it and others may not. I doubt many will speak the language of the great Lillooet." Cory chose his words carefully. They had saved his life, but one had to be careful not to offend. He knew the Lillooets' contact with the white man had been minimal and more often than not limited to French trappers who lived like the Indians. But he

141

didn't feel he could lie to Nkula. The people who would come would be gold rush men. They were a rough lot; they would not understand the Lillooet, nor even try.

"I will think on your predictions," Nkula announced. "Will you continue to look for gold in the ground?"

"If the great Lillooet allow me to," Cory replied.

"What do you intend to do with what you find?"

Cory smiled. "I will share it with the Lillooet to whom I owe a debt. And because it is in the ground, it should be shared."

Nkula nodded. "And can this gold be made into sacred gold like the gold that was stolen?"

"Yes," Cory answered. "Even though it comes from the ground, it is the same as the other."

Nkula grunted. "I am pleased," he conceded. "We will speak again of these matters."

With that, he turned and left.

It was the 1st of June, the date set for the departure of the wagon train from Independence. Twice Blaise had ridden the length of the wagon train with old Jackson, his assistant, a veteran of innumerable treks west over the Oregan Trail.

There were eighteen wagons in all, but three carried only supplies. The first passenger wagon belonged to the McGraths, the last to a brother and sister who were traveling with a single woman. The remaining thirteen wagons belonged to families with children, save one which held two newly married couples traveling west together.

Blaise was pleased with the passengers of the last wagon; seldom were there single women on a train, unless they were the blossoming daughters of large families. Of course, single women could cause difficulties as the tangled web of relationships developed on the long trek, and two single women traveling with one man would require additional help. He smiled to himself. Peggy McCree, one of the two women, was an attractive blond beauty. Not as ravishing as Mrs. McGrath, but certainly a woman he wouldn't mind assisting.

Blaise put aside his thoughts of Peggy McCree and

looked at the wagons. He had positioned them in a long line and drilled them repeatedly. Military precision was required, distance and timing were all-important. When a single-file wagon train needed to close its ranks, each wagon swung out alternately in opposite semicircles to form a corral. Each of the wagons' wheels were then jammed together in order to create a solid wall which could not be penetrated except for two openings. The maneuver took practice and skill.

But Blaise judged the novice drivers ready to begin the trip, and though they would not be going far this first day, a certain amount of excitement gripped the travelers as they prepared to follow his signal to begin the trek.

In the week since he had met them all, Blaise had tried to size up each of the participants and find out what special skills they had, what their experience was, and what kind of temperament each possessed. It was all part of a game he played with himself, a game of predicting who had leadership ability and who did not, who would cause difficulty and who would be cooperative.

He drew his horse up even with the first wagon. Ernest McGrath, the elected leader of the wagon train, sat up straight, holding the reins of his team of horses. He appeared to be a humorless man, and for the life of him Blaise could not imagine a woman like Mrs. McGrath having married him. She sat next to her husband, resplendent in a yellow gingham dress and broad-brimmed sunbonnet. Her hair was braided Indian style and hung beneath her bonnet. She's young, he thought, younger than I assumed she was when I first met her.

"Good morning," Blaise said, doffing his Stetson.

"When are we going to get started?" Ernest's dark eyes snapped with impatience.

"Soon enough," Blaise returned. He lifted his hand to his chin and rubbed it against his face. He was clean shaven now, but by the end of the trip he would have grown back his full beard.

Blaise studied McGrath. He had been elected leader by a narrow majority and only after a bitter struggle to make a compromise on the issue of drinking. Those who followed McGrath signed a morality pledge, but those who didn't sign were allowed to drink if they wished. It all amounted to the fact that those who followed McGrath were not quite as narrow-minded as the preacher himself. They voted for him on the grounds that the others be allowed to follow their own beliefs. But the fact was that Blaise felt uneasy. McGrath held considerable sway and Blaise considered a man as bigoted as McGrath to be dangerous. He spoke more like a god rather than like a man speaking God's words.

"As elected leader of this train, Mr. McGrath, you should ride back and make one check of the train yourself before we pull out."

Ernest glanced at Margot, who sat primly on the seat of the wagon, looking straight ahead. "All right. If you think it's necessary."

"You're the elected leader, Mr. McGrath. I think it's imperative."

Ernest climbed down off the seat of the wagon and unhitched his horse. He mounted and directed the horse down the long line of wagons. He was proud of how well he rode now; it was one skill he had truly worked on.

"Blasted inconvenience," he mumbled aloud. And what was he supposed to be checking for? He hadn't the faintest idea. Still, he supposed he was to be a sort of morale symbol. . . . Sent to enthuse the troops, so to speak. Cherishing the thought of the wagon train passengers as his new flock, he moved off.

Blaise remained by the McGrath wagon, allowing his horse to graze idly on the tall grass.

"Nice dress," he commented to Margot.

Margot looked across at him. She hadn't seen him except from a distance since the night he had joined her for dinner. And even on the day the train was being loaded, she noted that he spent most of the time helping the single women. Mr. Baron, she decided, was a ladies' man, a man who probably thought of little more than sexual gratification. She frowned slightly. Ernest had no interest in sexual gratification and this man represented the opposite extreme. Margot decided she was able to condemn both Ernest and Mr. Baron equally. Nonetheless, she accepted his compliment, even though she was careful to keep her voice cool. "Thank you," Margot replied.

"I enjoyed having dinner with you," Blaise told her. "I'm sorry we haven't had time to talk since."

"Well, you seem to have your hands full," Margot answered, "what with the single women and all."

Blaise grinned. Her voice was heavily laden with sarcasm, but her eyes were beautiful, hypnotic. . . He stared at her, noticing the curves of her body and conjuring up his fantasy of the redoubtable Mrs. McGrath unclothed.

Margot blushed under his bold gaze.

"I never asked your first name," Blaise said.

"Margot," she replied.

"I like your hair down." His eyes looked her up and down appraisingly and Margot touched her braid unconsciously. Ernest had ranted at her for half an hour about wearing braids, but she no longer cared what Ernest said or thought.

"Tell me, Margot, what do you want?"

Margot looked at him with a surprised expression. "I want to be a good missionary," she answered coolly.

Blaise Baron laughed. "I'm afraid you're not going to have an easy time of it."

"I shall do my best."

"And will your husband do his best?"

Margot's expression hardened a bit. "He will," she answered.

"Ah, here he comes now, inspection completed."

"Will you be riding up front?" Margot asked.

Blaise shook his head. "Jackson will ride up front today. I'll be in the rear with the single women for a time—just to make certain they get off to a good start." He smiled mischievously and turned his horse. "Good day, Mrs. McGrath."

Blaise paused and waited for Ernest to re-hitch his horse to the team. When Ernest was firmly back in the driver's seat, Blaise signaled to Jackson, who was fifty feet ahead of the first wagon. "Wagons west!" he called out in a booming voice.

Ernest let out the reins and the horses jolted forward, pulling off the wagon. Blaise remained where he was, signaling off each wagon in turn. Space between each was important. The novice drivers had to learn to leave stopping distances between one another's wagons. They had to be close, but not too close. The finer points of driving were a skill Blaise intended to see them all develop early on, since it made the train easier to handle later when the country became rougher.

When each of the wagons was rolling, he rode even with the last wagon.

"Nice day," he called out to pretty Peggy McCree who was driving with her brother.

"It is indeed," she replied with a warm, friendly smile.

CHAPTER XI

June 3, 1856

The wagons were circled for the night. Within the circle, dinner fires still flickered and men and women stood near the embers talking in hushed tones so as not to wake the children.

Margot stood on the step and peered inside her wagon. Its recesses were illuminated by a small lantern and the soft light gave the inside a warm, cozy feeling, like a small room. At one end was a straw-filled mattress covered with quilts; it was the bed she shared with Ernest. Their four trunks were arranged on either side of the wagon so that the weight was evenly distributed, and next to them were boxes and barrels containing the necessary foodstuffs and water required for the journey.

Margot entered the wagon and quickly readied herself for bed. She unbraided her hair and ran the brush through it as she sat on the edge of the mattress wearing her nightdress. Ernest was no doubt still talking with the men, or preaching one of his endless sermons on the evils of drink, the need for discipline, or the special frailty of women who, according to Ernest, were more likely to commit grievous sins because of their inferior intellect. Ernest's sermons tired her, his new ideas angered her, and she seethed when she thought of his arrogance, which seemed to grow with each passing day.

After a few moments, Margot heard the unmistakable sound of Ernest climbing up onto the wagon. He crawled through the drawn flap, then scrambled to his feet.

"Margot! Your hair is loose!" He gave her a dismayed look.

"I intend to leave my hair loose at night," Margot said stubbornly. With those words, she blew out the lamp and lay down in the dark, listening as Ernest fumbled about, taking off his clothes and putting on his red flannel nightshirt.

Ernest crawled into the bed beside her, as he had done each night since their wedding, but suddenly he reached over and grabbed her arm, roughly pulling her toward him. "Take off your nightdress!" he demanded in a low, threatening voice.

Margot sat up and bit her lip. "Ernest. . ."

"Sh! Take if off!"

"I don't want you to . . . to . . ."

She felt him turn in the bed and seize her shoulders, roughly pushing her back down to the bed.

"Ernest!"

"Sh!" He clamped his hand over her mouth. "You're my wife! Do as I tell you!"

Margot felt stunned by his sudden change of behavior, by his sudden lust. He tugged on her nightdress, but in order to do so he was obliged to remove his hand from her mouth. "I don't understand," Margot stumbled, aware that tears were forming in her eyes. She felt as angry at his advances now as she had at the lack of them on their wedding night.

"Don't scream," he warned. "People will hear."

Margot bit her lip. A woman could not refuse her husband. . . . She had believed this moment would never come. . . . She had initially hated Ernest for not making love to her, but over the weeks she had grown to hate him for other reasons.

"Ernest, please. . . ." She pleaded, but Ernest pulled off her nightdress and held her shoulders.

"It is time," he whispered urgently. "I must have you now."

Margot blinked up into his face fearfully. Her eyes had adjusted to the darkness; light from the surrounding fires cast strange shadows within the wagon. She could see Ernest's eyes. They seemed to be almost glazed, afire with desire and animal lust.

He ran his hand across her skin. "It burns," he whispered as he touched her breast.

"Ernest, be gentle. . . ." Margot felt the tears running down her face. Ernest pinched her roughly and she jumped.

"Lie still, woman! You're my wife!"

Ernest forced her legs apart and without a moment's hesitation penetrated her brutally. Margot let out a cry of pain, but again he clamped his hand over her mouth. She wiggled beneath him, trying to escape, but his large arms and heavy legs seemed everywhere. He withdrew and again plunged into her. Margot sobbed, "Oh. . . ."

He pumped up and down like a wild animal, he grunted and groaned and Margot could feel the perspiration on his body. Margot struggled, trying again to escape his painful, awkward groping. But Ernest continued to plunge into her. He arched his back and let out a sudden gasp; then, like a half-dead dog, he collapsed, rolling off of her, panting.

Margot sat up almost immediately, hot tears running down her face. She groped in the dark for her discarded nightdress. She put it on and wiped the tears off her cheeks. She had at least hoped for tenderness, but Ernest was like an animal. . . . He hurt her without concern, he was lustful and vile.

"There! Are you satisfied!" His voice sounded angry and tense.

"How could you?" Margot sobbed, aware that she couldn't stop the tears, and still shaking from Ernest's rape . . . yes, that was the word, rape, though of course no law existed that recognized the fact that a husband could rape his wife. . . . Margot felt violated and unclean. . .

"Women are not supposed to enjoy it," Ernest said meanly. "I have done what you wanted. I have done it because—" He didn't finish his sentence. Then, after a moment, he asked, "Did you enjoy it?"

Margot shook her head in the darkness, aware that Ernest could not see her. "Don't do it again," she said in a low, even voice.

"It's evil to enjoy it," he mumbled.

There was silence and then Ernest, in a completely different tone, his usual tone, muttered, "I couldn't respect a woman who enjoyed such activity."

Margot, still aware of the real pain she felt, lay down and crawled as far from Ernest as she could get. Ernest, she concluded, was more than dangerously self-righteous. He was a hypocrite . . . he was violent, he was not a man of God, as he proclaimed. Her mind filled with conflicting thoughts, with a renewed fear of the future and with anger over her own mistake in marrying him.

So Ernest could not respect her if she enjoyed it. She turned her head toward him. "Well, rest assured, Ernest, you can respect me," she said bitterly. "I most certainly did not enjoy it."

It was June 15. The wagons had been on the Oregon Trail for two weeks . . . two weeks across the flatlands of Kansas.

Blaise Baron sat apart from the rest of the wagoners. He had built his own small fire for light and was deeply absorbed in studying his list of passengers. Beside each name he had made notes.

Wagon one held the Reverend Ernest McGrath, age twenty-nine, and his wife, Margot, age eighteen.

"A strange, dark man," Blaise had written next to Ernest's name. "Many find him compelling. He appears strong and is fit for hard work; he can't shoot worth a damn. He is too strict with his followers, he speaks more as if he were a god, rather than speaking of the teachings of Christianity. Heaven save me from men who do things in the name of God! They're a dangerous lot!"

Beside Margot's name he had written nothing, although he was tempted to write, "attractive, looks unhappy, dresses to make herself appear older." But these were personal observations, not pertinent information. He needed to know if she had any experience outside of the small town she came from; if she knew nursing or had any other useful skill. He shook his head. He was so absorbed in her beauty and her haunted, unhappy expression—which seemed to have grown more unhappy in the past weeks—that he had failed to make any pertinent inquiries. He reminded himself to do so tonight.

Wagon two held the Palmers and their four-year-old child. Palmer, Blaise had noted, was a fine shot and a carpenter by trade. He appeared strong and capable. His wife was a fine cook and could also handle a rifle.

Wagon three held the Rathbones and their two adolescents—Prudence, who was fifteen, and Gideon, who was a strapping lad of fourteen. William Rathbone and his son Gideon were both good shots, and Gideon could handle a wagon team as effectively as any grown man. William had been a shopkeeper and was good at figures. Blaise intended to have Ernest McGrath put William Rathbone in charge of the purchase of supplies at Fort Laramie.

Wagon four held the Bryants and their two sons, wagon five held the Moores and the Wilsons. Wagon six held the Dillons and their three adolescents: two boys and young Cordelia, who was a bit of a flirt.

Wagon seven held the Bradleys and their children, Enid, ten, and Wakefield, nine. Wagon eight held the Keats, wagon nine the Roberts. Wagon ten held the Halls and their two infants, little Charlotte, two, and Ryan, one year. Wagon eleven held John Rutledge and his family; Rutledge was an assayer.

Wagon twelve held the Larkins and their two adult children: Filmore, who was twenty-three, and Herbert, who was twenty-two. Aiken Larken was a former soldier, Filmore could read, and Herbert, Blaise noted, seemed to be seeing a great deal of Cordelia Dillon.

Wagon thirteen held the Troyers, wagon fourteen the Carlows. Jessie Carlow was a midwife. Blaise also noted that they were the largest family on the wagon train and somewhat undersupplied, given the fact that they had four grown sons and a fourteen-year-old girl to feed.

Wagon fifteen held Bruce McCree and his lovely sister, Peggy, and Alura Alton. Bruce was a blacksmith and therefore in constant demand. Peggy, Blaise learned, much to his disappointment, was betrothed and on her way to join her fiancé, a young lumberman who lived near Fort Steilacoom. But, engaged or no, he liked her friendly manner and enjoyed talking to her.

Alura Alton was another matter entirely. Indeed, Blaise smiled at her name . . . it was most appropriate. Alura was brazen and somewhat hard. She pursued married men, and already many of the women on the wagon train didn't like her. She was, Blaise decided, trouble waiting to happen. He sighed. It wasn't just the real trouble that Alura herself might cause, but the possibility that Ernest McGrath would cause trouble for her. He had already preached a number of evening sermons on the evils of wanton women, and Blaise had not missed the fact that Ernest's eyes always came to rest on Alura, who stared back at him defiantly. There was always the possibility that Ernest would fire up the faithful to have her cast out. Then I would have to step in, he thought to himself. Alura had paid her way, after all, and she had a right to go west just like the others. "Bigotry!" Blaise said under his breath. Ernest McGrath was bigoted in the extreme and it occurred to Blaise that he would no doubt get on well with the governor of the Washington Territory— except of course that the governor drank.

Blaise folded his list and put it in his saddlebag. All in all, it was a well-balanced train, save its elected leader, Ernest McGrath, and the influence he had. There were farmers and carpenters, men and women with important skills. Men outnumbered women, of course, but the extra men were needed to drive the supply wagons that were positioned in the center of the train, and to stand guard duty. And all the men were of reasonably high quality. Most were good shots, and there were a sufficient number of necessary skills represented. They would be a fine group of settlers, assuming that they mellowed in their beliefs once Ernest McGrath left the train in the Yakima Valley.

Even Alura Alton would play a role. Every town on the frontier had an Alura. He knew, because he had availed himself of their services on more than one occasion. She certainly wasn't the most attractive woman on the train. That honor he accorded Margot McGrath. But Alura had a voluptuous, vulgar kind of raw sexual appeal. Her heavy breasts were too large for his own personal taste, though even he had to admit she had hips that drew glances. And she was open and obviously free with her favors, clearly willing. Yes, Alura had the look of a professional, and heaven knew, there were plenty of men in the territory who would be happy to pay.

Peggy McCree, Blaise decided, was the second prettiest girl on the train. But he knew when a woman wasn't interested in him. She was friendly, but she always talked about her betrothed.

Blaise stood up and stretched. As wagon master, he ate each evening with a different family. He and Jackson rotated, though they did not eat together with the same family. Jackson had begun at the beginning of the train and worked his way backward, Blaise had begun at the back and worked his way forward. Tonight, he would eat with the McGraths, although he knew Ernest would be late because he was on guard duty.

It will be nice to be alone with Margot, he thought. Without her strict, humorless husband.

Blaise thrust his hands into his pockets and stomped out the little fire. He could smell food cooking on the campfires in front of the circled wagons. He strode toward the McGrath wagon, noting with satisfaction that although it was not entirely necessary yet, the wagoners had learned to draw their wagons into a tight circle.

As he approached, he could see Margot McGrath in front of the campfire. It was a fine roaring fire, and because her husband had been on guard duty since the train halted, he assumed she had built it.

Margot had discarded her sunbonnet and her hair hung in braids. She was leaning over a pot, stirring the meal.

"Good evening." Blaise tipped his hat. "What am I having for dinner?"

"Fish soup. But not ordinary fish soup. It's my great-aunt Jenna's recipe. She always called it New Orleans fish soup."

"Bouillabaisse?" he asked enthusiastically. It was a rather special dish; he had sampled it in San Francisco.

"Yes, minus a few ingredients."

"It smells good."

"I caught the fish from the stream we were camped by last night. It was a boggy area and I was lucky enough to find crayfish."

"You're very inventive," he said admiringly. "Where did you learn to fish?"

Margot looked up, surprised. "I lived near a river, of course."

Blaise nodded, and winked. "What, no white wine?"

Margot frowned. "Ernest won't even let me cook with it. Ernest says wine is evil."

"Pity," Blaise said in a low, seductive voice. "Wine warms the spirit and the heart." He looked her over with his eyes and watched as her face turned pink. He found he enjoyed flirting with her and even shocking her.

"Please . . . My husband would be upset if he heard you saying such things to me. He'll be coming back soon."

Blaise sat down in front of the fire and stretched out his large frame. "Not that soon," he said knowingly.

Margot cleared her throat. "You really must stop behaving this way and talking to me as you do. I am a properly married woman."

"Regrettably," he grinned. "Properly married, but not happily married."

"Mr. Baron!"

"Your eyes are beautiful and sad. You yearn for love—"

"Stop!" Margot turned away, fighting back tears she did not want this ladies' man to see.

Blaise looked at her back. He saw her tremble and he decided to retreat. Teasing her was one matter, touching a raw nerve was another. "It's all right, Margot. I really treat all the ladies the same. I'm a born devil."

Margot inhaled and turned back toward him. She vowed she would not cry. Why had she looked forward to his coming? He was so rude, and what's more, he did flirt with everyone shamelessly.

"I should like you to treat me with respect," she answered, hating herself for even using Ernest's favorite word.

Blaise burst out laughing. "My dear young lady, you may

154

be married to a preacher, but you're a mere girl. If the first woman I ever slept with had become pregnant, I'd have a son or daughter your age! I'm sixteen years older than you, old enough to be your father!''

Margot's face burned with anger. Now he was calling her a child! "I'm a married woman!" she blurted out.

He smiled and winked at her. "That doesn't mean a thing. You have a lot to learn. Respect is earned, not given. Now from the smell of your cooking pot, I'd say there's no doubt that I will come to respect your culinary ability. But I have my doubts about your judgment and I don't know anything about what other abilities you possess.''

Margot tossed her head back. "You, Mr. Baron, are arrogant and rude, a most immoral man . . . an animal!" And so is Ernest, she thought in silent outrage.

"You really know little of my morals," Blaise answered calmly. He truly enjoyed goading her; it brought her buried spirit to the surface. He liked to watch her eyes flash. "As for my being an animal, let me assure you that I know how to make a woman happy.''

"And I gather you spend quite a lot of time making quite a few happy!''

Blaise laughed more softly. "Is that what you consider morals? Tell me, Margot, how moral is it to marry a man you don't love?''

"What do you mean by that?" She looked away from him. She knew she now sounded insincere.

"Exactly what I said. You don't love your husband.''

Margot returned to the fire, turning her back on him. She stirred the soup vigorously. "I will not discuss this with you," she said firmly as soon as she recovered her voice.

"All right." Blaise leaned back, his head on his arm. The stars were coming out, and a slight haze from the campfires rose over the wagon train. One of the little ones was crying. Blaise liked being on the wagon train, because it gave him the temporary feeling of being part of a large family.

"Perhaps you ought not stay," Margot said, interrupting his thoughts.

"What, and miss my dinner? I wouldn't think of leaving."

"Ernest will be here soon."

"And I'm certain we shall have a fascinating conversation."

"What about?"

"Well, we could discuss you," he suggested teasingly.

"No!" There was almost a tone of panic in her voice, and it suddenly occurred to Blaise for the first time that Margot McGrath might actually be afraid of her husband.

"All right, we'll discuss business."

Blaise heard her let out her breath. He found his curiosity was more piqued than ever now.

"Ah, Mr. Baron." Ernest emerged from behind the wagon and Margot visibly jumped at the sound of his deep voice.

Ernest leaned over and shook Blaise's hand. In a more friendly manner than Margot expected, Blaise accepted the handshake.

"Your wife appears to be a fine cook—judging from the aroma."

Ernest nodded. "One of the reasons I married her. Margot's mother died when she was quite young. She's had a lot of experience in homemaking."

Blaise made a mental note of Ernest McGrath's tone. He spoke of Margot as if she were some material object, rather than an intelligent, beautiful woman who should be respected and cherished. Blaise also sensed Margot's anger and frustration. She hadn't turned around; clearly, she didn't like her husband's attitude either.

"And she is a woman of true virtue," Ernest said proudly. "Not like some of the evil women traveling with us. . . . I tell you, the she-devil is among us." Ernest shook his head gravely.

Blaise didn't answer for a moment. The look in Ernest McGrath's eyes fascinated him. It was almost . . . yes, wild was the right word. "I don't think she'll cause any real harm," Blaise answered. Then, before Ernest could re-open

156

the subject, he abruptly asked, "Haven't you been on guard duty, Reverend?"

"Certainly, that's what kept me. But I see that dinner has not yet been dished up."

"Reverend McGrath, your lateness does not bother me. Your attire does. This is high grass country. I thought I mentioned that all the men should wear high boots. Don't you have high boots?"

"Of course I do. But it's far too warm to wear them."

"Reverend, this is rattlesnake country. The kind of shoes you are wearing are nothing short of dangerous."

Ernest looked down at his shoes. "They're leather," he said flatly.

"Your pants and socks aren't. A snake could easily strike you in the ankle. They're plentiful this time of year."

"Well, they do rattle first."

"Not always. Wear your boots."

"I feel uncomfortable in them," Ernest argued.

"Wear them," Blaise said authoritatively. "As elected leader of this train, you're setting a bad example."

"It would be an even worse example if a man of God were bitten by a snake," Margot suddenly said pointedly. Blaise wanted to laugh. Beneath her icy exterior of pretense there lurked a sharp tongue. She was spirited, though at the moment confused.

Ernest did not reply, but his face hardened.

Margot dished up three bowls of soup, angrily hitting the ladle against the sides of the tin bowls.

"Here," she said, thrusting Blaise's soup toward him. "And here, Ernest."

Ernest sat down awkwardly. Blaise sat Indian fashion. Margot took her own bowl and sat down on the opposite side of the fire. She ate in silence.

"It's very good," Blaise praised, "even without the wine."

Ernest grumbled.

"It's so peaceful on the plains," Blaise observed wryly as he looked heavenward. "Almost poetic, very romantic, such a lovely way to spend a honeymoon."

157

Ernest made a begrudging grunt and continued to slurp his soup. Margot maintained her stony silence. Blaise got up and walked to the stew pot. "Mind if I have some more?"

"No," Margot answered.

Blaise was the only one to have a second helping. When he had finished, he stood up and let out a yawn of satisfaction. "Have a nice evening," he said cheerfully.

Ernest grunted again and Margot nodded. Blaise suppressed his own smile. Nothing quite like a good, loving, Christian marriage. He shook his head and walked slowly away.

It was mid-June and the day had been warm and sunny. Cory inhaled deeply; he loved the smell of the mountain spruce and the sound of the evening breeze whistling through the trees. New Caledonia was a virgin wilderness—a land of snow-capped mountains, of fresh, clear streams rich with salmon—and it was alive with animals and birds. He smiled to himself, aware of his emotions. It was good to be alive. Somehow, his brush with death had made living even sweeter.

Cory sat by the fire with Nkula, the medicine man of the Lillooet. He had been allowed out of bed a week ago and for the past several days had been permitted the freedom of the village.

"I am well now," he told Nkula, who was not wearing his ceremonial mask. "I am well enough to leave."

Nkula did not turn and Cory could only study his craggy profile by the light of the fire. Nkula was a man of few words, but among the Lillooet he had absolute authority.

"Where would you go?" Nkula asked dispassionately.

"To my home."

"Across the water? What about the gold in the ground?"

"I would go home first, then return," Cory answered, his mind firmly on Anya.

"No," Nkula replied. "You find the gold first, then you can go home."

Cory didn't answer immediately. "Am I then a prisoner of the great Lillooet?"

158

"No, you are free to go when you have found gold and it has been divided between us."

"It takes a long time to find gold; when it is found, it takes a long time to get it out of the ground."

"But you know how?"

"Yes, I know the secret of the earth."

Nkula grunted. "I'll send two braves to help you."

Cory nodded. As anxious as he was to return to Anya, he realized that with the Indians' help his work would go much faster, and the terms Nkula had stated were not that bad. The Lillooet must want more sacred gold badly, he thought.

Cory did not wish to give an appearance of weakness. "I accept your offer," he said, as if he might have decided not to. "But I must warn Nkula that it will still take time. It is summer now, but in two or three moons it will be the time of the great snows. The earth does not yield gold when she is covered with snow."

Nkula nodded. "If it has not been found by the time of the great snows, you will winter with us. We have much patience."

Cory inhaled. It was June now. Snow in the mountains could be expected any time after mid-September. It would last until late April. . . . He would have to spend ten months among the Lillooet if he did not have success during the summer months. Nkula drove a hard bargain, and Cory admitted he had nothing to bargain with in any case. Nkula wanted his knowledge and clearly intended to have it. He was a virtual prisoner, albeit one who was well treated.

"I will stay as long as necessary," he announced.

"Yes," Nkula answered.

Cory shifted a bit to make himself more comfortable. If sufficient gold is not found by late August, I will have to find a way to convince Nkula to let me go, he silently decided. But for now I will stay. In any case, he reasoned, he needed rest. He was not yet ready for the rough journey back to the Hudson's Bay Post, and perhaps he was not ready to see Anya again either. Absence, he told himself, made the heart grow fonder.

CHAPTER XII

June 16, 1856

Margot jolted upright and looked at Ernest, who was visible in the half-light of the early dawn which filtered into the wagon. His hands were wrapped around his organ and his nightshirt was wrinkled and twisted, waist high on his body. He was bathed in sweat and his face was distorted in an expression which seemed to combine agony with hatred. Ernest groaned again and Margot, horrified at the sight of him, cringed on the edge of the bed.

"Jezebel! Evil temptress! Vile!" Ernest muttered in his sleep as his hands fell away, and Margot could see the white fluid which had come out of him.

"Devil!" Ernest mumbled, still deeply asleep.

Carefully, Margot lifted the cover which Ernest had kicked off and pulled it over him. "Ernest," she whispered his name, half afraid of waking him, half wanting to arouse him from his nightmare.

"Ernest!" she said a little louder.

He opened his eyes and they appeared glazed; he looked at her as if he didn't know her.

"Ernest, wake up!"

He blinked and a little spittle ran from his mouth.

"Ernest, you've had a nightmare." Margot did not mention his self-abuse—clearly, he had done it in his sleep and she decided to keep her silence.

"Nightmare?" He sounded like a child and his face was clearly pale. The expression of hatred he had had during his dream had disappeared and was replaced by sheer bewilderment.

"Yes, nightmare. You woke me up."

"I had a terrible dream," Ernest admitted. His calm seemed to be returning.

"Everyone has terrible dreams sometimes," Margot replied.

Ernest looked at her steadily. He remembered his dream full well. God knew he had it often enough.

He could feel the dampness between his legs. But he noted with relief that he was covered and Margot could not see. Nor had he apparently said anything aloud.

"I'm sorry I woke you. God was speaking to me. I know you will not understand that. It was a powerful dream, very powerful."

Ernest's eyes glistened and Margot looked at him, stifling her desire to laugh. God had spoken to him? Nothing of the sort. Ernest had been possessed of a lust dream—the very kind her brother Kevin used to have when he was thirteen. But Ernest was not thirteen—he was a grown man, and her legal husband. And his eyes, which had once seemed so thoughtful and so intriguing, now seemed wild and hungry.

Margot stood up. It was dawn and she could hear noises outside. "No matter," she said casually. "It's time to get up anyway."

Ernest breathed a sigh of relief. Clearly she believed him.

Margot turned away and, drawing the curtain that divided the wagon, dressed quickly. On the other side, she could hear Ernest dressing.

"I think the linen should be washed," Ernest suggested. He was thinking of the stained sheets—he wanted to remove all evidence of his lustful nightmare.

"I was going to wash tomorrow," Margot answered.

"I'll wash them," Ernest offered uncharacteristically. "It's the heat. I like the feel of clean linen."

"Very well," Margot replied, deciding not to cross him in any way.

"Are you dressed?"

"Yes."

Ernest drew back the curtain and looked at her. "You are different," he told her in a soft voice. "You are truly virtuous. Margot, no matter what you think, I do respect you."

Margot nodded, but kept her own council. Because I do not like to sleep with you, she thought. Because I cannot

162

stand it when you touch me, because I have no desire to touch you. She blinked and willed herself not to cry. I'm so confused, she admitted to herself. And in a split second, she also admitted that she was beginning to suspect that Ernest McGrath, to whom she was bound in wedlock, was not entirely sane.

The seventeenth of June . . . Margot marked the day off on her calendar. They had been on the trail for seventeen days and had traveled over two hundred miles. Soon they would be in the Nebraska Territory.

The landscape had already begun to change. The wagons no longer passed easily over dark, firm turf. Now they leveled bunch grasses, and the colors gradually turned from green to brown and tan.

Everyone complained of dry lips and sun-scorched skin. "I shall never again see a tree," Margot sighed. This land was even more barren than she had imagined. Having grown up in Canada West, which was so heavily forested, she realized she had taken trees and the welcome shade they provided for granted.

The animal life had changed too. She saw herds of animals she had never seen before; bison and pronghorns grazed lazily and eyed the sinuous wagon train with fear and suspicion. And there were colonies of prairie dogs which Margot found amusing. They were such peculiar little animals. They often sat up with their paws together, as if they were praying or begging, and they remained absolutely still, hoping the passersby would think they were small rocks.

The less delightful creatures Margot saw were called horned toads. They were grotesque, like some kind of diseased frogs. She had asked Blaise Baron about them one day when he rode alongside her wagon.

"They are simply well camouflaged," he laughed. "They match the ground they roam, making it harder for birds of prey to see them."

Margot admitted to herself that she wished Blaise Baron would ride alongside the wagon more often. He understood the land and its inhabitants, and she delighted in the bits of knowledge she gleaned from their short conversations.

"I suppose one cannot cook their legs," she surmised.

Blaise had laughed at the suggestion and shaken his head. "Do you like frogs' legs?"

"Yes, very much. But those horned toads are not really frogs."

Blaise smiled. "When we come to the Platte, you will have the opportunity to catch frogs. I'll help you, if you'll fix me a meal from them."

"All right," Margot agreed. It would be wonderful to have such a delicacy. But now, as she looked across the barren land, she could not imagine a river. Perhaps Blaise Baron was only teasing her.

This morning, Ernest was riding at the rear of the wagon train. Margot drove the team of horses, happy with her husband's absence. In the distance, she could see old Jackson. He led the way, and as long as he was in view, she had little to do but follow.

Margot turned as Blaise galloped even with her wagon. "You'll soon be able to see the Platte River," he told her. "Or the high reeds, in any case. It's a river like no other. Two miles wide and not even knee-deep."

"Will we camp near it?"

"At Fort Kearney . . . and we'll be on its southern bank for some days."

Margot smiled. "Have you forgotten the frogs?"

"Of course not!" He waved at her and galloped off, sending Jackson backward.

Jackson came alongside her wagon. "Morning, Ma'm."

"Good morning," she replied.

"How'ya bearing up?"

"Quite well."

"You really headed for the Whitman mission in the Yakima Valley?" He let his horse amble alongside the wagon, obviously intent on making conversation for a bit.

"Yes, we're following in the footsteps of Narcissa and Marcus Whitman." Margot said it with less enthusiasm than she had once announced it. Ernest was no Marcus, and she felt she was surely less than Narcissa.

"I remember them. . . . I was on that wagon train."

"You were?" Margot felt a sudden surge of interest.

"Damned if I know why you want to follow in their footsteps!" he laughed.

"Whatever do you mean?" Margot asked.

"Hell, they were just married and sharing a wagon with Narcissa's ex-fiancé and his bride. The four of them was all missionaries, but they fought like cats and dogs all the way to the Yakima."

Margot tilted her head. "Are you telling me the truth?"

"Yup. Got no cause to lie. Miss Narcissa was a real beauty. Not as pretty as you—and not as nice either, a real hellcat if you ask me. And Marcus, well, he was bullheaded like a stubborn old mule. Damn near killed himself taking that stupid wagon over the mountains. We all told him not to try it, but he did."

"I always thought that was a great accomplishment."

"Stupid, just plain stupid."

Margot looked at old Jackson, fascinated with his story and horrified with it at the same time. "What do you mean, Narcissa wasn't nice?"

"She was mean. She had old Marcus bamboozled, and everyone on the train said she was having a love affair with her ex-fiancé—right in front of his wife. One night the two of them got into a real wingding of a fight!" He laughed uproariously. "The hair was flying! Best entertainment I ever did see on a wagon train!"

Margot's mouth was actually open. "Mercy," was all she could manage to say.

"Well, ma'm, I'll be off. . . . but don't you go following old Narcissa too close, you hear?"

Margot nodded dumbly.

The wagons were neatly circled and the campfires burned brightly. In the distance, the watchtowers of Fort Kearney were outlined against the evening sky.

Margot inhaled and relished the smell of fresh water. Behind the fort, the River Platte and its hundreds of weaving channels cut through the sloping hills. It was as Blaise Baron had described it, wide and shallow. He joked that it was too deep to plow and too shallow for a boat. The river was surrounded by marshy land with tall reeds; it was alive with life, and the night was filled with the sounds of crickets, frogs, katydids, and other small animals and insects.

Ernest was meeting with the men and Margot sat by the fire alone, stirring it idly. She looked up when she saw Blaise Baron approaching, lantern in hand.

He smiled mischievously at her. "Have you forgotten our frog hunt?"

"Of course not."

"Well, the others are meeting. I see you are alone, and I can't think of a more perfect night." He pointed upward. "The moon is full . . . the frogs will be out in droves."

Margot stood up. She was wearing her high boots as Blaise suggested she should. Her skirts came above the ankle, and she wore a modest blouse, with a scarf around her neck. "I'm quite ready."

"Then come along." Blaise led the way with the lantern. "Do you know how to catch them?"

"Of course. You light a torch and shine it in their eyes, then they remain still and you can grab them. Oh, do you have a bag?"

Blaise nodded. "And a bound torch in my back pocket."

"Well, if you know so much about it, why did you ask?"

"I wanted to make sure you knew."

"Really," Margot mumbled.

"Listen, this river can be dangerous, even though it's not deep. There's quicksand and a great many insects."

"I'm sure I can take care of myself."

Blaise didn't reply, but continued to lead her into the reeds. Margot could feel the squishy ground beneath her feet.

"I'd say we'll be in the perfect area in about another half-mile."

"So far from the wagon train?"

Blaise laughed. "Are you afraid to be alone with me?"

166

"Don't be absurd! It's just that it might not be deemed proper."

Blaise laughed again. "I hardly see how a woman wading through a swamp in search of her husband's dinner could be improper. I promise not to try to seduce you, much as I'd like to."

"Mr. Baron, if you do not cease making such comments immediately, I shall return at once to the wagon train."

"You suffer from too much propriety and pride."

Margot remained silent. He sounded just like her father. And, she admitted, she yearned for her father and the rest of her family. She would have been able to unburden herself to him, to ask him about Ernest's dreams and about her own mixed emotions. Sometimes she hated Ernest, other times she pitied him. And there was no denying that at times— those moments when he claimed he was having visions—he terrified her.

"Here," Blaise said, turning. "Sh, listen. . ."

Margot stopped and listened. She could hear the frogs. "Oh, they sound like good-sized ones."

"Well, we wouldn't want small ones."

"Here, over this way. Give me the bag," Margot whispered.

Blaise lit the torch from the flickering flame of the lantern, then blew the lantern out. They were left with only the torch and the bright moonlight. He approached the rocks by the river and waded in up to his ankles. He held out the torch and on the rock a huge bullfrog fell silent, mesmerized by the flame.

Margot tip-toed through the water from behind, aware only of the slight sloshing noise she made. She approached the great rock and clamped the bag over the frog which jumped upward into it.

"I have him!" she called triumphantly.

"Good!" Blaise said smiling.

Margot started back toward him, but suddenly her legs flew out from under her and she landed with a resounding splash into the water, which was deeper in this spot—nearly two feet. She let out a cry and struggled, trying to stand, but her feet seemed caught in the mire, and though the water came only to her thighs, her feet seemed to be sinking into the mud.

"I'm caught," she gasped, "and drenched!"

"Stand still!" Blaise made his way carefully to the rock and spread himself out on it, reaching forward to Margot's outstretched hands. He grasped her wrists and pulled her toward him.

She panted with the effort of lifting her feet. She felt as if she were trapped in cement, but Blaise pulled her slowly toward him, and then she felt the ground beneath her feet. It was once again solid.

"Oh, my heavens!"

He laughed. Her clothes were soaked and clung to her figure. Even strands of her hair were wet and fell across her forehead. But she still held the bag with the frog. "I see you did not drop your prey," he observed admiringly.

He took the bag and tied it.

"Oh, my God!" Margot let out a scream that filled the silence of night. Her hands flew to her face, and she screamed again.

"What is it?" Blaise turned to her. She was ashen and looked terrified.

"Leeches! I'm covered with leeches!" She let out another shriek.

Blaise grabbed her hand and pulled her away. She was shaking and sobbing. "Get them off me, get them off me! I can feel them, get them off me!"

"I will, come on, we've got to get to a dry spot. I've got to get you out of the swamp!"

"I can't stand it! They're all over me!"

Blaise propelled her along in spite of her screaming protestations. They ran from the swampy area to the grassland beyond.

"Here," Blaise said. "Here, sit down!"

"I can't stand it! Get them off me!" She was quite hysterical and great tears gushed from her green eyes and she trembled.

Blaise lit the lantern and set it down. "Take off your clothes," he commanded.

"I can't do that!"

"Well, I can't get them off while you're dressed, woman." He looked stonily at her. Then, without waiting, he unbuttoned her blouse and pulled it open. "Damn! They are all over."

Margot's mouth was open and she was frozen with horror as Blaise pulled off her camisole, revealing her breasts.

Blaise fumbled in his shoulder pack and withdrew a small container of salt. He always carried it for leeches and ticks, as well as for heat sickness.

Margot shivered and covered her face with her hands. She felt him put the salt on her skin, she felt him touch her as one by one he lifted the leeches from her breasts.

He pushed her gently back on the grass and removed the rest of her clothing, examining it for leeches as he did so. Then piece by piece, he put it on the grass and returned to removing the blood-sucking creatures from Margot's body.

Margot felt him gently separate her legs and remove the leeches from her thighs. He rolled her over, and took them off her back. Then he turned her over and took one last leech off her left breast. His hands were warm and gentle. She quivered at his touch.

"There," he said finally. "They're all off."

"I'm shamed," Margot sobbed, still not removing her hands from her eyes.

"Why? You've got one of the most beautiful bodies I've ever taken leeches off of."

Margot groaned.

Blaise actually laughed. "Just because you can't see me, doesn't mean I can't see you."

She removed her hands and sat bolt upright, trying now to cover herself with her hands. "Where are my clothes?"

"Right there. It's all right; I took all the leeches off them."

Margot blushed under his bold gaze. His eyes utterly devoured her and her heart was beating rapidly. "Are you sure they're all off?"

Blaise reached out and caressed her breast. Her nipple hardened and she moaned slightly. Her lovely full lips were half apart, her eyes shimmered.

"They're all off. . . ." he replied, not moving his hand. He felt himself hard and strong. . . . "I am human," he said, after a moment. He leaned over and closed her mouth with a deep, probing kiss.

Margot struggled against him at first, pounding his back as he pushed her backward onto the soft grass. He ran his hand over her, touching her lightly, his fingers dancing on her skin. Her hands undoubled and she embraced him, aware only of his hands on her, floating in the sensations he was causing her to have, and responding to them.

"You're so beautiful," he whispered. "So white and soft in the moonlight, so loving." He kissed her nipple and she gasped and shivered when he drew it into his mouth and caressed it with his tongue. Simultaneously, he stroked her long white thighs, coaxing her legs apart, toying with her in a way which made her squirm beneath him. She felt she was no longer herself, no longer in control. His touch was sensual, his lips and hands were everywhere, drawing her to him.

He slid into her easily, and moved slowly in and out, kissing her breasts, then her lips, breathing in her ear, touching her hair. She felt him slide his strong hands under her buttocks and lift her to him. The base of his manhood moved across her most sensitive area with an easy rhythm until she thought she would cry out. Then Margot was plunged into the depths of pure sensation. Blaise arched his back and burst forth into her.

He did not withdraw immediately, but rather leaned over her, kissing her cheeks, running his hand through her hair. After a time, he rolled off her and stared up at the stars. Margot lay still, her eyes fastened on the sky, her heartbeat slowly returning to normal.

Slowly, tears began to run down her face. "What have I done?" she wept. "Oh, God, what have I done?"

Blaise turned toward her. "We," he said. "You didn't do it alone."

Margot sat up and reached for her clothes. She dressed rapidly and Blaise watched her, a smile of satisfaction on his face. She was beautiful, wild, full of passion . . . but she didn't want to acknowledge it. And, he thought proudly, though she'll never admit it, that's probably the first time she's ever enjoyed a man. And in spite of her protests, she had enjoyed it, that he knew for certain. Some women could pretend, but he had felt Margot throb beneath him, he had felt her respond not just with her body but with her heart.

"I am shamed," Margot murmured. "I am an evil, fallen woman, an adulteress."

"And damn good," Blaise said admiringly.

"Stop it!"

He shrugged. In truth, he felt totally frustrated at not being able to take her again. But he could sense her confusion and her strong feelings of guilt. She wasn't a whore, she wasn't even an ordinary woman. She was quite special. If I let her think I regard this experience lightly, perhaps it will help her feel less guilty, he decided.

"It's not that important," he said. "Don't make more of it than it was. You gave into passion, I gave into circumstance. That's all."

"You're terrible!" She stomped her foot in anger. "I hate you!"

"No, you don't. Look, no one will ever know. Forget it."

"I've committed a sin!"

"You'll be forgiven."

Margot looked at him in amazement. How could anyone be so callous! She obviously meant nothing to him and that seemed somehow to make it all worse.

"This must never happen again, never!" she said almost hysterically.

"As you wish," Blaise replied, trying not to sound as regretful as he felt.

She turned and picked up the frog bag. She marched off toward the wagon train. Blaise's eyes followed her silhouette in the moonlight. He picked up the lantern and followed her, aware that this was the first time he hadn't felt empty

171

and lonely after having a woman. But clearly, the situation was impossible. He cursed himself for the emotions he was feeling . . . for his dream of being with Margot not just once more, but for a lifetime.

In spite of the hot July sun and the hard work, Cory felt the old excitement of discovery running through his veins; for the past three days, the nuggets he and the two braves had found were of significant value. Now, he felt he had located the source.

"We dig here," he advised. He wanted to shout, "There is gold in New Caledonia!" but he kept silent.

The two braves scowled, and one wiped the perspiration from his brow. "Woman's work," he complained. "Braves hunt, fish, do battle. Digging is woman's work!"

Cory smiled. "Nkula wants you to dig for gold. Digging for gold is not women's work. Only men are allowed to take gold from the ground."

They grunted and began work. "Like this," Cory instructed. He had first stopped back to pick up his equipment at the camp he had originally established. The braves used his tools awkwardly, unsure of how to handle the shovels.

Cory began working too, aware of just how hot the sun was in mid-July.

"White man work too?" one of the braves inquired. His name was Sha Shan, or at least that was as close as Cory could come to pronouncing it.

"Of course. We'll finish sooner if we all work."

Sha Shan grunted. "White man does not have woman for digging?"

Cory could not keep from smiling. These two should know Anya. She was a fine example of why white men had to do their own work. "Nope," he answered.

"Never saw a white man work before," Sha Shan observed.

Doubtless, Cory thought. The only time the Lillooet saw white men at all was once a year when they went down the Fraser to trade with the Hudson's Bay Company.

"Well, let me assure you, white men do work."

172

"I've only see them make marks on paper. Then they move paper from one place to another."

Sha Shan was reasonably observant. Governor Douglas, who was also the chief factor of the Hudson's Bay Company, was a stickler for records. But he was also a just man, and the Indians of the entire region respected him.

"Does gold make white man wealthy?"

Cory nodded. "That's why they seek it."

"But they do not make sacred objects from it. How does it make them wealthy? They cannot eat it, they do not build houses from it. They do not even use it for their tools."

"They use it to trade," Cory replied. It was a difficult concept to explain to those who knew only barter.

"Is it more valuable than skins?"

"Yes," Cory answered truthfully.

"Good, skins are hard to find. The white traders want too many; the animals disappear."

Cory nodded and wondered if these Indians could even imagine what had happened to the Indians in the East, back in the Canadas.

"Here!" Cory said. He bent down and pointed to a rock. The vein is here!"

"Is that gold?"

"Yes . . . but I don't know if it's the main vein."

"It doesn't look like sacred gold."

"It will," Cory replied confidently.

CHAPTER XIII

July 20, 1856

Anya was dressed in her finest gown, and around her slim white neck she wore an emerald on a gold chain. Her long flaxen hair was drawn back, away from her face, and it tumbled loose over her shoulders.

She sat primly on the edge of the settee in the large, airy living room of Governor Douglas' mansion in downtown Victoria. It was a strange room, Anya thought. It was furnished with items from all over the world: oriental carpets, Turkish vases, elegant English furniture, and even some carvings which she had been told were from the Caribbean islands.

Sir James Douglas himself was as much a mixture as the furniture. Some said he was mulatto, others denied it in spite of his features. He was a stout man with an almost square face. His eyes were dark brown, his skin tawny. He dressed formally and his high white collar came up to his chin, giving him the appearance of a turtle.

Mrs. Douglas was considerably shorter than her husband. She had a round face, a broad nose, and an unsmiling mouth. She sat in a chair next to her husband's chair, her hands folded in her lap. There were as many stories about Amelia Douglas as there were about her husband. Amelia, it was said, was the eldest daughter of an Irishman named Bill Connolly. Bill Connolly was called a Nor'wester, and when he was eighteen he had married the daughter of a Cree chief at a place named Rat River. His wife became known as Susanne Pas-de-nom, Susanne No Name. It was well known that Amelia Douglas was part Irish and part Indian.

"It is kind of you to receive me," Anya said.

"It is our pleasure. Would you like tea?"

"That would be most pleasant," Anya smiled. The

Douglas mansion was a large three-story wooden frame house, the grandest in the Colony of Vancouver. And though its furnishings were exotic, its inhabitants were British to the core, or believed themselves to be.

In fact, everyone in the Colony could be classified as British, or so it seemed. Even the Indian women who had married settlers dressed like British ladies, affected their manners, and served tea and scones promptly at four o'clock as a matter of form. In attempting to satisfy their husbands and their neighbors, they had succeeded in becoming more British than the British themselves. But Vancouver Island was not an island like Britain; it did not face the civilized countries of Europe; it faced only high, rugged mountains on one side, an unsettled area that stretched thousands of miles, and on the other side, only the sea. Still, the community of Victoria had a cosmopolitan air about it. It was a flourishing little society, its charm born of isolation and tempered by its thriving sea-going commerce.

The butler brought in a silver tea service and delicate china cups. He set them on a table in front of the stony-faced Mrs. Douglas, who poured as though pouring for a formal party, her little finger extended, her mind on her actions.

"Sugar?" she inquired.

"No, thank you," Anya replied.

Mrs. Douglas handed her the cup and saucer.

"What brings you into Victoria?" Governor Douglas asked. He always avoided even trying to pronounce Anya's last name.

"I came to view my completed theater."

"Ah, yes! I am looking forward to a production. It's quite a handsome building. I passed it only the other day."

Anya smiled. "And because I wanted to discuss Mr. MacLean," she added.

"Cory? He has gone to New Caledonia, has he not?"

"Yes, some time ago. I was wondering if you had heard anything from him."

Douglas pressed his lips together and shook his head. "No, can't say that I have. But there's practically no communication, and Cory MacLean is a real wanderer—God knows where he is.''

Anya sipped a bit of her tea and leaned forward. ''I am rather concerned about him.''

''Oh, he's been gone much longer than this! Gone nine months the last time.''

''Yes, I know, it is just that he expected to be back sooner from this trip. . . . Is there no way to find him, to find out if he is all right?''

Douglas laughed. ''I shouldn't think so!''

''Well, he told me he was panning and digging for gold. Surely someone knows where he is?''

''I shouldn't think so.''

''Well, can someone go find him?''

''I'm afraid not. There just aren't any people who know the territory that well—I mean, Cory knows it as well as anyone.''

Anya leaned back. She felt defeated.

''Why do you want to get in touch with him?''

It was a question Anya really couldn't answer. She had found their last encounter both pleasant and unpleasant. When Rosa had run off and married Sir Fitz, she had realized that there was nothing real between Rosa and Cory; she had also realized her own jealousy and wanted to make amends. She even toyed with telling him the truth about herself, especially now that she was about to leave the farm and move into Victoria in order to be near the theater.

''Well, I am moving into Victoria,'' Anya said, with a little hesitation. ''To train a theater company, to be near the theater. Naturally, I wanted to thank Mr. MacLean for his immense kindness to me.''

''Naturally,'' Douglas beamed. ''But thanks can wait. He'll come back, no need to worry about that.''

Anya nodded. She hoped it would not be another nine months.

The land became a great plateau stretching toward the mountains in the distance. The wagon train was some twenty miles out of Fort Laramie, the last supply depot before the Rocky Mountains. Laramie was a desolate outpost of civilization on the Oregon Trail.

The earth beneath the rumbling wagon wheels was parched and great clumps of tumbleweed blew about in the unceasing winds that swirled up and blew themselves out against nature's wall, the famed and feared Rockies.

It was the end of July and the landscape consisted only of the dry red-brown earth, sparse bushes no more than three feet in height, jutting rocks, and an occasional patch of green or a nearly dry stream. There was only enough water to satisfy the needs of the sprinting jackrabbits and the herds of antelope that darted before the wagoners' eyes.

The wagon train stretched out, a long slow line headed for camp at the fort. On the last wagon, Alura Alton drove alone, her long, dark hair blowing slightly in the hot dry wind. She wore a long red skirt, somewhat stained and in need of a wash, and a dark low-cut blouse that revealed bare shoulders and accentuated her large bosom.

Alura looked up and waved as the Reverend Ernest Mc-Grath galloped toward the wagon. But she did not receive a smile in return. The Reverend McGrath's face was white, and he was biting his lip.

"Hold up! Stop your wagon!" He called out frantically, "Stop!"

Alura drew the horses in and the wagon jolted to a stop.

"Whatever is the matter?" Alura asked.

"A snake has bitten me!" Ernest virtually shrieked. "I'm dying! Oh, God, help me!"

"Tie your horse to the wagon. Come on. Quickly. Get inside!"

Ernest did what he was told. His hands shook violently as he tied his horse and scrambled into the wagon.

"Hurry, I know what to do!" Alura's deep voice carried a certain authority.

"Are you sure?" Ernest asked, shivering. "God almighty, I'm a dying man!"

Alura guided Ernest into the wagon. "Lie down," she commanded.

"What are you going to do?"

"Treat you for snakebite. Stop shaking, you'll be all right."

"I'm dying," Ernest whimpered. He was being punished for his dreams, he thought. He was being punished for giving in to lust and taking Margot!

"Where is it?"

"My leg, that one." Ernest pointed to his left leg.

Alura rolled up his pant leg and looked at the bite. "It's a snakebite, all right. You should have been wearing boots."

"Of course it's a snakebite!"

"What did the snake look like?"

"Like a snake! In the name of heaven, I'm dying!"

"I mean, what color was it?"

"Brown," he answered. "Sort of brown and orange. But I heard it rattle."

Alura shook her head. "What did its head look like?"

"Round, little beady eyes! Will you do something!"

Alura smiled. He was such a handsome man, but he didn't know a King snake from a rattler. "I'll have to cut you," she announced, producing a small, sharp knife. "Just a little, so I can get the poison out."

Ernest groaned. "I'll die," he muttered.

Alura expertly made a number of cuts around the bite. Ernest hardly felt them, he was so filled with terror. But he felt her long hair on his bared leg when she bent over to suck out the blood and poison. She sucked, then spit out the back of the wagon.

Ernest groaned again.

"Here," Alura said, handing him a bottle of whiskey. "Take some."

"Drink is evil."

Alura laughed, "This time it's medicine for snakebite."

Ernest frowned. He'd never had whiskey before. But men who drank were evil. "I can't," he finally stammered.

"You must!" Alura pushed the bottle into his hands. "You drink. I'll suck some more, just to make sure."

Ernest felt ill, a wave of nausea passed through him. He was certain it was the poison seeping slowly through his veins.

179

"Drink," Alura urged. Her voice was low and throaty. He took several gulps of whiskey. It burned his throat, and he could feel it as it trickled down into his stomach.

He could feel Alura sucking. The sound was nauseating. Again she spit out the back of the wagon. When she turned back to him, her sensuous mouth was still red with his blood.

"Drink some more," she suggested. "Here, come on, you haven't had enough."

Ernest drank more. He drank until the bottle was half gone, until the inside of the wagon was a blur of shadow and darkness and he was aware only of Alura's fingers as she cleaned and bandaged his wound.

Ernest groaned. He seemed to have no control over his body or his will. He stared at Alura's huge breasts; they seemed to be bursting out of her blouse.

She was kneeling beside him, wiping the sweat from his face. Ernest felt himself getting hard as he watched her. Lust! He inhaled deeply and tried to fight his growing desire to possess her.

She reminded him of the slithering snake that had bitten him; she wove in front of him.

"Oh Lord!" Ernest yelled, and he reached out for her breasts.

Alura jumped up and took a step backward. "No!" she shouted.

Ernest's mouth was open. "You tempted me!" he gasped. His fingers were stretched toward her, his face was contorted. "You're a whore," he breathed angrily. Then he shouted, "An evil, filthy whore possessed of the devil!"

Alura blinked at him. "I didn't touch you!"

Ernest pointed his finger at her menacingly, "You'll be driven from this wagon train! You should be branded a whore! Devil!" He stood up and staggered toward her, but she ran for the front of the wagon and, climbing into the seat, urged the horses forward with a crack of the whip.

Ernest staggered, then fell backward.

He shook his head and crawled forward as the wagon jolted onward across the rutted land.

"Where's my horse?" he demanded angrily.

"Tied to the back," Alura answered without turning her head.

"Stop this wagon! I want to get on my horse, I want to leave you . . . you . . ."

Alura pulled in the reins, bringing the wagon to a halt, but she held the whip tightly in her hand.

"You shouldn't be among decent men and women," he shouted at her. "Look at you . . . your hair . . . your blouse . . ."

"Go away!" Alura shrieked. "I know your kind. Get out!"

Ernest turned and staggered to the back of the wagon. He unhitched his horse and then mounted, almost falling because the animal was still moving along with Alura's wagon. He rode off, cursing under his breath.

The campfires burned brightly and in the center of the circle the wagoners gathered. They sat on blankets on the ground and they sang hymns. At the end of the third hymn Ernest rose to give a sermon.

"I have spoken of temptation before," he began. His voice was booming and he waved his arms around in the air. Margot stared at him and felt a chill run through her . . . something in his tone and mannerisms made her especially apprehensive.

"I have spoken of wanton women and of how they tempt men into evil. There is such a woman among us . . . a she-devil, an emissary of evil!"

Margot stiffened. Ernest's arm was outstretched, his finger was pointing. She half expected it to stop and rest on her. She shivered and hovered in the shadows, her eyes automatically seeking the figure of Blaise Baron. He was across the circle, standing straight and watching Ernest himself.

But Ernest pointed at no one for the moment. "Today! Today I encountered this woman. . . . I encountered her first in the guise of the serpent. Yes, the serpent condemned to slither on its belly for its sins! This serpent struck out at

181

me and when I sought aid I was again in its vile company. Yes, my friends, the evil fallen woman on this wagon train tried to seduce a man of the cloth! Brazen! evil! She bared herself!''

A hum of whispers passed through the assembled, and Margot's mouth opened.

"Such a woman is not fit to be among you!"

On the far side of the circle, Blaise moved his foot in the dust abstractedly. Shit, he thought to himself. The bastard was going to go too far. He would have to intervene if anyone tried to bother Alura. He stuffed his hands in his pockets and looked at the crowd. They were all whispering among themselves, waiting for McGrath's next revelation. Singly, they were reasonable people, but even reasonable people were not always reasonable in a group. It was something that always amazed him; he had seen his share of mob violence, and he knew he could be dealing with a very unpleasant situation indeed.

Ernest took a step toward one of the fires and from it he lifted a red-hot branding iron. "Such a woman should be branded! What she is should be seered into her flesh! I say that such a woman should be driven from the company of decent folk! She should be marked and sent away!''

Blaise stared at McGrath. The man was a raving lunatic! But those assembled before him seemed to agree with his fanatical ravings.

"Send her out!" one of the women shouted. Blaise couldn't see who it was.

And the men . . . Blaise could see the enthusiasm on their faces. "Sadistic bastards," he muttered.

"There she is!" another shouted.

Two men rushed Alura and dragged her forward. She screamed and struggled.

"Sinner! Sinner!" Ernest cried out, his finger pointed at her.

"Far enough . . . too far . . ." Blaise said as he strode forward. But to his surprise, Margot reached her husband before he did. Her voice rang out clearly, clearly enough to silence the assembly.

182

"Christ said sinners were to be forgiven!" Margot faced Ernest, looking up at him almost defiantly. "Didn't he say that?" she demanded.

"He said that! Amen!" someone shouted.

"Forgive the sinner!" another chimed in.

Blaise halted in his tracks. He could see the look on Margot's face and he bit his lip. She's asking for her own forgiveness, too, he thought sadly. What a woman—she's trapped her husband on his own ground.

Ernest stared back at her. He took a breath, then looked around. He had lost momentum, the people were no longer with him.

"Yes," he quickly agreed. "Yes, sinners are to be forgiven!"

Margot dropped her eyes and grasped her skirts. As quickly as she had come forward, she ran away, back toward her wagon. The congregation broke into song, and Blaise slumped to the ground and sat down.

Margot sat on the edge of the bedroll in the darkness. She buried her face in her hands and wept for a time; then, having no more tears, she wiped her face on her arm. Not only was Ernest not the man she had once thought, he had actually changed in the past months. He had always been strict, but tonight's display was something different, something more extreme. And people listened to him! Lord, they had almost hurt Alura and certainly they would have sent her packing. Margot shook her head. She almost wished Ernest had known about her and that he would send her away.

"Margot!" Ernest's voice startled her and she jumped.

"I see you there!" he sounded angry, but restrained.

"Yes, Ernest," she said, trying to sound normal.

"Why did you do that?" he demanded.

"Do what?" Margot answered, wary.

"Interfere. You interfered."

"Did I?" she answered innocently.

"That woman should not be allowed among decent folk!"

Ernest advanced on her and he jolted her upright by the

183

shoulders and shook her. "Don't ever do that again, Margot! I will not tolerate it!"

Margot stared into his eyes defiantly. "Let me go," she said evenly. "Let me go or I shall write the missionary society and tell them—"

Ernest dropped his hands immediately. "Tell them what?"

Margot stared at him. In truth she had no answer. Tell them he had nightmares? Tell them he had raped her? Tell them he was a hypocrite? She shook her head, but did not reply. Everyone had nightmares. A husband taking his wife was not rape, and Ernest was not the only preacher to hound women of easy virtue; her would-be accusations had no foundation.

"You will learn to obey me," Ernest said menacingly.

Margot lifted her head proudly. "I am your lawful wife, Ernest. I am bound by a vow that cannot be broken, but I do not agree with you."

Ernest stared at her and she was certain that if there had been light she would have seen the hate in his eyes.

Cory watched as Nkula examined the gold with a jaded eye. It was mid-August, and if he was to leave the Lillooet village it would have to be soon. It was a long way down the river and across the mountain range to the coast—a long way back to Victoria.

"It is not enough," Nkula concluded.

Cory leaned back against the base of the giant pine tree. The Lillooet camp was filled with the aroma of fish as the women prepared dinner. The children of the camp played noisily among the trees, the braves sat in circles around small fires and talked. Everyone in the village is related, Cory thought, and between all of them there was trust and a shared belief in the stories of the tribe's beginning. Under other circumstances, he would have been happy to remain here indefinitely. He might even have taken an Indian woman. But his mind was too much on Anya, and he felt no urge for the companionship of one of the Indian maidens.

"Nkula, within a month the snows will come to the

mountains. We cannot dig for gold when the ground is frozen.''

Nkula nodded silently. ''You will stay, you will begin again when the spring rains come.''

Cory considered the situation. There was gold where they had been digging; the problem was equipment. The Lillooet had no real knowledge of what was required. The only metals they possessed were knives and pots and pans they had obtained from trading with the British.

''We need more shovels, more equipment to dig with. Without the proper tools we will not recover sufficient gold to replace Cloya's sacred gold.''

Nkula looked at him suspiciously.

Cory smiled. ''Yes, I know of Cloya.'' The bluejay, or Cloya, as the bird was called by the Indians, was an intrinsic part of the beliefs held by most Salish-speaking tribes— Cloya was both the creator and a trickster.

Nkula grunted. ''For a white man, you are wise in the ways of my people.''

''Nkula, let me go back across the great waters. Let me go home to get the tools to dig for the gold. Trust me to return with the spring rains.''

''You will not return.''

''I will return, I swear I will.''

''No, you will stay, I will give you a woman for the winter.''

Cory shook his head. ''I have a woman,'' he lied.

Nkula grunted again. ''You cannot have two squaws?''

''Two squaws are much trouble.''

''Only for the white man.''

Cory smiled; Nkula managed well with three. But of course, the marriage laws among the Lillooet, who were a plateau people, were quite different than the marriage laws in white society. Among the Lillooet, a man could have many wives, but if a woman tired of her husband, she could simply leave him and return to her family—she could even remarry. And every chief had a female advisor. Women could even become tribal shamans. But among this group, Nkula was both shaman and chief.

185

"How can I prove to Nkula that I will return?"

"You would leave all the gold you have found?"

"Yes."

"I will think on it," Nkula allowed. "I will consult with the ghosts of the forest, who can see into your heart. I will give you my decision seven suns from now."

"I am satisfied," Cory replied.

Nkula rose and walked away from the fire. He moved with dignity, and Cory knew he was wondering if a white man could be trusted.

Cory waited a few minutes, then he too got up and headed for the hut he had been given. It was small, half above the ground, half subterranean as a shelter against the snows of winter. On the far side of the village he could see the steam fires rising from the sweathouse where the women cleansed themselves after their flow. It was adjacent to the menstrual hut where they were confined during their unclean period. Abstractedly, Cory looked upward to the tall tree tops where the beautiful blue scavenger jays nested. "Be on my side," he whispered. "Let Nkula read the signs correctly."

CHAPTER XIV

August 16, 1856

Blaise was thankful that the South Pass trail was so difficult that it distracted the settlers from further thoughts of Alura Alton. The physical difficulties of the trip produced a weariness which had a gradual calming effect. Then, too, Ernest hardly preached at all in the evenings. Still, the whole incident left a bad taste in Blaise's mouth. He found he avoided the settlers and kept more to himself than ever.

Margot rested uneasily on his mind as well. She was cool and distant, seemingly distracted with personal guilt and so obviously miserable in her relationship with her husband that his heart ached for her as much as his body longed for her.

This was the night he was to eat with Margot and Ernest, but again Ernest was on guard duty and would be until the early hours of the dawn. Blaise scowled. He didn't relish a meal in stony silence, nor did he wish to hurt her further. She was a woman absorbed in her own confusion, a woman whose naturally passionate nature warred with her morality. Although, he conceded, Margot certainly did not share her husband's extreme views.

Blaise picked up the string of mountain trout he had caught earlier and headed for the McGrath wagon on the far side of the circle. He could see Margot from a distance, alone by her fire.

"Good evening." He tried to sound casual, as if there were nothing between them and never had been. It was an attitude he had affected since the night he had possessed her—or perhaps, he thought, the night she had possessed him.

"Good evening," Margot returned. As usual, she did not meet his eyes.

"I caught some trout this morning. I brought them for you."

"That's very kind of you."

"My pleasure."

"If you had told me sooner, we could have had them for dinner. But I've already begun the stew."

Blaise smiled. "I like stew. . . . Anyway, the trout are for you. Fix them tomorrow when I'm not here."

Margot nodded.

Blaise sat down near her. She automatically moved a bit, creating between them a greater distance.

"Margot, for heaven's sake, can't you even talk to me? I know how you feel—or I suppose I know how you feel."

"We are talking."

"Like two perfect strangers."

Margot whipped her head around and he could see tears forming in her eyes. "That's the way it must be," she whispered. "Don't torture me further. I beg you."

Her eyes looked haunted, and Blaise noticed that she had lost weight. "The last thing I want is to torture you," he told her softly. "But I just can't help feeling that something else—something besides that night—is troubling you."

"Is that night not enough?" Margot's hand trembled and again she turned away.

"I should like to be your friend," he ventured.

Margot was silent. It wasn't, she concluded, only that night that troubled her. It was Ernest. His nightmares had grown more frequent and often he woke up sobbing like a small child. And his self-abuse continued. Once, she had lain awake half the night watching him, frozen as if she herself were dreaming. He tossed and turned, he mumbled and cursed. His face became contorted in fear and agony. Then, after a time, he seized himself and caressed himself until he was satisfied. He awoke with a scream about the devil. More often than not, Margot pretended to be asleep.

But she was grateful for one thing. He kept his promise; he never touched her, he never came near to her. He once spoke of her virtue, but for the most part he ignored her completely.

I am not virtuous, Margot thought. I am a fallen woman.

And in spite of it all, she couldn't look at Blaise Baron without wanting him to hold her as he had that night. In his arms she had felt secure, and from him she had derived the pure pleasure of love. It is my punishment, she thought. I will forever long for what is totally forbidden.

"Are you and your husband still planning to leave the wagon train in the Yakima Valley?"

"Yes, at the Whitman mission."

"You will not find the Indians friendly."

"So I have been told, but I'm sure that with a little kindness they can be won over."

Blaise smiled. "You're an idealist. If you're kind, it will be the first kindness they have known in some time. And what about your husband? Will he be kind?"

Margot opened her hands and stared at them. "I shall ask him to be kind," she said softly. In truth, she wasn't sure that once she was alone with Ernest her threat would have any meaning. Clearly he was appalled that she might have witnessed his dreams. She suspected that while he feared her knowledge now, he seethed with anger internally, an anger that would soon be turned on her.

"The governor of the territory is a bastard," Blaise said. He didn't really want to talk about Ernest.

Margot did not flinch at his choice of language. "I have heard he does not keep his promises."

"That's the least of it."

"Some white men can be cruel, some Indians can be cruel."

"I can't disagree with that." She seemed to be relaxing a bit, Blaise thought. Perhaps if they stayed off personal matters, they could at least have a conversation.

"How long do you plan to stay at the mission?"

"Until our replacements come next year. It is a sort of training period. After that, Ernest wants to head up toward Fort Victoria, or perhaps to the mainland. He says most of the missionaries in that area are Papists. He thinks there is a need for Protestant missionaries there. Personally, I don't want to remain in the United States."

Blaise smiled. He did not bother to tell her that he often made his home on Vancouver Island, near Fort Victoria.

"I have a friend there," he said vaguely.

"What's it like?"

"God's country—the most beautiful place on the entire continent. It would be wholly perfect without the British."

"My father says that the colonies will unite and that one day there will be one nation."

"And will this nation allow the people of Lower Canada to speak their language?" Blaise's voice held just a bit of sarcasm.

"I hope so," Margot answered truthfully.

"The last time a unification of the Canadas was considered, in 1822, that was not the case, and even now, from what I've heard, under this Act of Union there is no representation by population and English is the official language. The British seem to decide these issues for us. Are we children in their wilderness?"

"My father believes we should be the masters of our own house."

"Your father sounds like an unusual man."

"He is," Margot said, unable to disguise her longing.

"I hope your father has his way. But make no mistake, I will never trust the British."

Margot looked at him, and Blaise relished the intensity of her eyes. He saw in them her desire to understand.

"Why don't you trust them?"

"Because I come from Montreal . . . because I lived through . . ."

"Lived through what?" Margot pressed.

"Through a bad period."

"You're being intentionally mysterious. Tell me about it. Tell me why you left Montreal?"

"When I was young, my mother died of cholera, a disease brought to Montreal by British immigrants."

"You cannot hate the British for that! My mother died of typhus when I was ten. A lot of people blamed it on the Irish, but the Irish died, too. And many of the English died of cholera as well!"

"It's more than that. . . . We wanted representative government; a government in which the French-speaking majority had a voice, a strong voice, and French as an official language. I don't expect you to understand."

"I do understand."

"No, you don't! It was denied, there was a rebellion . . . I was part of that rebellion! My father was murdered by British soldiers—shot in cold blood. I killed two soldiers, but I escaped arrest. Others were not so lucky. They were hanged . . . not shot as soldiers, but hanged!"

"You were part of the Papineau rebellion!"

"Yes, and I cannot go back."

"But you could! There was an amnesty long ago!"

Blaise shook his head. "I know that, but there would be retribution . . . and I could never go back to a Quebec under the thumb of the British. I could never go back to find a fat British merchant living in my father's house, owning my father's business, and spending my father's money." His voice was low and bitter and he wasn't at all certain why he had told Margot all this. Perhaps, he thought, she will feel less guilt and less pain if she knows me for what I am.

But her reaction was not what he expected. She looked sad and she shook her head silently.

"You are another kind of prisoner," she finally said. "You're a prisoner of your past and of your bitterness."

Blaise wanted to reach out and take her in his arms. He tried to change the subject. "Would you tell me about your past?" he asked her.

Margot nodded.

"What was your name, before you were married?"

"Macleod. . . . We live on a farm, a very large farm outside Niagara-on-the-Lake. It was originally founded by my great-great-grandparents, Janet and Mathew Macleod."

"That's a lot of 'greats,' " Blaise joked.

"Janet came from Scotland in the 1740s; Mathew, too. Their's was a great, long love story. It's sort of a legend in my family. Then Mathew came to Fort Niagara—that's in the United States now—and he founded Lochiel across the river, which opens onto the lake. Janet was in Quebec during the Battle of the Plains of Abraham, but her brother-in-law—I think he came from Scotland with her . . . he was the brother of her first husband—brought her back to Mathew. Janet's brother-in-law was a famous woodsman, and so were his sons and grandsons. One of his sons married Janet's daughter, Jenna Macleod, so the two families are forever united.'' Margot sighed with homesickness. ''I have a very large family,'' she concluded.

''I thought some were French?''

''Oh, some are. Janet and Mathew adopted three children. The family was called Deschamps.''

''That's a well-known name in Montreal. I know many Deschamps.''

''Yes, they went back to Montreal, except for my great-great-aunt Madelaine. She married Mathew's son. She's dead, of course, but I grew up with her grandchildren.''

''You know a lot about your family.''

''On long winter nights we tell tales. It's a tradition among the Macleods. My great-aunt Susanna knows the most.'' Margot leaned over conspiratorily, ''She sits for hours and drinks elderberry wine and tells stories about lost lovers who were reunited, and how our family was tangled with the MacLeans.''

Blaise smiled. Cory was a MacLean. But then, it was a common name.

Margot nodded. ''Oh, it's one of great-aunt Susanna's longest stories! I don't know if it's really true, or if it's the elderberry wine, but she's a wonderful story teller.''

Margot looked thoughtful. ''Aunt Susanna's stories occurred long ago.''

''Long ago,'' Blaise repeated solemnly. The Papineau rebellion had been a long time ago too, he thought.

The afternoon sun filtered through the trees and a warm breeze rustled the bushes along the dirt trail. Cory and the two braves headed back toward the village. It is the day of the seventh sun, Cory thought, and Nkula will give me his answer. He will let me know if I can leave the Lillooet and return to Victoria.

Cory wondered what Anya was doing. Indeed, he wondered if, now that he had decided to pursue her, she would have him. She was a strange woman, unpredictable by any standards.

The ever-present aroma of the cooking pots greeted them first, then a group of little girls, who ceremoniously brushed the pathway with sticks in front of Cory and the braves as they walked.

Sha Shan poked Cory in the ribs. "What do you think of her?" He motioned toward a slender young woman dressed in drab garb. Her face was painted a bright orange, her hair tied in a bun. She had been standing near the well, drinking from it through a sort of tube. But when she had seen them approaching she had darted away with the agility of a deer, quickly running into the compound of the menstrual hut.

"It's hard to tell," Cory answered honestly. "I cannot see her hair nor her face with all that color on it."

"She's very pretty," Sha Shan said, smiling. "She is undergoing the rites of womanhood, because she has just had her first blood. She is not allowed to drink directly from the well, and she is not allowed to touch her hair. The color on her face identifies her as one on the brink of enlightenment."

"What must she do?" Cory asked curiously. He had only the vaguest ideas concerning the rites of womanhood among the Lillooet. He knew more about the rites of manhood.

"She will remain in the compound with the unclean for a time. When her blood is past, she will go to the mountain to fast and she will fast until the ghosts of our ancestors speak to her, until she has seen the visions that bring enlightenment. Then she will return to the village and recount her experiences."

"And then?"

"Then I will marry her," Sha Shan announced.

Cory nodded and smiled. "I'm certain she is an excellent choice."

"It is her brother, Mkan, who was keeper of the sacred gold."

"What became of him?"

"When the gold was taken, he was taken, too. He may be dead, he may be a slave. It is hard to tell. We do not know how those related to the Flatheads treat prisoners. We did not find his body, so we only assume that the Flatheads have the same custom as we, and that young braves may be taken as slaves."

"Who stole the gold?" Cory asked curiously.

"Warriors of the Yakima, they say. It is said they hoped to use it to pay off white men. They say white men treat the Yakima badly. It is said the white men demand gold for hunting grounds."

Cory looked up and saw Nkula approaching. He wore a long, tailored robe that was brightly colored. He also wore a broad-brimmed hat of woven tree branches. He looked stately as he signaled Cory to come over to him.

Cory waved good-bye to the two braves and greeted Nkula formally. "Good day."

"It is the day of the seventh sun."

"Yes. Has the wise Nkula made a decision?"

"I have consulted Cloya and I have spoken with Coyote. I have listened to the ghosts in the rustle of the trees and I have seen an omen of great importance."

"And what is the omen?"

"Things must be told in order. Please come into my hut."

Cory followed Nkula into his large hut. "Sit, please." Nkula directed him to a pile of furs. Cory sat down, but Nkula remained standing. It was the custom; the teacher stood, the student sat at his feet.

"Cloya is not given to trust the white man, but Coyote, who is almost as mischievous as Cloya, argues for trust. After I spoke with them, I spoke with the Great Spirit and the ghosts of our tribal ancestors. . . . They see all, they know what will happen in the future, and in that way they look after us.

"While I was standing by the edge of the pond created by the river's deviation, a small animal crawled out of the ground and as it emerged from its nest it left a trail across the

194

soft earth; but the trail was a message given to salamander by the Great Spirit. It told me that Coyote was right and that if you left you would indeed return. But it also told me another fact; it told me that shortly after you returned, our sacred gold would be returned. When I related this to Cloya, he said that you should leave, for if you do not leave, you cannot return, and if you do not return, our sacred gold will not be brought back to us.''

Cory nodded. "I give Nkula my word that I will return."

"You may begin your journey tomorrow."

"I thank Nkula for his trust."

Nkula's face remained a bit of chisled stone. "It is more appropriate that you thank Coyote."

"I will," Cory replied.

Cory hurried along the main street of Victoria. It was mid-September, but the weather was still warm. Vancouver Island had a much milder climate than the interior of New Caledonia, which was ringed by high mountains that were often snow-covered year round.

It had taken him twenty-three days to reach the Hudson's Bay Post and another day to sail by steamer to Vancouver Island. Still, he had made the trip in record time.

Cory paused in front of the theater. He had gone to the farm first. Then, learning that Anya had moved into Victoria, he had gone to the small house where he was told she resided. There he learned from her Indian maid that this was the opening night of Anya's production of *Romeo and Juliet*. Cory had rushed directly to the theater.

He pulled open the door to the lobby and went in. Clearly the production was already in progress. He opened the little door between the lobby and the theater and walked in, pausing in the aisle while his eyes adjusted to the darkness.

On stage, two men were acting out one of the early scenes of the play. Every bench in the theater was filled and every person, Cory noted, sat in absolute silent rapture.

In the front row he spotted Governor Douglas, Amelia Douglas, and their thirteen children. Everyone was dressed in their finest; this appeared to be a real event.

Captain Langford was there, too, as was Dr. John Sebastion Helmcken, The Reverend Cridge, John Muir, Thomas Skinner, James Yates, Dr. John F. Kennedy, Joseph Pemberton, and J. W. MacKay . . . the latter were all members of the newly elected Legislative Assembly.

Cory glanced to one side. John Tod was there with his wife. She was a stout Indian woman, dressed as any proper English lady might dress, complete with a splendid high feather bonnet. Her hands were folded primly in her lap, her stony face was utterly devoid of enthusiasm. Her official name was Sophia Tod, but her nickname was 'Singing Lola'—although it was well known that not only didn't she sing, she rarely even smiled. She was staid and strict, a model of British decorum.

The entire establishment of the Colony was present. In addition, there were rows and rows of miners, of gold seekers, and of men who were more usually drunk and raucous. But they too were dressed in their very best clothing, incongruous as some of the outfits were, and they too sat enraptured.

The curtain drew to a close and there was a round of applause. Cory clapped too.

There were sounds of things being shoved about behind the curtain. The curtains parted and Anya appeared standing on what looked for all the world like the used scaffolding of a mine shaft. The stage also sported a number of dying shrubs, presumably to indicate a garden.

There was an immediate round of loud applause from the rows of miners, and a certain amount of whistling and foot stamping as well.

"Hush!" Mrs. Douglas proclaimed in a shout that could be heard the entire length and breadth of the theater. Instantly, a hush fell over the audience.

Commander Arlen stepped onto the stage. Raising his arm toward Anya, he began, ". . . But soft! What light through yonder window breaks?. . ."

Cory made a face and listened as Arlen completed his first speech. He himself had memorized the entire play, at his mother's insistence.

Anya stepped to the edge of the scaffolding. "Ay me!"

Arlen dropped to one knee. "She speaks! Oh, speak again, bright angel! for thou art as glorious to this night, being o'er my head, as is a winged messenger of heaven unto the white-upturned wond'ring eyes of mortals that fall back to gaze on him when he bestrides the lazy-pacing clouds and sails upon the bosom of the air."

"Oh, Romeo, Romeo! wherefore art thou Romeo?"

"Wait!" Cory shouted, running down the aisle on sheer impulse.

Anya straightened up. Governor Douglas laughed.

"Sh!" Mrs. Douglas demanded.

The miners broke into hysterics, and someone was heard to comment, "God, an Anglo with the heart of a Latin!"

Cory climbed onto the stage. He looked at Arlen and grinned. "I'll take over now," he said authoritatively.

Arlen was red-faced. "You don't even know the role!"

Cory winked. "I do, too, and I'm type-cast."

The clapping continued. "You're absurd," Arlen fumed. Grumbling, he retreated to the side of the stage. Cory grinned again and waved at Anya. "Go on. Say the rest of your lines!"

Anya lifted her head proudly, and without missing a beat continued.

The curtain closed after the final scene and the audience clapped wildly. Then the curtain opened, and the cast, Cory included, took their bows. Two more curtain calls, flowers for Anya, and the curtain closed for the final time.

Cory turned to Anya and grinned. "Surprised you, didn't I?"

She gazed at him unsmilingly. "That was an absurd thing to do."

"Well, I do know the role."

"But you nearly ruined the production!"

Cory laughed. "I'm not sure it's possible to ruin the first play ever shown in the Colony. People are starved for entertainment."

"I know that."

"I'd like to get out of here. I have to talk to you." Cory

197

looked around. He was well aware that the eyes of the rest of the cast were on them. Arlen stood some distance away, a bemused expression on his face.

"I doubt I should go anywhere with you! You are without doubt the most . . . most—"

"Unpredictable person you know." Cory took her arm and guided her away. "Have you a dressing room?"

"Yes, and I am going into it alone. When I come out, I am going to the home of Governor and Mrs. Douglas for a reception. It is the custom to have a party after opening night."

"I'll come with you."

"As you wish."

Anya turned and disappeared, leaving Cory amidst the other players.

"What are you up to, old man?" Arlen came over and slapped him across the back.

Cory scowled. "I just want to talk to Anya."

"Doesn't everyone!"

Cory turned away. "Damn!" he swore under his breath. Somehow this was not how he had envisioned his homecoming.

Anya returned, magnificent in blue taffeta. Her eyes looked huge, but Cory could not read them.

"I stand proudly, ready to escort you to the party, Juliet," Arlen told her, stepping up and taking her arm.

Cory quickly took the other. "It's not every Juliet who has two Romeos," he smiled.

The three of them crammed themselves into Arlen's carriage and drove, mostly in silence, to the Douglas house.

Mrs. Douglas herself opened the door, frowning slightly to see that Cory was not dressed formally. "I didn't have time to change," he mumbled, knowing how much manners and form meant to her.

"No matter. You're quite welcome."

Cory followed Anya and Arlen into the parlor where the cast and the elite of the colony were gathered. He felt like a fish out of water . . . or, more appropriately, like a bear out of the woods.

"You certainly have made a spectacle out of yourself," Anya whispered. She turned away from him to accept a compliment from the Tods, smiling at them radiantly.

Governor Douglas tapped Cory on the shoulder. "You have absolutely no patience, my friend. She will be done here soon enough," he whispered.

Cory flushed. "This will go on forever."

"Oh, not that long. We like to get to bed early."

Cory's eyes followed Anya around the room. People surrounded her, and that stupid Arlen was at her side. Cory wished he were dressed more presentably.

"Excuse me," he said. He fought his way across the room and took her arm. "I have to talk to you. Now!"

Anya allowed him to pull her off into a corner. "Well? What is it?"

"Not here. Come out into the rose garden with me."

"I can't leave now. It would be impolite."

"Will you let me take you home? After all this is over?"

She sighed deeply. "I suppose so, if it's that important."

Anya broke away from him and floated back to the guests. Cory went to the punch bowl and had a drink. He watched her for more than an hour until finally the guests began to leave.

He waited until several had departed, then walked over to her and took her arm. "I think we should go," he told her firmly.

Anya smiled. "All right, I'll come now."

They bid good night to their hosts, and Cory arranged to borrow the governor's carriage.

"Shall we drive around a bit?" he asked.

"I think I would prefer to go home."

"As you wish."

He drove through the streets of Victoria to her house several blocks away. Anya wrapped her shawl around her and walked rapidly toward the door. Cory followed her, stopping her at the doorstep with a hand on her arm.

"I was worried about you," she told him, without meeting his eyes. "I asked the governor to send someone to look for you."

"I doubt anyone could have found me."

"That is what he told me."

Cory inhaled deeply. "Nice night," he commented.

She looked straight at him. "You burst into my first theater performance and took over the role of Romeo to tell me it was a nice night?"

Cory laughed. "You're a beautiful Juliet."

"You're impossible." She opened the door. "I suppose you intend to come in."

Cory didn't answer, but simply followed her through the door and watched as she lit the lamps.

"It's very nice," he said, looking around approvingly. The room was tastefully furnished with goods that had quite obviously been imported from the orient. "Captain Arlen manage all this?"

"Some of it," Anya allowed.

Cory felt a surge of jealousy, "What's going on between you two?"

"Why is that your concern?" she asked coldly.

Cory took a step toward her, and she stood looking at him. He pulled her into his arms and lowered his mouth to kiss her. She struggled, against him, then went limp. "That's why it's my concern," he said softly into her ear.

Anya trembled against him, but she didn't try to move. "You wanted to marry a rich man," Cory said. "I'm a rich man."

Anya pulled back and looked into his handsome, rugged face. "Riches do not concern me as much as you think."

Cory didn't answer, but instead lowered his lips to hers again.

"Stop it!" Anya shivered and drew away, her large blue eyes filled with tears.

"You want me to kiss you," he insisted. "As much as I want to kiss you."

Anya shook her head. "You do not know me, you do not know about me!" Her voice was high-pitched; tears tumbled down her face.

"I know you are beautiful, proud, and intelligent."

Anya steadied herself against the small table. "I am a thief," she said softly. "I am also a used woman."

Cory studied her face. It was filled with pain and with a humility he hadn't seen there before.

"Tell me," he pressed. "I don't know what you mean."

"I am not fit to marry anyone!" Anya sunk into a chair and dabbed at her eyes.

Cory came to her side. "Tell me, Anya."

She began in halting tones to tell him about her uncle and how he had abused her. She sobbed incoherently and clenched her hands into fists as a flood of memories returned to her.

Cory was quiet for a moment. Then he asked, "Why did you lie?"

"Because you might have sent me back. . . . Because once a woman is no more a virgin, she is ruined!"

Cory knelt beside the chair and took her lovely hands into his. "I don't think so," he said quietly. "Anya, I still want you. I want to marry you."

He reached up silently and wiped her cheeks. She seemed more appealing now than she ever had before. She had survived a physical and emotional ordeal with an unbroken spirit.

"Every day I was away, I thought of you," he told her.

"Then why were you gone so long?" She was still sobbing with the emotional upheaval that her memories had brought to the surface.

"It's a long story. I came as soon as I could."

He stood up and, taking her hands, pulled her up, too. "You will marry me?"

She looked at him almost uncomprehendingly. "You do not mind that I am used?"

He smiled and shook his head. "I'm not entirely new myself," he joked.

"It is different with men."

Cory drew her into his arms and pressed her close. "Not so different," he told her. "I love you. . . ."

Anya let her head rest on his shoulder. "I am yours," she whispered.

CHAPTER XV

September 16, 1856

The plain little houses of the Whitman mission stood like a cluster in the midst of the lush, seemingly uninhabited Yakima Valley in Washington near the Walla Walla River. The wagon train had circled for the night. Tomorrow, September 17, the wagon which had held the McGraths and their belongings would be driven by the Carltons, who presently lived in the Whitman mission but who were now going on to Fort Steilacoom while the McGraths stayed to replace them.

Blaise Baron stood by the McGrath wagon and looked across the valley. He shook his head dejectedly and wondered why no Indians, save those who lived at the mission, had appeared. This was their territory; he considered their absence an ominous sign.

For the past hour Ernest and Margot had been emptying their wagon so the Carltons might fill it with their own belongings. Young Gideon Rathbone helped, while the other settlers took advantage of the fine water supply and washed themselves and their clothing.

Margot came out of the neat little cottage that was soon to be her home.

"Almost done?" Blaise queried.

Margot nodded. "A few more things, that's all."

"How do you like the house?"

"It's fine." She looked miserable, almost on the verge of tears, he thought. And, he admitted, he didn't feel much better. He fought the urge to take her in his arms and tell her she couldn't stay with Ernest because she didn't love him. You love me, he wanted to tell her.

Instead, he smiled and said, "It's a beautiful valley."

Margot nodded, unable to speak.

"Margot, are you sure you want to stay here?" It was as close as he could come to telling her what was on his mind.

"I must," she said without looking up, as he'd expected her to say.

She turned and climbed into the wagon.

Mrs. Carlton appeared with an armload of bedding.

"Mrs. Carlton," Blaise said, "may I speak with you a moment."

She was a round little woman with wispy gray hair that apparently defied all efforts to manage it. She wore a plain housedress and the traditional bonnet.

"As soon as I put these things away," she replied. Blaise nodded. She looked more a missionary than Margot. He envisaged Mrs. Carlton in her kitchen making endless apple pies and eating all of them herself. She and the Reverend Carlton had fourteen children, ranging in age from four to twenty-two. But Mrs. Carlton did not look miserable or harrassed. She managed her brood like a drill sergeant, holding them in line with constant quotes from the Bible and vague threats that nastiness would freeze on their faces and make them forever ugly.

She emerged from the wagon and wiped her hands on her apron. "How can I help you?" she asked.

"I haven't seen any Indians since I entered the valley. I consider that unusual. Do you know what's become of them?"

Mrs. Carlton shrugged. "They all disappeared about two weeks ago. I heard from one of the mission Indians that they were having a big pow-wow way over on the far side of the valley."

"Any trouble?" Blaise asked.

"One family on the edge of the valley was attacked and the soldiers came in. They shot a few Indians and there's been no trouble since then. But the Indians don't bother us."

"Can you find the mission Indian for me? I'd like to ride over there and talk to the chief."

"I don't know if that's a good idea."

"I'll be the judge of that," Blaise returned.

Mrs. Carlton shrugged. "His name is Paul. You'll find him over in the barn doing chores."

"Thanks." Blaise turned and walked toward the barn. Damned if I'm leaving Margot here if there's any danger, he vowed to himself. Briefly his mind returned to his disturbing encounter with Governor Stevens nearly a year ago. Things were bad enough then; what were they like now?

"Paul?" Blaise peered into the barn.

"Yes, sir," the young voice replied.

"My name is Blaise Baron, I'm taking the wagon train to Fort Steilacoom. I'd like to go across the valley and meet with the Yakima chief. Will you lead me to their camp?"

Paul stood in the doorway of the barn. He was quite young, maybe fourteen. Possibly a tribal outcast, Blaise thought. Many of the mission Indians were. Sometimes they were one of twins; tribal belief often caused the Indians to abandon twins, considering them a bad omen. Or, perhaps he had white blood or he was illegitimate by tribal law. Whatever the reason, he looked mildly troubled by Blaise's request.

"You don't have to take me all the way," Blaise said, hoping to make it easier. "Just near to where they are camped, then you can return."

Paul agreed, but refused to lead Blaise into the camp itself.

They rode for nearly two hours before Paul drew in his horse. "The camp is two miles that way," he pointed off. "You will see the fires."

"Thanks," Blaise replied. "I'll go alone from here."

Paul turned his horse and spurred it. He took off, riding rapidly back to the mission. For a moment, Blaise followed the retreating figure with his eyes.

Half a mile from the Indian camp, Blaise was intercepted by nine braves who surrounded his horse, their bows drawn.

Blaise reined his horse in and held out his hands, palms up. "I come in peace," he told them in their own language. "I come to see your chief, Kamiakan."

"I have seen this man before," one of the braves told his comrades.

"You will give us your weapons if you come in peace," another brave said to Blaise.

Blaise nodded. He unfastened his gun belt and handed it over. Then he lifted his rifle from its holster on the side of his saddlebag, handing it over as well. Then he gave them his hunting knife.

"Fine knife," one of the braves commented as he admired it. The knife was Blaise's only connection with his past, having been a gift from his father. It was a finely honed knife, of the sort used by the voyageurs.

"A gift from my father," Blaise told the brave.

"You will have it back if Kamiakan wishes."

Blaise nodded and followed the braves into camp.

"Sit here," the braves instructed. Blaise sat down in front of the fire. He waited for some minutes before the elderly Kamiakan appeared, dressed in full tribal regalia. Silently, the chief sat down and lifted his pipe. He filled it and lit it from the fire, inhaling deeply. Blaise smiled at the smell of the pleasant mixture; it was wild tobacco and bayberry leaves, commonly smoked by many of the plains Indians.

"How may I be of service?" Kamiakan asked.

"I come to see how the Yakima are, how all the friends of the Yakima are, too," Blaise said after a few minutes.

Kamiakan shook his head. "Many have been killed by white militiamen. We will have war."

Blaise bit his lip. "On whom will you war?"

"On the white man who takes our land and who does not keep promises."

"On all the white men?"

"On those who keep guns. On those who kill our people."

"Kamiakan, I have left new missionaries at the mission. They know nothing of war."

Kamiakan nodded. "If they leave us alone, we will leave them alone. I have no concern with missionaries. I have concern with settlers who allow animals to graze on hunting grounds and who kill braves who try to hunt. I have concern with the militia who come and kill, and with those settlers who abuse our women."

"I understand Kamiakan's words."

"It is not just Kamiakan, Chief of the Yakima. It is all the chiefs of our brother tribes. We rise together as one."

"But you will not harm the missionaries?"

"If they do not harm us, the messengers of the white man's Great Spirit may remain. They teach, we learn."

"I will be taking the wagon train from the valley in the morning."

"That is good."

"I thank Kamiakan," Blaise said. "I hope Kamiakan does not need to war."

Kamiakan nodded silently, then added, "We will suffer." He turned to his braves. "Give this man back his weapons. He travels in peace."

The morning sun streamed through the window of Anya's cottage. Cory lay in bed, watching Anya as she slept peacefully. They had been together all night. It was, he reflected, the best night of his life.

She curled on her side like a child, her flaxen hair spread out on the white pillow. Her skin looked like alabaster and Cory marveled at the lovely curves of her body. Impulsively, he leaned over and kissed her smooth, soft shoulders. She stirred slightly, then, still asleep, rolled languidly over onto her back, exposing her small, white, pink-tipped breasts to him.

Cory touched her nipple softly and watched as it turned to a hard pink rosette. She blinked open her huge blue eyes. Cory smiled and ran his hand over her flat belly, lingering for a moment on her tuft of blond hair.

"Again," she breathed heavily, lifting her arms and embracing him.

"In the morning light?" Cory teased, increasing the pressure of his hand and toying with her until she squirmed beneath his touch.

"You should be tired," Anya whispered.

He lowered his head and drew her nipple into his mouth, playing with her other breast until she moaned with delight. "I don't get tired," he breathed into her ear, before he

207

moved to kiss her throat and nuzzle between her neck and shoulder.

Her hands encircled his manhood. "You're strong, but you don't hurt me."

Cory closed his eyes, reveling in her touch. "I can't go so slowly, if you do that."

She laughed seductively and he stroked her mound until she pressed herself closer, almost reaching for his hand, which came and went. "You drive me mad," she whispered, returning his kisses.

"Good," he answered, again withdrawing his hand and stroking her belly instead. He drew small circles on her with his fingers, tickling her and teasing her.

"Please," she whispered, clinging to him.

Cory covered her full mouth with a long, deep kiss. He moved his leg across her, and he continued to play until he heard her breathing deepen and felt her aflame beneath him.

He returned to stroking her mound, then gently parted her and slipped in. Together they moved, while Anya's breath came in short gasps. Cory lifted her to him in the final instant and felt her wild spasm even as he himself shook.

For a few moments he remained entwined with her. "We are one," he said into her ear.

"Yes," Anya murmured. "I did not think it possible to know such joy."

Cory slid from her, but he drew her close, covering her breast with his hand. How many times had they made love in the last eight hours? Happily he admitted he had lost count.

"We'll go to the governor's today and be married," he said with determination. "Next time I leave, I will leave a wife."

"Leave?" She looked up at him, distressed.

Cory smiled. "Not till spring, my darling."

"Then I will go with you."

"It's too rough and too long a journey. The dangers for a woman are too great."

"Then I won't let you go."

"I have to go. I gave my word."

208

Anya snuggled in his arms. "To whom?"

"To the Indians. I have to keep my word."

Anya nodded. "Then I will go with you," she insisted.

Cory kissed her blond hair, "No, you will not, but you have my promise that I will not be away one day longer than necessary."

Ernest was in the mission house lying down. He did not even feign interest in the departure of the wagon train. "I've been with those people too long," he complained. But Margot knew it was more than boredom. Since the night she had challenged him, he had been sullen and unhappy with his flock of followers. He had lost his hold over them and, as a result, had also lost interest.

Margot stood outside the house and watched as the circle unwound and once again became a long line of white-tented wagons. Blaise rode up to her and looked down from his mare.

"Our moment of parting has come," he said in a hushed voice.

Margot lifted her eyes; they were great green pools, misty and contemplative. "Yes," she said. "I shall miss you."

Blaise stroked his beard. "I'll come back if you ever need me," he finally said.

"No. It cannot be, I am married to Ernest. It cannot be." She lowered her head and looked at the ground.

Blaise fought his every instinct to try once again to convince her to leave. Instead, he gave her one last, longing look, and when she did not respond, he spurred his horse and rode to join the wagon train. It was September 17, and one more mountain range had to be crossed before the snows came.

He called out the signal, and the wagon train began to pull out. Margot stood and watched, feeling as if her heart would break, longing to run after him. She stood for nearly an hour until the line of prairie schooners was far in the distance and the lone figure of Blaise Baron on his horse had long disappeared. Wearily, Margot turned and went into the mission house. "Here I will stay," she said aloud.

Margot sat down and put her feet up. It was strange to be in a house after so long in a wagon. In the other room, she could hear Ernest's snoring; the sound irritated her.

I've made such a mess. I was only infatuated with Ernest! I wanted him because the other girls wanted him, she admitted to herself. I didn't listen to my father and I should have. She thought briefly of home. She had spent her nineteenth birthday on the trail; it had gone by unnoticed, even by Ernest. At home there would have been a party and Highland games. Her father would have still tried to toss the caber, and her great-aunt Susanna would have been into the brandy and full of tall tales. But on the trail there was only dust and hard work. Margot wondered if her father had received any of her letters. She had sent one from each fort along the trail. She described the journey and the scenery; she spoke in detail about her fellow passengers. When she mentioned Ernest she tried to be casual. If her father knew how unhappy she was, if he suspected Ernest's cruelty and unnatural ways, he would have worried terribly.

"No," Margot said aloud. "It is I who made the mistake, and I who must somehow live with it." I'm trapped, she admitted to herself. And the man I have fallen in love with has gone away, forever. Tears filled her eyes, and for a few moments she let herself sink into misery.

After a time, she got up and walked around the house. It was a large house that befitted the Carltons and their many children. Margot looked into one of the bedrooms and sighed. "At least I can sleep alone," she whispered to herself.

Doggedly, Margot began to unpack and put her personal belongings in the small bedroom once inhabited by two of the Carltons' children. She spent several hours unpacking and putting things in their place; she worked, trying to forget her situation.

"I see you've been busy," Ernest said as he emerged from his long nap. He yawned.

"Did you sleep well?" Margot looked at him. In spite of his nap, he still looked tired. She knew he had had one of his nightmares the night before; they came almost every night and in the morning he awoke with great dark circles under his eyes.

"Yes," Ernest replied. "I'm hungry."

"I'll get supper. I've just finished putting the kitchen things away."

Ernest grunted.

Margot went into the pleasant little kitchen. The Carltons had left it well-stocked, and Mrs. Carlton had even left freshly baked bread.

Ernest followed Margot into the kitchen and plopped himself down. He tapped the table nervously and his eyes followed her every move.

She fixed some greens and prepared some dried meat, adding them to a large cauldron of soup stock that Mrs. Carlton had left. "If you're so hungry, have some bread and butter," Margot suggested.

Ernest tore some bread off the loaf and thickly buttered it. Margot continued to stir the soup, still aware of him watching her with his staring, vacant eyes.

Margot set down the soup spoon and turned. "Why are you staring at me?" she demanded.

"It was bad of you to interfere, Margot." His voice took on a curious tone. "And you threatened me, too."

"I just believe in forgiveness," she replied, trying to hide the feeling of panic that was starting to grow in her.

Ernest tore off some more bread. "You must never interfere again, Margot. You must never threaten me. You are my wife, and you must obey me."

Margot steadied herself by leaning on the sinkboard. His voice sounded mean and ominous, but his eyes looked strangely calm.

"Do you promise never to interfere with my mission?"

Margot nodded.

"Then I shall consider forgiving you. I shall consider it an act of ignorance, rather than an act of disobedience."

Margot let out her breath. "This is a large house," she observed, trying to sound casual. "Ernest, don't you think you would sleep better if I slept in one of the other rooms?"

Ernest nodded and indeed, he almost looked relieved.

Margot returned to the soup, feeling somehow that they had achieved a temporary truce.

"Tomorrow we'll meet with the mission Indians," Ernest announced, tearing off another hunk of bread.

"And can I begin teaching?" Margot asked. Perhaps, she thought, it will help me forget.

"I should think so." Ernest took another bite, then looked across the table at her. "Margot, are you pregnant?"

Margot shook her head. The question shattered her. He had only just told her she could sleep alone. . . . She had told him after the first time that she didn't want to couple with him. . . . "But women shouldn't enjoy it," is what he had said. Did his question mean he intended to exercise his husbandly right in the near future? Margot shuddered at the thought.

But Ernest didn't say anything. He remained silent and continued to eat.

Margot only looked at her food. Ernest is always talking about hell, but I, she thought, have found it.

The butler showed Cory and Anya into the living room of Governor Douglas' house in Victoria.

Anya squeezed Cory's hand. "They're so formal!" she whispered.

Cory winked at her. "Everyone in this colony thinks it's important to keep up appearances."

Governor Douglas strode purposefully into the room, Mrs. Douglas waddling behind him.

"Cory! Let me tell you how much I enjoyed your stage debut!" The governor was clearly in a fine mood. He roared with laughter, while Mrs. Douglas fidgeted with the edge of her peplum.

"I found the play edifying," she said, without looking up.

"I'm glad you enjoyed it," Cory replied.

"Do sit down," Governor Douglas urged. "I'll ring for refreshments."

He went to an ornate cord and pulled it. A bell tinkled and within a second the butler reappeared.

"Tea," Mrs. Douglas ordered.

"Perhaps Cory doesn't want tea, my dear," the governor intervened. "Bring some brandy as well." He turned back to Cory. "As you know, I'm a moderate man. But I sometimes like a pinch of brandy. I don't think it's too early, do you?"

"Certainly not," Cory allowed.

"I must say, my boy, you're looking a bit wan. Was your performance too much for you?"

Thinking of his night's—and morning's—activities, Cory smirked. "I suppose it was, sir. I find performing, well, quite taxing."

"Well, let me tell you, a theater is a fine addition to the colony! A fine addition indeed. A man gets tired of parties."

"I enjoy entertaining," Mrs. Douglas cooed.

"I know you do, my dear, but think of it! Now you can have theater parties as well."

The butler appeared with a silver tray on which was a bottle of fine French brandy and glasses.

"The tea will be a moment, sir. It has to steep."

"Wouldn't want unsteeped tea, would we?" Douglas went right to the brandy. "Let's all have some," he suggested, pouring four snifters. He passed one to Anya and one to his wife. Then he handed Cory a snifter and took his own, sipping it instantly. "Ah, delicious!" he mumbled appreciatively.

Cory leaned back against the settee, his hand still holding Anya's, an act that did not go unnoticed by Mrs. Douglas, who eyed them suspiciously—almost as though she had been peeking in their bedroom window.

"We'd like to be married," Cory said abruptly.

"Married!" The governor's voice boomed through the room and Mrs. Douglas actually looked relieved, as if she were glad to be spared the chore of having to spread gossip about the new love affair in the area.

"Congratulations, my boy! Good Lord, I've been waiting for you to marry for years!"

"Congratulations," Mrs. Douglas repeated.

"And when will the ceremony be?"

"Well, we'd like to be married as soon as possible. Perhaps even today."

"Oh, heavens!" Mrs. Douglas came to life. "Dear, dear no! First, the Reverend Cridge should marry you, and second, oh my goodness, we shall have to have a reception!"

"Well. . . ." Cory started to say.

"My little flower is quite right! When one of the most important men in the colony marries practically the only beautiful woman in the colony"— he looked at his wife uneasily, then corrected himself —"the only beautiful single woman, he cannot ignore the social graces! It simply would not do at all, not at all."

"I do believe I could manage to have everything in order within a month," Mrs. Douglas put in. "But certainly not a moment sooner! I'll have to organize the flowers and the refreshments. And Governor Douglas will give the bride away—oh, how terrible that Mr. Baron is not here to be the best man! Well, I'm certain you will think of someone else. Now there's the question of the wedding dress. I have a wedding dress, but I doubt that it will fit you, dear. But perhaps we can get someone to alter it. Yes, that may be a solution. Now, I really think you should be married in Christ Church Cathedral, it's quite lovely when it's decorated. Of course, there is the question of flowers this time of year . . . dear, dear, I shall have to give that one some thought. . . ."

Cory smiled at Anya. The usually quiet Mrs. Douglas had suddenly turned into a babbling brook. She was full of endless words and plans.

"I suggest we allow the ladies to plan this affair," Douglas said, smiling. "Mrs. Douglas is really very good at this sort of thing."

"So I see," Cory replied, rather dreading the whole thing and realizing that he and Anya would have to remain apart for the month, if only for the sake of form.

Anya sighed happily. "I always wanted a proper wedding," she said dreamily.

* * *

214

By mid-October the days at the Whitman mission in the Yakima Valley seemed to be getting shorter. The sun had fallen over the distant hills, and they looked like giant purple mounds against the darkening sky. "It's all going well," Ernest said to himself as he went into the barn. Last Sunday, twenty-three Indians had turned up for Sunday services in the little mission chapel, and there were several new children in school. So anxious to receive salvation! he thought.

Ernest felt a mild exhilaration. He'd been sleeping a little better, but even when his nightmares came, he was more relaxed because Margot was not in the same room; now she could not see or hear him. He hoped that his nightmares would vanish with the activity of his new life.

He shook his head and thought sadly, if only his father had not made him marry! If only the missionary society had not insisted on married missionaries. Ernest cherished the thought that he could have been quite happy single without any possibility of feeling tempted.

But of course, as it turned out, Margot was the best of all possible choices. She practically never stopped working, she didn't talk much, she made excellent meals, and she cringed as any woman should before all contact with him. It now troubled him only a little that she had threatened him. He had wanted to scream at her that he was not responsible for his dreams. After all, he was totally in control of himself when he was awake. He had fallen only once—that night he had taken Margot in pure lust. And of course, there was Alura. . . . He had been tempted, but that, he told himself, was the drink. And Alura was a she-devil! But it was all in the past. He felt calm about the future.

Distractedly he rubbed his stomach, thinking of dinner. Lately he had been eating a great deal, and he noted that he was putting on weight.

Ernest opened the barn door and blinked into the darkness. Margot had shown him how to milk the cow; now she insisted he perform the evening milking. Well, he thought, she did practically everything else. It was the least he could do, though he resented the time away from preparing his sermons and his lessons. His new flock was challenging, different from all others he had preached to. They did not say "Amen" in unison. The mission Indians seemed passive in the extreme, but he felt rewarded that they seemed to listen so closely to him; never had he experienced such rapt attention.

Ernest held up the lantern to illuminate the darkness of the barn and gasped.

In the hay were two Indians, one a young girl totally without covering, the other a young man, his loincloth well up to his waist; his condition was quite obvious.

"What!" Ernest shouted. The brave scrambled to his feet and darted past Ernest at breakneck speed, through the half open barn door and right out across the field. Ernest, mouth open, turned back to the girl; she cowered in the straw, trying to cover herself with her hands.

"Shameless!" Ernest shouted at her as he moved closer. She was one of the young women in Margot's sewing class. She was, he surmised, no more than sixteen.

"Shameless whore!" Ernest chastised her.

She hung her head. Her long, straight, dark hair was loose and fell over her bare shoulders; her breasts were full and her nipples still hard and firm—no doubt from being fondled by the young man. Her skin was copper colored and damp with sweat; it glistened in the lamplight. Ernest's eyes fell to her mound and with amazement he noted that the hair there too was straight.

Ernest felt beads of perspiration forming on his brow. He stepped toward her, driven by a force he didn't seem able to control. He stopped in front of her and rolled his eyes heavenward. "Whore!" he shrieked. He drew back his hand and struck her with all his strength across the face. "Devil!" He shouted. "Foul woman! Devil!"

The girl blinked up at him with terror-filled eyes and Ernest seized the horse whip and lashed out at her. "You must be punished!" he yelled as he beat her. "Evil must be punished!"

Her terrified screams of pain filled the barn. She squirmed this way and that, trying to escape the lash that cracked against her bare flesh.

216

"You shall not escape the wrath of the Lord!" Ernest screamed incoherently. She was Alura Alton! She was all the whores on the streets of Chicago! She was Eve tempting Adam in the garden! She was the accomplice of the evil serpent, the handmaiden of the devil! And as he wielded the whip, he could feel the lashes his father had applied to him. "It is for your own good!" he shouted. "The evil must be purged from you!"

The girl, bleeding and sobbing, struggled to her feet. Ernest let loose with a vicious blow that opened the flesh across her back. She tried to run for the door, but blood ran into her eyes, blinding her, and she tripped and fell lifeless in a small pitiful heap.

Ernest advanced on her with the whip, and though she did not move, he continued to beat her. "Whore! Can you hear me?" he screamed.

She did not move. Ernest stared at her. Her head had hit the edge of the steel plow, and blood gushed from a great gash on the back of her head. The whip dropped from Ernest's hand and he touched her with the tip of his boot. She still did not move.

For a moment, Ernest leaned against the cow's stall. His mind seemed to have gone blank. The only reality was the lifeless, bleeding form in front of him. "I didn't kill her," he said aloud. Still, the reality was there before him. He shivered. No one must find out. After all, he rationalized, she was only an Indian, and evil. But Margot mustn't find out. He ran to the barn door and looked out. He sighed with relief. Margot was still off in the schoolhouse. She couldn't possibly have heard. No, no, it would be all right, Ernest convinced himself.

He looked around quickly. There was no time to take the girl's body to the river tonight. He would have to hide her somewhere in the barn until he could find the time to get rid of her. He summoned himself up and buried the body in piles of straw, then he washed away the blood and tidied up. "An accident," he repeated.

CHAPTER XVI

October 17, 1856

Margot finished teaching her classes and watched with some satisfaction as her pupils scattered, leaving the little schoolhouse and hurrying away. Her students were all girls, ranging in age from nine to sixteen. Margot read to them, told them Bible stories, and instructed them in health care, sewing, and even some cooking, though she suspected that most of them could cook quite well.

It was late in the afternoon, and the mission Indians returned to their huts on the outskirts of the farm. Those who came from the tribal village returned to it, though they were fewer in number.

This was the time of day when quiet descended over the compound; it was the time of day Margot dreaded most. With her students gone, she was not only alone with Ernest, but with her persistent thoughts of Blaise Baron.

"How did it go?" Ernest's voice from the doorway of her small classroom startled her, and Margot jumped.

"You walk too quietly," she said, trying to smile.

"Sorry," Ernest replied.

Margot looked at him carefully. He had looked terrible at breakfast, he looked even worse now. His eyes were rimmed with dark circles, his cheeks were puffy; he looked like some stuffed animal. Ernest had put on a great deal of weight, she noticed. Small wonder! He ate ravenously at all three meals, filling himself with second and third helpings.

"Well, how did it go?" Ernest asked.

"Fine . . . I do have one less student, though."

"Who?" Ernest's eyes opened wider, and Margot thought he looked almost fearful.

She smiled. "Well, you know, they come and go. Just one of the older girls. I haven't seen her for two days."

"Probably no loss," Ernest uttered.

"On the contrary, she was a very pleasant young lady."

"None of them are ladies—they're heathen savages—they have no god and no morals!"

His tone amazed Margot, who took a step backward. He sounded utterly hateful, and his face had flushed almost crimson. She was so surprised by his outburst that she couldn't say anything for a moment.

Ernest steadied himself on the side of one of the tables. He said, more softly, "I'm not feeling well."

"Should we send for a doctor?" Margot asked.

Ernest shook his head.

"Well, I'm going to the barn to pick up some eggs."

"No!"

"What do you mean, no? Why shouldn't I go for the eggs? I shouldn't think the hens would want them forever."

"No, I mean, I'll go."

"Don't be silly, Ernest. I want to go. I haven't checked on my prize layer for two days. You insisted on doing all the chores yesterday—which is very nice—but really, I want to go."

Margot lifted her skirts and started for the door. Ernest grabbed her arm.

"Ernest, stop being foolish. Let me go!" He dropped his hand dejectedly and watched as Margot walked out the door and headed for the barn. He stood frozen. Then, when he saw her go into the barn, he followed silently.

"Ah, chick, chick, chick . . ." Margot reached under the hen and removed two eggs. "What a good chick, chick." She always talked to her hens, even at Lochiel where she had known each one by name. She put the eggs in her basket and leaned against the hutch. A wave of nostalgia swept over her. She remembered the Sunday her father had killed Annabell, the oldest hen in the clutch. He had insisted on boiling her for chicken soup, but Margot, only nine, wouldn't eat a bite and stood in the kitchen and wailed, "How could you kill Annabell!"

She smiled at the childhood memory. Her father had comforted her and talked to her for hours. He had held her and

220

explained that farm animals had to be killed sometimes; that farmers couldn't make pets of their animals. "That's not what farming is about," he told her.

Margot sniffed. "It smells awful in here," she said to the chickens. "This barn doesn't smell the way it should."

Margot set the basket down and sniffed again. It was the odor of decay. She bit her lip and wondered if some small animal had died somewhere in the barn. She moved off a bit, sniffing and trying to follow the foul odor. She came to a great pile of hay.

"Yes," she said aloud. "That's where it is."

Margot walked over to the pitchfork and returned to the hay. She began to move the hay, but the fork struck something firm just beneath the surface—something large.

Margot raked the hay away and a brown arm fell out. "Oh, my God!" She stood for a moment, then quickly removed the hay. "Dear God!" Margot whispered. "Oh, the poor girl!"

Margot looked at the young girl's face. It was the one they called Juna, the one she had not seen for two days. "Dear God in heaven." Margot stood up. Juna's face was encrusted with dried blood and her bare back bore the unmistakable marks of a whip.

"Who would have done such a thing?" A shiver of pure terror ran through Margot. Her mouth was partially open and she shook convulsively as she thought of Ernest. Margot seized her skirts and whirled about to run from the sight of the dead girl. She let out a scream when she saw Ernest standing in the doorway of barn. His eyes were glazed, he stared at her vacantly.

"Ernest, did you . . . ?"

"I see you found her," Ernest said, shaking his head.

"Ernest!" Margot could hardly control her voice; he looked like a wild man, and though she hadn't heard it from his own lips, she knew he was responsible.

"You killed her!" Margot whispered. "You beat her!"

"I found her with a man! They were, they were—"

"She was only a child! An innocent child and you beat her and killed her!"

221

"I didn't kill her!" Ernest shouted. "She fell!"

"You! You're a murderer! Ernest, she was an innocent child!"

Ernest's face hardened. "She was with a man! Her clothes were off, they were like two animals!"

"So you killed her. Ernest, you're not God! You've taken a human life."

"She was an Indian."

Margot's mouth opened. . . . This was the man who had supposedly come west to help the Indians, to teach them. She blinked back tears of anger and fear. The man who stood before her was surely mad. She shook her head. "Ernest, you'll have to go to the authorities. You've committed a crime."

"Authorities?" Ernest glared at her. "I am the authority here! This is my mission and I am the word of God to these wretched, immoral people! I've made an example of a whore. That's not a crime!"

Margot stiffened. "Then I shall go to the authorities." She pressed her lips together. "Ernest, I'm leaving you. You are bigoted, self-righteous, and a murderer. You have done something that only God can forgive you for. I'm leaving and I intend to write the missionary society and tell them you are not only totally unsuited for this work but unsuited to be a minister as well!"

Ernest's face contorted. "You are no better than the others!" he shrieked. "You threatened me once before! You are interfering with my mission, my mission, Margot!" Ernest seized the whip and took a step toward her. "You will have to be punished, Margot. A woman has to learn to obey her master!"

"Stop it! Don't take another step!" Margot backed up and held him at bay with the pitchfork.

"I knew you were like all the others," he hissed. "Disloyal! Filthy! You're all filthy!"

Margot retreated yet another step, but Ernest stepped to one side and with his long arm reached out and seized the pitchfork above its deadly prongs. He whipped it with such unusual strength that Margot tumbled backward. Ernest advanced on her and lashed out with the whip. Margot screamed as it lashed her legs. She rolled to avoid it, closed her eyes, and covered her ears, trying to block out the pain and prepare herself for the next blow.

Then Margot heard Ernest wail like a banshee, and she opened her eyes. The barn was full of Indians in full tribal dress. They surrounded Ernest, their bows drawn.

"You will come," Kamiakan said to her.

Margot shook her head to clear it. She felt almost like throwing herself into the Indian's arms, but his face was stony and unmoved by her situation.

"You are the squaw of this vermin?" Kamiakan poked Ernest roughly in the stomach with his bow.

Margot nodded. "He's mad! He tried to kill me!"

Kamiakan nodded. "He killed a woman from our village; a woman married to this brave." He pointed to one of the men.

"I demand you let me go!" Ernest suddenly seemed to find his voice.

Kamiakan again poked him, but this time more roughly. "You will be cut into a thousand tiny pieces—slowly." Ernest shrunk back, quivering.

"Oh, no."

"He is full of evil spirits," Kamiakan proclaimed. "He will die."

"But . . ."

"You will come. You will be escorted to your house and you will get warm clothes. You will return to our village."

"What for?"

"Perhaps to serve as a wife to this brave. Your husband has deprived him of his wife."

Margot opened her mouth to speak, but one of the braves prodded her with his hand.

"Go!" Kamiakan ordered.

Margot walked to the house between two braves. She hurriedly pulled on her boots, and she brought her heaviest coat, her great long scarf, and her gloves. As she passed through the kitchen, she picked up several loaves of bread and stuffed them in her satchel. "I am ready," she said.

223

Outside, Ernest had been put astride a horse. His legs were tied underneath the animal, his hands were tied tightly behind him. One of the braves held the horse's reins; the other flanked him.

Ernest could say nothing; they had stuffed his mouth with a kerchief. But great tears ran down his face and he trembled uncontrollably.

The ride to the village was long and silent and Margot, still shaken from her ordeal with Ernest, found it impossible even to think about her own fate. The man who was obviously the leader had said only, ". . . perhaps to replace the brave's wife." Margot assumed that meant he hadn't made up his mind. She deemed it prudent not to talk.

When the troop entered the village, hordes of women and girls came out of their huts bearing switches. From the moment the braves moved away, they beat Ernest, hovering over him, bringing down their switches over and over. His face was a mass of scratches; his clothes were soon in shreds and the blows fell mercilessly on his bare flesh.

"This is inhuman!" Margot cried.

Kamiakan seized her arm and propelled her away from the sight. "Inhuman! Your husband murdered a young girl; a young girl with child; a young girl who should have lived through many summers! And other white men do the same! Inhuman?" The chief's voice was angry and low, solemn. He pulled Margot into a hut full of steam. On a cot above the smoldering pyre was a young woman. Her face was contorted in pure agony, her legs held far apart and tied to a table.

Margot covered her mouth with her hands. The girl was quite nude, but her entire internal area—her womb—was a mass of hideous burns.

"*This* is inhuman," Kamiakan told her in a low voice. "She would not yield to the drunken soldiers, so they thrust a hot branding iron into her and now she lies dying."

Margot shuddered and felt the vomit rising in her throat. Her head pounded and she turned, flinging open the hut door. She retched on the ground outside.

Kamiakan put his hand on her shoulder. "Come," he said

quietly. "I must think of what to do with you. You will either be a wife to the brave, or remain in servitude. But you will not be harmed."

Margot followed him as if she were in a trance. They came to a small compound that was entirely surrounded by a twelve-foot-high spiked wall. Guards were posted outside.

"This is where we keep prisoners," he said matter-of-factly. "There is one slave in there now, but he will not hurt you." Kamiakan gave the signal and the small door was opened. Margot, satchel in hand, was shoved inside.

The ground inside the compound was barren and its only inhabitant was an emaciated young man, older than she, but probably no more than twenty-two. In front of him was a pan of water. He looked up at her suspiciously and Margot sat down on the ground in the opposite corner of the small space.

After a time, the young man motioned to her and, as much out of curiosity as anything else, Margot walked over to him and sat down.

"You slave?" he asked.

Margot tilted her head. She could not understand any of his language. It was true that she spoke very little Yakima, but she was certain he did not speak Yakima and besides, tribes usually had slaves from other tribes.

She shrugged, trying to convey the fact that she did not understand.

The young man opened his mouth and pointed inside. Margot studied his facial expression. He looked half-starved; perhaps he was asking for food. She opened her satchel and handed him one loaf of bread.

He smiled and patted her arm, then he devoured the bread like a famished animal. When he finished, he drank water and wiped his mouth with satisfaction. Then, pausing, he handed the water to Margot. She sipped some and smiled. He put the water down.

"Mercy, you were hungry," Margot said.

"*Merci? Merci beaucoup,*" the Indian replied.

"You speak French!" Margot immediately began speaking French to him.

"What is your name?" she asked. "Why are you here?"

"I am Mkan, warrior of the Lillooet. We live far to the north on the great river the English call the Fraser."

Of course he spoke French, Margot thought. Most of the trappers in that territory were either French-speaking Metis or from French-speaking communities in the West.

"I am here because I was kidnapped when our sacred gold was taken."

Margot nodded, trying to understand. But she was distracted by a piercing shriek. She realized it was Ernest who had screamed. As lucidly as she could, she tried to explain her story to the young Indian, who looked at her sympathetically.

"They will make a slave of you, too," he warned.

Margot nodded. At the moment she didn't care, she only wished she did not have to listen to Ernest. The images she conjured up were at least as bad as his reality. They were most certainly going to torture him to death.

She closed her eyes and covered her ears. She stayed that way for a long while, until Mkan tapped her on the knee. "Have they stopped?" she asked.

"For now. They will go back to him later and cut off his organs and shred his skin piece by piece from his body."

Margot shuddered.

"You will come with me," Mkan said.

She looked around, thinking she had misunderstood him.

He leaned over and whispered in her ear. "You have been kind to Mkan, you will come with me tonight."

"We are prisoners," she replied.

He shook his head and pointed to a large rock on one side of the compound. "Beneath is a tunnel," he whispered. "But tonight is the time I have waited for. They will be busy with your husband. We will go."

"I can't . . . I can't leave him."

Mkan shook his head. "He is half dead now. You come. I hear bad things in this village. The white men are cruel; the Yakima will war. You come, I'll take you out of Yakima country."

Margot studied him carefully. He meant to help her and

226

she decided to take the help. The chief was a bitter man—not without cause—but bitter and angry.

"I will come," she said after a time. "I will go with Mkan."

Darkness fell over the village, but from the compound one could see the light of the flickering fires. And again Ernest's screams began.

Mkan motioned to her and Margot, clutching her satchel, followed. Silently, he moved the rock and slipped into the earth. Margot followed. She squirmed through the space and felt Mkan's hands take hers and pull her from the hole. He motioned her to follow and Margot did. When they came to a cluster of rocks, he bid her sit down.

"I go back for gold," he said, smiling. "The tents are empty, no one guards it."

"You mustn't!" Margot pleaded.

But Mkan pulled away from her. "Wait until the moon is high. If I do not return, run. Go back to your home, get a horse."

Margot nodded. Her home was at least ten miles away. She leaned against the rock and watched as Mkan disappeared like a shadow into the darkness.

Margot leaned against the rock. It was still warm from the sun, and strangely she closed her eyes and dropped into a light sleep as her energy seemed to flee, leaving her exhausted.

She jumped and almost screamed when Mkan jostled her. "I have it!" he beamed, holding up a sack. He opened and withdrew a gold bird. It glistened in the moonlight.

"It is very heavy," he said. "But it will keep the Great Spirit with us. We will be safe."

"It's beautiful," Margot admitted. She tried to see more of it, but the moon was not bright enough to illuminate the detail.

Mkan thrust it back into the sack. "We must hurry," he urged. "When the sun comes up, they will discover we are gone."

They walked until the dawn broke in the western sky and until the sun blazed over the mountains.

"I smell smoke," Margot said.

Mkan nodded. "Good smell. You could be Indian."

"It's coming from that direction."

Mkan led her through the woods.

"It's a farm," Margot said. She paused and peered out from the bushes. "It's burning."

"They will kill all the white men in this valley," Mkan told her. He looked around warily. "Long gone. They don't burn same house twice. We will look for horses."

"Wouldn't they take them?"

Mkan shook his head. "The Yakima have too many horses. They have more horses than braves. They leave them wild to breed in the valley."

"How long have you been with the Yakima?"

"Many summers," he said, shaking his head.

He led Margot across the clearing. "There," he pointed. "See?"

Near the house was a pile of bodies—a woman, a man, four children. Their throats were slit. "Oh, God!" Margot murmured. She wanted to vomit, but there was nothing. She hadn't eaten since yesterday noon. But more than that was a hardening of her emotions. She had been through so much in the last twenty-four hours and she was so exhausted, no horror could move her.

"Over there, in the field!"

Margot turned from the dead and saw the two horses. "The barn's on fire; there are no saddles."

Mkan laughed. "You cannot ride without a saddle?"

"I can . . . it's just been a long time."

Mkan ran to the horses and seized them. He led them to her. "We are fortunate, they have reins," he said.

Margot mounted with Mkan's boost. She took the reins and put her small satchel in front of her. The horse's back was warm from the sun.

Mkan mounted easily with a leap. He signaled the direction and they galloped off to the north, paralleling the great Cascade mountain range in the distance.

The weak October sun broke through the billowing clouds

228

long enough to dry off the steps of Christ Church Cathedral and allow the smiling guests to leave the church. Their exit was made to the accompaniment of music provided by the newly formed Victoria Philharmonic Society.

Amelia Douglas fulfilled the duties of doting mother-of-the-bride with all the concern for detail Anya's real mother would have shown. And to everyone's delight, the ceremony went perfectly.

The entire community of Victoria was there to watch Governor Douglas give away the blushing bride; Cory allowed Captain Arlen to be the best man in place of Blaise Baron. The Reverend Cridge performed the ceremony in a booming voice. Indeed, Cridge even went so far as to explain—both to the bride and to those present—the similarities between the Anglican Liturgy and the Russian Orthodox Liturgy.

The only outburst during the ceremony occurred when the Reverend Cridge proclaimed loudly, "You may kiss the bride!" When Cory lifted Anya's veil and planted a long, deep kiss on her lips, the woodsmen, traders, and miners let out a loud "Whoopee!" It was instantly silenced with one of Mrs. Douglas' commands to "Hush!"

Cory held out his hand to help Anya down the steps of the church. "You look beautiful," he whispered.

"And you look very handsome!"

Cory ran his finger around his high collar. Mrs. Douglas had seen to it that he was appropriately dressed in tails, stiff collar, and bow tie. "I feel absurd," he mumbled.

But Anya did look breathtaking, Cory thought. Her flaxen hair was done up in braids that were pinned on top of her head. Her white veil danced in the breeze and her low-cut bodice pushed her bosom up, though her cleavage was covered with thin gauze that made the dress both seductive and modest. The full, silken gown clung to her. She was a sight to behold—certainly the most beautiful woman in the entire colony.

When they reached the bottom of the steps, Cory pulled her to him and kissed her neck, whispering in her ear, "I can hardly wait to get you alone, Mrs. MacLean."

229

Anya hugged him. "Later . . ."

Cory squeezed her hand. The last month hadn't been easy. Mrs. Douglas had insisted that Anya stay with them until the wedding; thus, she and Cory had been separated the entire time since their first and only night together. But such was life in the Colony. Now he would have to endure the reception before he could take Anya home with him.

Governor Douglas' carriage pulled up in front of the church. "Come, come, we must get to the house before all the guests arrive." The governor was red-faced and feeling exceptionally cheerful.

When they arrived, they found the grounds of the Douglas mansion decorated with Chinese lanterns, colored paper, and large tents which had been set out on the lawn. Wind chimes tinkled, and on a raised platform the members of the Victoria Philharmonic tuned their instruments, preparing for yet another performance. Governor Douglas himself was to play the cello, and Augustus Pemberton, the Commissioner of Police, was going to play his flute; he had brought it from Ireland and insisted that Irish flutes were by far the best.

It seemed as if Mrs. Douglas must have made every woman in the community do a share of the cooking. There were, under the tents, tables laden with fresh breads, apple pies, cakes, and scones. Over the huge grill, fresh salmon was being cooked, while large Canada geese turned on spits.

Captain Arlen outdid himself by providing Russian caviar and fine wines from Europe—and champagne as well.

Mrs. Douglas fussed about having too much alcohol, but Captain Arlen assured her he would monitor the drinking.

The guests began to arrive shortly after Cory and Anya, who at the insistence of Mrs. Douglas were made to stand in a receiving line.

First came the Muirs with their family, Dr. Helmcken and family, Thomas Skinner, James Yates, Captain and Mrs. Langford, Dr. Kennedy, Chief Justice Cameron, Rosa and Sir Fitz, and then an endless string of oddly dressed miners from Naniamo and the men from the Hudson's Bay Company.

The whole lawn was a sea of colorful gowns and parasols, black coats, sparkling jewelry, and ornate bonnets. And there was a dance floor! Cory shuddered. He and Anya were going to have to waltz in front of all these people!

Mrs. Annie Muir sidled up to Cecilia Helmcken and whispered, ''Her gown is a trifle risque for a virgin bride.''

''Well, she is supposed to be a Russian princess! And since she ran away from home, she may not be so virginal! Besides, she's an actress and you know how they are!''

''She's wearing a ruby necklace.''

''It's probably not real. Not that it makes much difference with all Cory's money.''

''He's a gem, isn't he?'' Annie rolled her eyes and cooed.

The orchestra began to play *God Save The Queen,* and everyone turned and stood at attention. When it was finished, Captain Arlen, glass in hand, raised it high in the air and shouted, ''To Her Majesty, Queen Victoria! Long live the Queen!'' Everyone joined the toast, and there was a chorus of ''Here! Here!''

''Let the party begin!'' Arlen called cheerfully.

Such a good Englishman, Cory thought. The English are such good losers.

''My dear,'' Governor Douglas said, bowing from the waist, ''I believe the honor of the first dance is mine.''

He waltzed off with Anya.

''Oh, Cory!'' Mrs. Douglas came up in a flurry. ''Could you go over there and cool some tempers? Those men are annexationists and they refused to toast the Queen and then those other men from the Hudson's Bay Company started to argue with them and, well, I just don't want any fights.''

Cory went off obediently. ''Come on, lads, let's leave the politics behind!'' Cory put his arm around Sean McBride, the most strident of the annexationists present. ''This is hardly the place,'' he said. ''You know that these people believe in the British Crown and its institutions. They don't want to be part of the American Republic, man.''

''Do you?''

''I'm a Scots. Truth be known, I'd rather be free of both

231

of them, but that's something for another time and place. Right now, you toast my bride, McBride."

McBride nodded. "A pleasure, my friend."

Governor Douglas returned Anya to Cory's arm. "Your turn, my boy."

Cory took her to the area cleared for dancing and the orchestra struck up a waltz. "Oh, it's easy," he said, taking her into his arms.

"You're holding me rather closer than modesty permits," she whispered.

"Not as close as I'm going to hold you," he whispered back.

The party continued until nearly midnight and was finished off with a fireworks display. "Come home with me, Mrs. MacLean," Cory said hungrily. "I've been waiting a long time."

She kissed him. "So have I."

CHAPTER XVII

November 1, 1856

Blaise Baron had dispatched his final duties as wagon master and had collected his fee. Under normal circumstances, he would have returned instantly to Fort Victoria, but he lingered in Fort Steilacoom, drinking with lumbermen and trying to clear his mind. He fought the desire to go back to the Yakima Valley. He knew Margot would reject him. At the same time, he couldn't bring himself to go back to Victoria. The result was that he did nothing.

Blaise emerged from the bar into the early evening light. He thrust his hands into his coat pocket and began walking. The smell of freshly cut timber was in the air; the evening was crisp and cool.

"Mr. Baron!"

Blaise turned to see a young man running toward him.

"Mr. Baron?" the lad repeated, a questioning look on his young face.

"Yes," Blaise stopped. "I am Mr. Baron."

The young man was panting as if he had run a long distance. "I've been looking all over town for you! Went to your room and to three bars. In the last one, they said you just left."

Blaise smiled, "And so I have."

"I've got a message from the governor of the territory. He wants to see you. He wants to see you right away."

Blaise raised an eyebrow. He didn't relish seeing the boorish governor; the man was beneath contempt.

"Can you come now?" the boy asked.

Blaise sighed. "Is it important?"

"The governor says so. Says he has to see you. Says you might pick up a pretty piece of change."

"Oh," Blaise replied. And he thought to himself, if the

governor thinks I'm going to start doing his dirty work among the Indians, he's mistaken.

"Can you?" the boy pressed. "I have the authority to bring you right away."

The young man looked so earnest that Blaise almost laughed. "I'll come," he agreed. "Right now."

They walked along together toward the governor's house.

"Sure am glad I found you. I wouldn't get paid if I hadn't found you."

"I'm not really that hard to find."

"You move around a lot."

"Guess I do," Blaise agreed. The boy had a winning smile. It's nice to talk to someone who isn't drunk, Blaise thought. He was thoroughly disgusted with the atmosphere in Fort Steilacoom. It seemed as if all the inhabitants were as crude, stupid, and prejudiced as the governor. They all talked of the Indian war as if they were actually looking forward to it.

"Here we are," the boy announced. He walked ahead of Blaise and knocked on the door. An elderly Indian woman opened the portal and peered out.

"Is that Baron?" The governor's voice boomed out from inside the house.

"It is!" the boy called.

"Well, bring him in and collect your fee, lad. Hurry up!"

Blaise followed the boy into the house and they went directly to the parlor where the governor sat in his usual chair, whiskey in hand. He dug into his pocket and handed the boy some coins. "Good lad!" he praised drunkenly.

"Good evening, governor." Blaise tipped his hat.

"Sit down, Baron. I'll come right to the point."

Blaise sat down. A tray of whiskey sat on the table in front of the sofa.

"Help yourself," the governor said, waving to the whiskey.

Blaise poured himself a drink. "How can I help you?"

"No, no. It is I who am going to help you."

"Oh," Blaise said cautiously. This, he knew, was a man one had to be careful with.

234

"Got a message by pony express yesterday. Labeled 'Important!' Mind you, it wasn't all that important, but I thought it might interest you—I mean, you're more or less personally involved."

Blaise cocked one eyebrow. "Tell me about it."

"There's an uprising out in the Yakima Valley. . . . Hell, I don't really know how serious it is, all I know is that those missionaries you delivered seemed to have started it all."

Blaise froze. "What do you mean?"

"Seems that Ernest McGrath killed some Indian bitch and the Indians went on the rampage. Took McGrath and his wife, then they wiped out half a dozen farms."

Blaise drew in his breath. Ernest had killed an Indian girl! The full implications of what Stevens was saying flooded his mind.

"Course I can send in the militia, but there ain't near enough of them. I've been waiting for troops to arrive, going to be another two or three weeks anyway. Thought I might hire you. I hear you talk pretty good with Indians. Thought you might cool them down till I can get the troops in there to clean out the whole filthy lot."

Blaise stood up abruptly and shouldered his pack. "I'm going back to the Yakima Valley."

"Well, I didn't mean you had to go tonight. Hell, it will wait 'til tomorrow."

Blaise's features hardened. "I'm going back to find Mrs. McGrath, if she's still alive." He spoke the words, but they had a kind of unreality. He felt strongly, instinctively, that she was alive. He knew Kamiakan would not harm an innocent woman.

"Oh, I see. Pretty, is she? Good lay?"

Blaise turned to the governor, whose face bore a lecherous expression. "Get that look off your face, you slob! Or I'll knock it off!"

"I could have you arrested for talking to me like that!" Stevens face went purple with rage.

"But you won't, because I'm going to go talk with the Indians."

With that, Blaise stomped from the room.

"Good luck," the drunken governor called after him.

Blaise drew in his horse and dismounted. His eyes were red from lack of sleep—he'd been riding day and night with little rest for four days. Early that morning he had traded his horse for a fresh one at a farm on the trail. No animal could keep up the pace he'd set. Fortunately, there were farms every now and again. He knew the route and most of the settlers along the way.

He led his horse down to the stream, where she quenched her thirst. When the horse had had her fill, he tethered her so she could graze. He himself lay down in the grass, determined to sleep a few hours before heading on.

He stared up at the darkening sky, praying for sleep, but knowing that every part of him was still flooded with energy. Margot was in mortal danger. The sense of foreboding he had had since morning swept over him again. He felt powerless and stupid. I should never have left her with that man! I should have known that anyone who even suggested branding a woman was mad. Ernest McGrath, he suspected, was a man who had been severely repressed, a man who believed natural acts to be evil. Yes, that was it. Ernest was a misogynist, a woman hater, a man who probably blamed women for his own weaknesses.

Blaise tried to think. Certainly, the Yakima would have killed Ernest. But there was an excellent chance that they had taken Margot prisoner and would keep her as a slave. Margot was a beautiful woman, and Kamiakan was not a wasteful man. Blaise shuddered at the implications of his thoughts, forcing himself to concentrate on the fact that she might well be alive. "We'll be together, Margot," he vowed. It was not the first time he had admitted to himself that he was truly in love with her, but it was the first time he had allowed his dreams of the future to have substance.

"She loves me, too," he said with conviction. Blaise turned restlessly on his side. He put his arm under his head and forced himself to close his eyes. The darkness was peaceful and he badly needed sleep.

Blaise rode as fast as he could. He had been traveling for eight days, and as he drew closer to the Whitman mission he passed burned-out farms. Doubtless Kamiakan had killed Stevens' Indian agent; that, Blaise decided, was no loss, save the fact that it would give Stevens the excuse to bring the U.S. Army down in force. But then, Stevens needed no excuse.

Blaise approached the Yakima village warily, waiting for the braves to greet him. But he stopped short before a horrible sight. On a pole by the road was the shrunken, shriveled body of a man. His eyes had been plucked out by birds, his arms and legs were missing, as were his ears and sexual organs. This was a man who had died slowly in a death reserved for the enemies of the Yakima.

Blaise approached the hanging body slowly and peered at it. "Oh, Lord," he mumbled. There could be no mistaking the body; it was Ernest McGrath's. Blaise closed his eyes and crossed himself. Margot. Where was Margot? He tried to steady himself.

Blaise rode down the road another few feet, and the braves emerged out of the bush.

"It is Blaise Baron," he called out. "Friend of the great chief of the Yakima, Kamiakan."

Two of them recognized him, and again Blaise turned over his weapons and followed them into the village.

He dismounted and waited as he always did. He forced himself to be patient. The Yakima were probably in no mood to be pressured by a white man.

Kamiakan appeared from his hut as stony faced as ever.

"You come in spite of the warning on the road."

"The man died the death of an enemy of the Yakima. I am a friend to Kamiakan, so I did not think the warning was for me."

Kamiakan lifted his hand in a sign of peace. "Come, smoke with me," he requested, walking to his traditional spot beneath a tall tree. There he sat down and quietly stuffed his pipe.

"You may sit," Kamiakan invited.

Blaise sat down and drew his own pipe from his pocket. He filled it.

"What brings you to the village of the Yakima?"

"I came for the man on the post—I came to take him back to the white man's justice."

"The white man has no justice. The Yakima have justice."

"So I see," Blaise said, trying to sound dispassionate.

"The white man—the missionary—he killed one of the maidens of our tribe. A young woman with child. She was lying in the barn with her husband who came to see her while she was studying. Her husband ran away so she would not get into trouble. When he returned he found her dead, her body bloody from the whip.

"He was an evil man," Blaise confirmed.

Kamiakan nodded. "He was trying to kill his squaw when we intercepted him."

Blaise breathed a sigh of relief. She wasn't dead! "Where is his squaw?"

Kamiakan shrugged. "She was put into the slave compound while I gave some thought as to what should be done with her. I felt she should listen to her husband dying."

Blaise didn't wince, though he wanted to. Poor Margot. Even if she hated Ernest, she must have suffered terribly.

"Is she still here?"

Kamiakan shook his head. "In the compound was a young Indian of the Lillooet nation. He had been our slave for some time, but I planned to let him escape and steal the sacred gold of the Lillooet back. I did not realize he would choose that night and take the white man's squaw with him."

"She went with him?" Blaise asked incredulously.

"Quite willingly. If she had resisted, there would have been noise, we would have heard."

Blaise nodded. "But why were you going to let him escape?"

"The gold belongs to his tribe. I no longer want war with them. So I let him build a tunnel to escape; it is bad for a man's pride to be let go. It is better for a man to believe in his wits."

238

Blaise agreed. Kamiakan understood pride.

"And you didn't follow them?"

Kamiakan shook his head. "One day, we may need the friendship of the Lillooet."

Blaise breathed a little easier, though he was still very concerned about Margot. It was a long way to the Fraser; a long way over incredibly rough country. But Margot had a will to survive; she must have felt that going with the Indian was her only choice.

"What kind of man was this slave?"

"A young warrior. He will not harm her. But of course, she is probably not strong like an Indian squaw."

Blaise agreed. But Margot was resourceful. He could only pray that she would endure the long journey back to the Lillooet—that is, if they do not try to cross the mountains in the winter.

Margot and the brave had a head start, and the young Indian would most certainly stay off trails known to the Yakima. There was absolutely no chance that Blaise could track and find them. His only hope of ever seeing her again was to go directly to the Lillooet and wait. And, he admitted unhappily, it could be a long wait.

"Will you stay with us for a time?" Kamiakan asked.

Blaise shook his head. "I will go back to Fort Steilacoom, and from there across the great water to the British community of Victoria. There I will get supplies and head for the Lillooet nation."

Kamiakan smiled, one of the few times Blaise had ever seen him smile.

"Tell the Lillooet of our troubles. I will give you tribute to take them. Tell them we want no more war with them, that we have enough war with the white man."

"They will accept your friendship," Blaise returned. Wars among the Indian tribes were, he knew, limited affairs, often restricted to the theft of such things as sacred objects. The tales were woven into the folklore; they were part of the traditions of nomadic peoples. But war with the white man was something else. It was devastating for the Indians

239

and it often resulted in the resolution of difficulties between tribes since they banded together against a common enemy.

"Guard your women and children," Blaise advised. "The white man does not distinguish them from warriors in battle."

Kamiakan nodded. "Go, Blaise Baron. Return when you can."

"I am honored by Kamiakan's trust and friendship."

"I am honored to know one with white skin who does not lie."

Blaise got up and stretched. "May the Great Spirit guide your actions and protect your people."

Kamiakan did not answer, but his look of sadness revealed his inner thoughts. Honor demanded that the Yakima and the other tribes fight; common sense told Kamiakan they would lose.

Blaise left the village and headed back toward Fort Steilacoom. The Indian war would be a terrible tragedy, and for the first time he looked forward to leaving the United States and returning to British North America. He bit his lip and silently prayed he would find Margot. But regardless, he swore, he would put his prejudice towards the English behind him and return to live in British North America. I'll settle in Victoria and confine my travels to New Caledonia and the great mountains called the Lion's Gate. That's where I belong, he admitted.

Margot wrapped her long scarf around her neck. The cold wind whipped across the valley, heralding the end of fall and the beginning of winter. It was late November; it would snow soon.

Mkan had built a small shelter and was now at work on a fire. Margot scaled the fish she had caught, and looked forward to eating them. Theirs was a journey of shared experiences and shared work. Mkan said little, but obviously admired her ability to fish and trap. These, Margot assumed, were the duties of a squaw and she performed them with all the skill her father had taught her as a child. For his part, Mkan built the shelters in which they slept, plotted the trail, and built the fires. Periodically, he instructed Margot on what leaves to gather for making tea and what berries were edible. He asked once where she had learned the ways of the woods and she explained that her father had taken her and her brother to live with Indians for two summers; she stressed, though, that the eastern Indian tribes were different and now had many tools obtained from the white man.

"But it is all different here. There are mountains and fish in the rivers I do not know. Everything is different. I do not know this land," she told Mkan.

On a personal level, Mkan treated her well. He promised to return her to the white man—but to the British, not the Americans. He said the tribes in the United States were warring; it was unsafe there and the white men who ruled the land were not to be trusted. "When we reach my village," he told her, "you will be escorted down the great salmon-filled river; there the British come to meet us and you will be free to go with them to Fort Victoria."

Margot accepted Mkan's plan without hesitation. She wanted to return to British North America. She knew that Blaise had a friend in Victoria and she felt she might be able to find the friend and through him find Blaise. In her heart, she carried her love for him, wondering if fate ordained it to be.

We are good traveling companions, Margot thought, as she watched Mkan blow gently on the flame of the fire. Mkan spoke often of his wife and child. Margot, in turn told him about herself and about Blaise Baron. Between the two of them language was no longer a problem. His French improved, and he began to teach her a few words of Salish.

The small fire grew as the flame from the twigs caught on the larger pieces of wood. Margot walked to the fire and sat down, drawing her coat around her.

"Soon it will be ready to cook on."

"It's getting colder every day," Margot noted.

Mkan nodded. "And everyday you look and act more like an Indian woman."

She smiled warmly at him. It was true. Her normally pale skin was tanned from sun and wind. Her long black hair hung in two Indian braids and only her somewhat tattered clothing and the color of her eyes betrayed her heritage.

Mkan pointed off toward the purple mountains that were etched against the blue gray sky. "Soon the soft blanket of white will cover them." He shook his head. "We cannot cross the mountains now; it is too cold and soon the snow will be too deep."

Margot nodded. "But it is not so cold here, not as long as we follow the river valley."

"We are near the line which cannot be seen. The line which divides the white nation of the south from the territory ruled by the Hudson's Bay Company."

Margot thought of asking him how he knew, but she didn't. He had without error led her to the Okanagan, the river he called after another Salish speaking people who, he explained matter of factly, lived on both sides of the invisible line.

Mkan shrugged. "The white men draw pictures of the land and draw lines; my people do not understand lines that cannot be seen."

"They are borders between nations."

"We have many nations and no lines. We know the territory where others hunt and they know ours. But the land belongs to no one—it belongs to all."

Margot nodded. She could not explain to the Indian how Europeans regarded land. No greater chasm existed between white man and red man than the concept of land.

"If we cannot cross the mountains, what will we do?"

Mkan waved his hand in the air. "The Great Spirit guides us. We will go to the chief of the Okanagan and ask for shelter until we can cross the mountains in the spring."

"Is he friendly to the Lillooet?"

Mkan nodded. "There will be no difficulty," he said confidently.

"When will we reach the Okanagan nation?"

"In a few days' time. That is why I tell you now that we must seek shelter there, that we cannot continue."

"I will follow Mkan," she answered.

"You are a good squaw. You shared your bread with me

242

when you did not know if it would be your last bread. Life in an Okanagan village will not be easy for a white woman; you will have to work with the other squaws. But there may be white trappers there; you may find company."

"Are there missionaries?"

"Perhaps a priest."

"Tell me about the Great Spirit," Margot asked. She liked Mkan's stories. At night he spoke to her about the stars and told her tales about the bear in the sky. He also told her about Cloya and Coyote. But she did not tell Mkan about the Bible; she found herself unable to discuss it or anything connected with being a missionary. In her mind, the memory of Ernest loomed large. He had not destroyed her faith, but he had damaged it severely. She admitted now to herself that the Indians had their own religion, and that they accepted the white man's religion less for what it brought them spiritually and more for what it brought them materially. She felt she was coming to understand a faith outside the narrow confines of her own beliefs.

"He dwells everywhere," Mkan replied. "In the trees, in the rivers, in the mountains. He sends us animal messengers who sometimes play tricks on us. Coyote and Cloya are great tricksters!"

Margot's eyes fell on a tall fir tree. Her father had always said that when he wanted to talk to his Maker, he went and sat under a tree. His beliefs, she realized, were not unlike Mkan's.

"Tell me about Cloya's tricks," she requested.

Mkan stirred the hot coals of the fire. "After we eat," he promised. "I will tell you how he makes his nest from the hairs plucked from the heads of the best and bravest warriors."

"Blaise!" Cory flung open the door to his farmhouse before Blaise even dismounted. He ran outside, his face all smiles.

"Pining for me?" Blaise called out cheerfully. Cory looked in fine condition and in excellent humor.

"No, but damn glad to see you. It's the middle of December; where have you been?"

"You look fit," Blaise commented as he slid from the saddle and greeted Cory with a bear hug.

"I owe that to married life!" Cory watched for Blaise's reaction.

"Married life! My God, what's happened in my absence?"

Cory grinned. "So much it will take me an age to tell you."

"Married? I can't believe that! I thought you were a confirmed bachelor."

Cory shook his head, "No more, my friend. Those days are over."

"Does that mean no more journeys to the mainland?"

"Not at all; in fact, I have to go back in the spring. That's a part of what I have to tell you. I'd like company."

"You'd like help, you mean."

"That, too," Cory admitted.

"I have to seek out the Lillooet," Blaise told him. "I intend to go myself in the spring."

"The Lillooet? Those are the people I have to return to!"

"Partners again," Blaise smiled, slapping him on the back.

Cory took his arm and led him toward the house. "Anya's inside. She's Russian; you'll like her."

"I like all women."

"I'm glad to see you haven't changed, even if I have."

Blaise winked. "But I'm afraid I have changed. If she is still alive, I believe the woman I intend to marry will return to the Lillooet. So, you see, I have a story, too.

Anya appeared at the doorway. Her long flaxen hair blew gently in the breeze, and she smiled warmly.

"This is Anya," Cory said proudly, taking her arm. "Anya, this is Blaise Baron, of whom I've spoken so often."

"Now I understand," Blaise said admiringly.

Anya reached out and took his hands. "I'm pleased to

meet you. I've heard more stories about Blaise Baron than I can remember."

"Your English is very good," Blaise noted as he kissed her on both cheeks.

"I study all the time, but I think I will never lose my accent."

Blaise released her, saying, "Nor I mine, so be proud of it. In the West, we all come from somewhere else. Just one big *mélange*, eh?"

Blaise turned to Cory. The love Anya and Cory felt for one another was evident in their eyes. It made him happy to see Cory so contented, but it also made him look into his own heart and ponder his own dilemma. He was still haunted by his feeling of helplessness, his feeling that he ought to have tried to follow Margot after all.

"Have you eaten?" Cory asked.

Blaise shook his head. "I came directly here."

"Let's eat then, and talk."

Blaise sunk into the chair. He felt as if he had spent his life astride a horse. "You start," he suggested. "Something tells me your story is happier than mine."

Ronald Macleod leaned back in his chair and folded the somewhat battered parchment letter. It had been written by Governor Douglas, Governor of the Colony of Vancouver, on December 30, 1856. It arrived some weeks after Ronald himself had sent messages through the United States in an attempt to find out if Margot was all right. He had received one letter from the Whitman mission; then, mysteriously, all communication ceased.

The letter from Douglas explained everything and nothing. It explained about the Indian uprisings, it explained that Ernest had been killed and Margot taken prisoner, it explained that she had escaped the Yakima and was headed for New Caledonia with an Indian warrior, and it explained that one Blaise Baron—"a respected man"—was looking for her. The same Mr. Baron had come to the governor and requested he write to Mr. Macleod in Niagara-on-the-Lake. Surprisingly, the letter was actually addressed to Lochiel.

245

The governor verified the fact that Mr. Baron was to be trusted and that he knew Mrs. McGrath well since he had led the wagon train on which she was a passenger.

"Naturally, things which occur in the United States are not normally my concern," the governor had written. "But since you too live under the British Crown and since Mr. Baron has requested it, I have done my best to relate the facts concerning your daughter."

Ronald bit his lip and fought back tears. What was not written by the governor was as important as what was. It was believed she was still alive, but, good Lord! she was traveling across a wilderness!

Ronald forced himself up out of the chair. He walked to the mantle and took down the tattered, ink-stained diary of Janet Cameron Macleod. He returned to the chair and began reading its brittle pages. Tears streamed down his face. "Be as brave and as resourceful as your great-great-grandmother," he said aloud. And then, to the spirits he was certain inhabited Lochiel, he muttered, "You watch over that girl."

CHAPTER XVIII

June 15, 1857

Margot and Mkan stood near the two horses they had purchased from the Okanagan. Margot had traded them her gold wedding ring, and though Mkan had objected at first, she assured him it meant nothing to her. The horses they had begun their journey with had been turned loose when Margot and Mkan crossed the border in British North America and began to travel up the Okanagan River by canoe.

Margot was now dressed in Indian garb—clothing she had made over the winter from elk skins or ''Wapiti'' as the Okanagan called them. Mkan made moccasins for her and she continued to wear her hair in two long Indian braids.

The entire village came out to bid them farewell. Groups of braves encircled them; behind the braves were the women of the village and behind them innumerable children.

''We bid you farewell.'' Okana, the chief of the Okanagan, lifted his hand in parting. ''May the Great Spirit guide you through the mountain pass and deliver you unharmed to your people.''

''We thank Okana for his hospitality,'' Mkan returned. Margot maintained her silence. It was not the custom for women to speak to the chief unless spoken to. That was not to say that the women of the tribe did not have a voice; they did. One of Okana's chief advisors was a woman, as was the tribe's shaman.

''We will go now, while the sun is high,'' Mkan announced. He turned and helped Margot onto her horse. Mkan too mounted and without further farewells or ceremony they turned their horses and headed for the tall mountains.

Mkan's pack held the extra blankets, the sacred gold, and rope. Margot packed the food given them by the villagers.

They rode for some hours before they stopped to water the horses and eat. The foothill lands were rolling, edging up to the peaks that lay ahead.

"It's a long way," Margot sighed.

Mkan nodded. "It will take us many weeks to reach the river, but from there it is a quick journey.

"And how long will it take for me to reach the British ships at the mouth of the Fraser?"

"They come to trade when the leaves fall from the trees. You will go then."

Two or three months, Margot thought. It seemed like a short enough time after the long winger with the Okanagan and the long months spent in misery with Ernest. Truly, she could not say she had been unhappy with the Indians. The work was difficult and her hands were calloused, but she rested well; she found she enjoyed the Indians, whose way of life was so different from all that she had known before. And although she did not ask Okana to treat her differently, he did. He asked her to teach the young braves and the children of the village some of the white man's language, so trading might be made easier. She dwelt with the chief's second wife, and though she taught during the days, she was expected to cook for Mkan, who took responsibility for providing the meat. While the men of the village hunted, it was the women who were expected to fish and to gather what vegetation was available. It was the women who skinned and dressed the animals that were caught, and it was the women who tanned the skins and prepared them for their varied uses. At night, the women of the village sat by the fire and chewed the wapiti skin, softening it as part of the tanning process.

"Why does your brave not visit you at night?" the chief's second wife had asked Margot. Margot had not been able to explain that while Mkan took responsibility for her, she was not his squaw. There was not enough language between them, so Margot had merely shrugged and allowed the chief's second wife to believe she was in some unstated way unsatisfactory.

"You yearn to return to your people as I yearn to return to mine," Mkan said, breaking into her thoughts.

248

Margot nodded. She still dreamed of Blaise. She wondered if she would ever find him.

She and Mkan traveled on. By nightfall they would enter the mountain range itself, and the difficult part of the journey would truly begin.

June had been a rainy month in New Caledonia and, as a result, Cory and Blaise did not reach the village of Lillooet until the tenth of July. Nkula stood and raised his hand in greeting. "You have come later than expected, but you have returned. Coyote was correct."

Cory dismounted. Blaise craned his neck, looking about the village. Of course, he could not expect to find Margot yet, but he could not control the anticipation he had felt all winter.

"We've brought equipment for digging; it is heavy and difficult to transport," Cory said, pointing to the pack mules and sledges. "There was heavy rain in the coastal mountains, mud and rock slides delayed us."

Nkula nodded.

"This is my friend, a blood brother, Blaise Baron."

Nkula raised his hand in greeting.

Blaise dismounted and wasted no time in asking the question he had waited to ask for so many months. "Does the great chief of the Lillooet know of a warrior called Mkan?"

Nkula looked surprised. "Yes. How do you know his name?"

"I have heard of Mkan from Kamiakan, chief of the Yakima nation."

"He is a prisoner of the Yakima. They stole our sacred gold. What do you know of him?"

"Kamiakan has allowed him to escape with the gold so he might return it to the Lillooet."

"Why would Kamiakan do this?"

"He wars with the white man. He no longer wishes to war with the Lillooet or any of the Salish nations. I bring tribute from Kamiakan."

Nkula smiled. "Many moons ago, when I consulted the ghosts of the forest, an *ethkay* emerged from its hiding place by the shore of the river. As it travelled across the wet mud,

249

it left a message. The message told me that if our guest was allowed to leave, Cloya's gold would be returned to us. The *ethkay* wrote the truth."

Blaise smiled, knowing that the *ethkay*, or salamander in English, was a respected oracle among the Lillooet.

"We shall continue to dig," Cory told Nkula.

"That is as it should be. The sacred gold is not yet restored to Cloya. There are many hardships on the trek across the great mountains. One does not know what tricks Coyote might play on the bearers of the gold."

"Mkan travels with a white woman who is known to us. She too was a prisoner of the Yakima."

"It is a difficult journey for a white squaw, but Mkan is a brave warrior. He is honorable and he will look after her."

"May I deliver the tribute from Kamiakan?"

Nkula agreed. "Let us smoke together. You will tell me what you know of the Flathead tribes to the south."

Blaise and Cory joined Nkula and Blaise presented the tribute.

"I thank you," Nkula said. "But I do not forgive Kamiakan until the gold is returned. When it is returned I will speak to you of these matters again."

Cory and Blaise returned to their mules and unloaded the equipment they had brought.

"When do you think they might come?" Cory asked Blaise.

"*If* they come. I don't put quite as much store in visions as Nkula. But if they are alive, they would have begun their journey as soon as the snow melted. It is a difficult and unpredictable trail. It could take them all summer."

"Do you know, in all the time you've been talking about your Margot, you've not told me her last name."

"Macleod was her maiden name."

"Macleod? Where is she from?"

"The Niagara," Blaise answered distractedly.

Cory beamed. "If she's from the Macleods of Niagara, she'll survive the journey."

Blaise looked up, "She mentioned there were MacLeans in her family. You're not related, are you?"

Cory laughed. "It's more than likely. My father's mother was Jenna Macleod, from the Niagara."

"Her aunt Jenna! She told me about a great-aunt Jenna."

"Then she *is* my cousin." Cory said, slapping Blaise on the back. "You've fallen in love with my cousin."

Blaise questioned, "Why do you say she'll survive the journey? Is being related to you enough to survive in the wilderness?"

Cory laughed and shook his head. "No. It's just that I know the family. First off, she comes from a family of woodsmen who settled the frontier. The whole family has always set great store in knowing the ways of the Indians. Second, she's a Macleod woman, and my father always said that no more stubborn and more spirited women existed."

"I'd say that description fits," Blaise was able to smile at that. "But she was reared on a farm in a small town."

Again Cory shook his head. "You gain strength from what has come before. Margot will cling to the stories of her ancestors and she will know that if they survived, she can too. The lore in my family is strong. Margot and I share the same roots, and those roots are deep."

"I wish I had your faith," Blaise told him. "But I can't let myself hope too much."

The August sun blazed down as Margot and Mkan picked their way along a narrow rock-strewn pathway. The gorge below was deep and filled with stones; above them the mountain loomed, a wall of solid granite.

Somewhere, Margot thought, there's a valley. And when I get to it, I'm going to lie down in a meadow for hours and hours. She wiped the perspiration from her brow. It was hot and dry, and there were no tall pines to offer shade. She glanced upward and saw only rocks jutting from the sides of the mountain. They were above the tree line in a world of stone. But, she consoled herself, they were descending, and her valley and mountain meadow could not be far away.

Margot moved as close to the side of the mountain as she could. She became dizzy if she looked down into the gorge. She led her horse; the path was too steep to venture riding.

251

The horses moved as slowly as Mkan and Margot, testing the ground as they went.

"It's steep!" Margot said.

"Dangerous," Mkan agreed. "But this is the worst part. When we descend, we will be close to the river."

Suddenly, Margot's horse reared and whinnied; Mkan's horse did the same.

"Whoa!" Margot said, holding the bridle and trying to control the beast. "Whoa!"

"Get back!" Mkan's shout came simultaneously with sounds and vibrations—the ground moved beneath Margot's feet and the two horses reared up again.

But before Margot even had time to think, huge rocks rained down on the pathway and the earth trembled violently.

Margot screamed. She pressed herself to the side of the mountain, aware of small rocks pelting her.

Margot whirled around and clung to the mountain, her eyes closed. She screamed again and again. A large stone hit her shoulder and she winced in pain. Seconds? Minutes? She couldn't even think, but was aware only of scratching at the granite, of trying to claw her way inside the mountain. Then it stopped as it had begun, and there was only deathly silence.

"Mkan!" Margot called out. She turned slowly, painfully, clutching her bleeding shoulder. "Mkan!" He lay on the pathway, his head cut and bleeding, the lower part of his body buried in rocks. "Mkan!" Margot screamed.

One of the horses remained standing—he, too, was bleeding, but not too badly. The other had bolted over the edge; its body lay askew a hundred feet below.

Margot looked up. All the rocks on the side of the mountain looked jagged and ominous. She knelt on all fours and scrambled to Mkan's side.

"Mkan," she said, gently cradling his head in her arms. He blinked and opened his eyes.

"Oh, thank God, you are not dead!"

He groaned, and Margot began to lift the heavy stones off the lower part of his body. She worked feverishly, pulling, pushing, and prodding.

"Where is the gold?" Mkan asked haltingly.

Margot glanced up. It was her horse which had gone over the side. "It is all right," she answered, "but you are hurt."

Mkan shook his head. "You cannot help me, I cannot feel my legs. You must take the gold and hurry down the mountain before the earth speaks again. You will find the river . . . follow it." He groaned and winced in pain.

"I will not leave you!" Margot said, struggling with the last boulder. Mkan was bleeding, and clearly his legs were broken. "There!" she exclaimed as she rolled it off.

"The earth seldom speaks just once; I beg you, save yourself and the sacred gold, more rocks will fall."

"I will not leave you. I must get you on the horse and when we are down the mountain, I will build a litter."

"My legs are crushed. You must go!"

Margot shook her head. "No, Mkan. Not without you."

"A squaw should do as she is told," he said firmly.

"Put your arms around my neck," she insisted.

Mkan did as she bade him and Margot struggled to lift him. He staggered to his feet and cried out with the pain. She half dragged him to the horse.

"I shall have to build a step of stones . . ." She lay him down and scurried about collecting debris into a tall mound.

"That will take too much time," he groaned.

Margot didn't answer. She kept adding to the pile, using as many large stones on the base as she could move. Her arms ached, but her shoulder had stopped bleeding. She worked for over two hours, and blessed God when the sun disappeared behind a cloud.

"Now," she said. "I know it will hurt terribly, but you must try to get across the horse."

Mkan nodded, and again Margot pulled him up and hoisted him.

Mkan groaned in agony but managed to pull himself across the horse's back. Margot took a bit of rope and tied him loosely to the horse. Then she began to lead the animal down the winding path, aware that it was already twilight.

An hour and a half later, the ground leveled out and Margot breathed a sigh of relief as she saw a small stream and tall trees; an ideal campsite.

253

Margot tethered the horse and Mkan slid into her arms. She nearly fell backward under his weight. She laid him out on the grass, and took a cloth out of the pack and hurried to the stream, then washed Mkan's wounds and put cool cloths on his face. He lost consciousness.

Margot left him, and in the semi-darkness hurried to gather wood for the fire. She lit it and breathed a sigh of relief when it caught. Soon the fire roared, and the sight of the flames made her feel better. She built a shelter over Mkan as best she could.

Wearily, Margot unpacked the supplies and prepared a broth from balsam root. She took the broth into the shelter.

"Eat," she said propping him up with two pieces of log.

"I cannot go on," he whispered hoarsely.

"You will go on. Tomorrow I will make splints for your legs and build a litter. You will rest and the next morning we will resume our journey."

"You are not a shaman."

Margot smiled. "But I know what to do."

With the morning sun, Margot was up collecting heavy rounded bark pieces for splints. She tended first to Mkan's legs, binding them securely to the heavy bark. She thoroughly washed all his wounds and bathed them with a tea made from the leaves he told her to collect. Then she set about making the litter with rope and with strong green tree branches, which she cut with Mkan's knife.

When she finished that, she cooked their meal of fresh fish and berries.

"You would make a fine Indian," Mkan praised.

Margot smiled. "Cloya does not want you to die."

She was pleased to see that Mkan ate the fish with relish. "And you know how to catch big fish," he told her. "If I did not have a squaw and you did not have a brave, I would take you for a wife."

Margot smiled. "You are kind," she told him. "But I am not so good a squaw. It is only that the Great Spirit has filled that stream with many fish."

"You long after your brave," Mkan observed. He pointed to the heavens. "See, there is a full moon. The

254

Sepass people say that the sun god longed after the daughter of the moon and created the earth for her. They say the sun god and the daughter of the moon sat in the heavens with their arms outstretched to one another and then, in the shadow of evening, they leapt to earth and became the first man and the first woman. All who long and wait are united. They inherit the earth.''

"That's a beautiful tale.''

"It is a tale for lovers. You will find your brave.''

Margot nodded. "Not without your help, Mkan. Do your legs feel better?''

"Yes. You *are* a shaman, and blessed by the daughter of the moon.''

Blaise and Cory worked tirelessly at the vein. As each week passed, Blaise became more and more anxious.

"Time weighs heavy,'' Cory observed.

"I feel helpless.''

"You couldn't have followed them; you'd never have found them.''

"I should have done something other than just come here to wait for a miracle.''

"You did about all you could.''

Blaise bit his lip, "But damnit, I should have done more!''

"I don't think you should give up yet.''

Blaise shook his head sadly. "But soon I will. It has been too long; it's already the middle of August.

"I suggest we call it a day.'' Cory put down his shovel and signalled the braves. "It's a fine vein, you know. Even after it's divided with the tribe, we'll have a great deal.''

"I'll be rich and lonely,'' Blaise said bitterly.

The two of them walked side by side back to the village. Blaise could not shake the thought of Margot's death from his mind. I'll never see her again, he thought. The reality came to him over and over. Perhaps they had been killed by the warring tribes of the area; perhaps they had frozen in the winter snows. . . . A hundred possibilities haunted him night and day; friend or not, he found it increasingly difficult to talk about what was in his heart with Cory, whose heart and thoughts were more often than not on Anya.

"I'm going to go wash," Blaise said, heading for the hut. Once inside, he filled a small basin and splashed cold water on his face. "Damnit! If I have to ride every inch of this territory to find her, I will!" he said out loud, and ran his hand through his wet hair.

He jolted to attention at the sound of shouts from outside. The women were all shrieking and the children screaming. Blaise hurried out of his hut and stood for an instant, staring at the sight.

Sitting astride a horse was Margot. Her long black hair hung in braids and she wore the Indian dress of the Okanagan. She rode bareback with only a blanket for a saddle. And the horse bore a litter to which a man was tied. The crowd of villagers surrounded the horse.

"Mkan has returned!" the children shouted.

Blaise's mouth opened. For all his misgivings, Margot had not only survived, but she had returned bearing Mkan, who appeared badly injured. He burst into a run across the compound.

"Margot!"

She turned to the sound of his voice, slipped from the horse, and ran toward him.

Blaise threw his arms around her. "Thank God! You're safe! I wanted to follow you! I came here to wait!"

Held close in his embrace, Margot clung to him and began to cry.

Blaise kissed her and pressed her to him, aware of the noise of children and the weeping of Mkan's wife who sobbed as she embraced her husband.

"Everyone is looking at us," Margot said, brushing the tears from her eyes.

"Who cares?" Blaise kissed her again and to his joy he felt her returning his passion. Then she pulled away reluctantly. Blaise continued to hold her hand.

Nkula stood quietly, a bemused look on his face.

"Where is the chief of the Lillooet?" Margot asked.

"Here," Nkula replied.

Margot returned to the horse and carefully lifted down the leather bag. "Mkan and I return the sacred gold of the Lillooet," she said, smiling.

Nkula accepted the satchel. "It will be returned to the sacred place."

"She is responsible," Mkan called from the litter. "She refused to leave me for dead."

Nkula looked at Blaise. "I compliment you on your choice of a squaw."

Blaise laughed, "I'm a man of great experience and good taste."

Cory approached Margot and bowed slightly. "Congratulations, cousin."

Margot looked at him quizzically.

"I'm your great-aunt Jenna's grandson," Cory told her. "Cory MacLean!"

"The same," Cory said, smiling broadly.

Blaise's arms circled Margot's waist protectively. "And my partner as well," Blaise said, laughing.

"We're also neighbors back in Victoria," Cory added.

"Oh, Blaise, when can we go to Victoria?"

Blaise glanced at Cory, who in turn looked at Nkula.

"The gold has been returned. You are free to go. You may return when you wish to dig in the ground."

"We can leave tonight," Blaise said.

"Well, you two may be in love enough to travel by night, but I'd rather wait until morning," Cory told them.

Blaise looked at Margot's face. "Let's walk," he suggested. "I know a secluded spot not so far from here."

Margot took his hand and looked up at him lovingly. "Yes, let's."

"I suppose this means our family reunion will have to wait," Cory said good-naturedly.

"First things first," Blaise answered.

Blaise and Margot walked a long way through the woods together, talking as they went.

"Here," Blaise said. "Here, sit down with me."

He sat on the grass and pulled Margot down beside him. She leaned her head on his shoulder.

257

"Do you see that stream coming out of the ground over there?" Blaise pointed off to what looked like a stream.

"It's a hot spring. Over there, is a cold one," he told her. "The Indians say they were a married couple who wanted to be together always, even though they were quite different and wanted to retain their individuality. So the transformer—Cloya, the Bluejay—made them into two springs."

"Your tales are as good as Mkan's."

"Margot, I know about McGrath," Blaise began, wanting to spare her the pain of explanation.

"How?" Margot asked, turning to him with a serious expression.

"I heard in Fort Steilacoom. I went back to the valley and spoke with Kamiakan."

"He was mad," Margot said sadly. "He killed an Indian girl—he tried to kill me, but the Yakima intervened. They killed him. I can't even talk about how . . . it was horrible. I know he was mad, but no one deserves to die that way. No one."

"You mustn't think about it anymore. It's over."

"Blaise, someone must have notified my father . . . He must think I'm dead."

"I had the Governor of the Colony of Vancouver write him with as much information as I myself had."

"Oh, Blaise, I must get a message to him, to set his mind at ease."

"All things in good time. You can send a letter in Victoria. It goes by steamer across the Isthmus of Panama to New York and from there by mail. . . . It takes a long while."

They were silent for a while, content to be together and listen to the sound of the nearby springs.

"I brought you to this spot on purpose, Margot."

She looked up at him with her great luminous green eyes.

He took her in his arms, letting her fall back on the soft grass. "I love you, Margot. I want to be by your side always. I want to marry you."

Margot lifted her arms and put them around his neck. "I love you, too," she whispered. "Make love to me now, by the two springs, so we will be like them, lovers for eternity."

CHAPTER XIX

December 25, 1857

Outside, a gentle rain fell, and though it was cold, it was far milder than any winter Margot had ever known. Christmas in Victoria, she discovered, was green rather than white and frosty.

She sat by the fire while Anya sat on the settee and Cory and Blaise occupied the two chairs in the parlor.

"It was a lovely party," Margot said wearily, "but tiring."

"Mrs. Douglas' Christmas reception is always a show," Cory replied. Then he added, "Tell me, now that we've settled down, what are we going to do with ourselves?"

"Build a lumber mill," Blaise replied. "Lots of new people coming into the territory. There's need for lumber."

Cory nodded. "Partners?"

Blaise grinned. "Always."

Anya leaned back awkwardly. She was pregnant and she patted her stomach. "It's moving again."

Cory laughed. "Restless. Shows that it's a MacLean. Which reminds me, we should be off soon."

"Not yet," Blaise said as he stood up. He walked to the closet and returned with a package. "This came yesterday," he said, looking at Margot. "But it says on the outside 'not to be opened until Christmas.' Far be it from me to disobey the instructions of my father-in-law."

Margot jumped up. "It's from my father?" Her face was alight with anticipation.

Blaise handed her the battered parcel and Margot tore it open.

"Oh, look!" she exclaimed with delight.

Blaise and Cory examined it and Anya leaned over curiously.

Margot shook her head. "That's Papa," she said, pointing to the picture of Ronald Macleod, ". . . and great-aunt Susanna, and Aunt Peggy, and Kevin. . . ." They were all present, together, against a dark background, standing formally. "It's not as good as a good painting," Margot said, unfolding the letter that was also in the package.

"It's some sort of miracle," Anya said, examining the picture.

"It's a carte-de-viste," Blaise said. "Done with a camera. I have heard the army was looking into the process to replace illustrations."

"Read it out loud," Cory suggested. "Unless it's too private."

Margot laughed. "It's not at all private." She began reading.

"My darling Margot,
    I received your letter from Victoria with great joy. Your Blaise Baron sounds like a man after my own heart.
    I am writing this letter on the 30th day of October, in the year of our Lord 1857. This night, the entire west field of Lochiel was given over to the gathering of the MacLean and Macleod Clans and to all our friends. Tonight, as you know, is the 100th Anniversary of the founding of Lochiel.
    We had a huge bonfire that lit the night sky and we ate all the harvest foods and played all the traditional highland games. I myself tossed the caber, though I lost to a younger, stronger MacLean. There were one hundred and fifty people present.
    Your great-aunt, old Susanna, refused to sit down for a single minute—she danced the night away because, she said, Hell, son I'm not going to sit down! People in this family have a way of dying during celebrations. Trouble was, they all sat down. They're going to put me in my grave vertical! I'm never going to sit down.
    Your brother Kevin brought John MacDonald,

leader of the coalition government with Etienne Cartier, and Kevin toasted the Scots for settling this country from Nova Scotia to the mouth of the Fraser River. MacDonald pounded the table and said that one day this would be one nation from sea to sea. I thought of you, then . . . I thought how very much like your great-great-grandmother you are. Margot, I'm proud of you.

Enclosed you will find a reproduction of the family. I think I like paintings better, myself. . . . We all look a bit strange. This a new invention and a photographer came all the way from New York to take this picture. He is one of Trace MacLean's sons who learned the art in Paris from someone called Nadar. He says it's the latest thing and that soon everyone will be using a camera instead of a pencil or brush to make pictures. It's all rather new and odd, but I thought you would like to have it.

My love to you, my darling Margot. Put down strong roots in your new home, Victoria, and one day your great-grandchildren's children will remember your trek just as we have just celebrated Janet Macleod's. Carry Lochiel in your heart, Margot. Remember, though we Scots once lost our land and our language, we still have our spirit and our lore.
Love,
Papa''

Margot refolded the letter and made no attempt to wipe the tears from her cheek.

Blaise put his arm protectively around her shoulders and took the picture from her hands. He smiled as he looked at her family.

"I have something for you, too," Cory put in. He pulled the silver chain from around his neck and handed it to her. From it dangled an ancient Roman coin.

Margot took it from him and touched it reverently. "For me?"

"It's rightfully yours. This is *the coin*. The coin that

Mathew Macleod gave to Janet Cameron. There were once two, as you probably know. One was lost with my great-grandfather, Robert MacLean, when he drowned. This is the other. It was given to me by my father, who got it from his mother, your great-aunt Jenna. Jenna was a Macleod, and rightfully this is the Macleod coin.''

Margot turned it in her fingers slowly, tears still glistening in her eyes. "I don't know what to say."

"Say nothing. Wear it and pass it on to your youngest child."

"Last born and not first born?"

"That's the tradition," Cory confirmed.

"It'll be years before she has to part with it!" Blaise joked. "You know how we French are! We have a reputation for fertility."

Margot blushed.

Cory stood up and took Anya's hand. "We'll be going now."

"Merry Christmas," Margot said again.

Blaise and Margot extinguished the lamps and went to their bedroom. He watched Margot undress as he lay on the bed waiting for her. For a woman who was once so prim, she managed to undress rather seductively, discarding one garment at a time and enjoying the expression on his face.

"You have a very lecherous look," she told him. "It makes me warm all over."

"I always remember the first time. Gives me an excuse to like leeches."

"They're not very likeable."

"Depends on who they're on."

He reached out for her. . . . She was always irresistible to him. Milk-white skin, jet-black hair, green eyes. And since they had been home, she'd put on a little weight. Not too much, but just enough. Her hips were once again rounded and firm, her breasts were full and lovely, her waist still small enough to circle. And her legs! He felt he could write poetry about her legs . . . more so when she wrapped them about him.

"You're so anxious."

He took her arm and pulled her down on top of him, feeling her curves and kissing her face and neck. "God, I love you! You make up for everything!"

Margot returned his kisses. He was so gentle and yet so strong; so slow in his lovemaking and always the romantic. "We were made for each other," she said, kissing his eyelids. Slowly, Blaise ran his hands over her, kissing her breasts, taunting her until she clung to him and breathed deeply. He slid into her and they moved as one, reaching together for pleasure, each aware of the other, each caring.

Margot arched her back and moaned. Blaise felt himself tumble into that void of sensation. He continued to rock her in his arms, to caress her, to hold her. Then they lay side by side.

"I have a Christmas present for you," Margot whispered.

Blaise gazed across at her. "You're present enough."

Margot smiled. "We are going to be three."

Blaise's mouth opened. "You're pregnant!"

"Well, we make love enough! It had to happen sometime!" she laughed.

He took her in his arms and rocked her. "I love you! I love you!"

"It makes you happy?"

"Of course it makes me happy!"

Margot smiled, "And if it's a boy, can we name him Mathew Baron, for his great-great-great-grandfather?"

"And he'll be a giant of the new West. I like that. 'The Barons of the West!' "

"It has a nice sound to it." Margot reached up and kissed him. "Make love to me again."

Blaise kissed her nose. "My pleasure."